THE MEMOIRS OF
CHANCELLOR PASQUIER

1767 – 1815

The Memoirs of
Chancellor Pasquier
1767 – 1815

TRANSLATED BY DOUGLAS GARMAN

Introduction and notes by Robert Lacour-Gayet

Fairleigh Dickinson University Press

Rutherford · Madison · Teaneck

Fairleigh Dickinson

First American Edition 1968

Fairleigh Dickinson University Press
Associated University Presses, Inc.
Cranbury, N.J. 08512

English translation © Elek Books Limited 1967

Originally published under the title
Souvenirs du Chancelier Pasquier
© Librairie Hatchette 1964

Printed in England by
Unwin Brothers Limited
Woking and London

Contents

Illustrations

TRANSLATOR'S NOTE

The present volume is a translation of SOUVENIRS DU CHANCELIER PASQUIER: 1767–1815 (Hachette, Paris: 1964), a selection of extracts made by M. Robert Lacour-Gayet from Pasquier's HISTOIRE DE MON TEMPS. In accordance with the author's wishes the original work, covering the period 1767–1830 and completed during the reign of Louis Philippe, was not published during his lifetime. For thirty-two years the manuscript remained in the hands of his heirs at the Château of Sassy, where it still is, and it was not until 1894 that its publication was authorised by the then Duc d'Audiffret-Pasquier. This edition, in six volumes and comprising some three thousand pages, appeared under the title of MÉMOIRES DU CHANCELIER PASQUIER and, apart from one or two omissions from the original manuscript, remains the only complete one. Unfortunately, despite the fact that the Duke was a member of the Académie Française, he allowed it to be published without Notes or Introduction.

This defect is admirably remedied in M. Lacour-Gayet's volume. His Notes especially, largely derived from contemporary sources, add continually to the interest of the text and, together with the summaries with which he skilfully links the extracts, help to overcome the discontinuity in the narrative that such drastic compression makes to some extent unavoidable.

Inevitably, however, being primarily addressed to the French reader, these Notes assume a familiarity with the principal historical events and personalities referred to by Pasquier which can scarcely be taken for granted in an English reader. In making the present translation, therefore, while retaining the great majority of M. Lacour-Gayet's footnotes (occasionally subsumed in his commentary), I have added one or two others in the hope that they may add to the interest and pleasure of the general reader. In order to accommodate these additions, and with the same general aim in view, I have also ventured to omit two or three pages from M. Lacour-Gayet's Introduction, where he quotes at some length from French reviews of the MÉMOIRES at the time of their first appearance.

Introduction

BY ROBERT LACOUR-GAYET

Not many people live to be ninety-six. But to have been born in the time of Louis XV, on 21 April 1767, and died under the Emperor Napoleon III, on 6 July 1862, confers a special interest upon such a life-span, as may be seen from the following brief summary.

Counsellor in the Parlement of Paris at the end of the *Ancien Régime;* in hiding during the first years of the Revolution and imprisoned under the Thermidorean terror of 1794; unemployed until 1806, then, at the age of forty, beginning his administrative life as a member of the Emperor's Council of State and Prefect of Police; confirmed in the latter post under the First Restoration, and subsequently appointed Director General of Roads and Bridges; banished from Paris during the Hundred Days but, having proved himself a master of the art of waiting, appointed Minister of Justice and of the Interior in July 1815; dismissed in September, then appointed Minister without Portfolio and Member of the Privy Council, and rewarded by the Grand Cross of the Legion of Honour; elected to the newly constituted Chamber of Deputies, where he was the active representative of the Liberal minority; President of the Assembly in 1816; Minister of Justice for the second time in 1817, then Minister for Foreign Affairs from 1819 until 1821, and in the latter year created a peer of France; President of the Chamber of Peers from the time of Louis Philippe's accession to the throne as a result of the 1830 Revolution; Chancellor of France in 1837; elected to the French Academy five years later; granted a dukedom in 1844, by which time he had retired, though he was still to live through the 1848 Revolution, the short-lived second Republic and eleven years of the Second Empire—such was the life of Etienne-Denis Pasquier.

It is scarcely surprising that such a varied experience should have given him the idea of writing his memoirs, a task which he began in 1822 during his last month as Minister of Foreign Affairs.[1] To start with, the objective he set himself was a

[1] It is possible that he was urged to do so by Mme de Boigne, who says: 'During the last months of his Ministry (at the end of 1821), and especially after

limited one. He proposed to write 'the history of the French cabinet, and of the principal events that occurred in the kingdom and in Europe, from the end of 1818 to the end of 1821. The need to make known and to set in its true light the attitude adopted by myself and my friends with regard to the major issues of that period decided me to devote my leisure time to this purpose ... '

Soon, however, the nature of the project changed: Pasquier decided to write an account not only of his whole life but also of the entire epoch. This was a considerable undertaking, probably inspired by a desire to imitate Chateaubriand, whom he disliked. What title should he choose? 'Memoirs is too commonplace; besides I myself do not play a sufficiently important part, and the events I am writing about are on such a scale that it would be unbecoming to put myself in the forefront. On the other hand, to call it a HISTORY would be somewhat pretentious and I doubt whether I could justify such a title: there is so much that I have passed over in silence; at times I have written so hurriedly. ... However, after reflecting upon the best way to describe what is to be found in these pages I came to the conclusion that the most appropriate title would be: HISTORY OF MY TIMES.'

The manuscript of this immense work, running to fifteen folio volumes, has been preserved in the Château of Sassy near Argentan, where the present Duc d'Audiffret-Pasquier, a descendant of the Chancellor, has graciously permitted me to make use of the archives. ... It covers the period 1767 to 1830, and was completed under the July monarchy. Later it was supplemented by a volume of SOUVENIRS, and a SUMMARY OF MY LIFE, written in November 1843; while the Revolution of 1848 provided him with the material for yet another work.[2]

In the Foreword to the HISTORY, the Chancellor expressed the wish that, if it were to be published, this should not be until

his resignation, M. de Richelieu often used to visit me. He brought M. Pasquier with him, and it was then that my close relationship with the latter began'. (For Pasquier's friendship with Mme de Boigne, see the final chapter.)

[2] While a few passages of the manuscript *Histoire* were omitted from the printed *Mémoires*, the latter drew to some extent on the later *Souvenirs*, though the *Summary* remains unpublished. Another work, published in 1944 under the rather misleading title *La Révolution de* 1848 (193 out of 295 pages in fact deal with the July monarchy), takes the story further. For Pasquier's other works, see the final chapter.

some time after his death. His wish was respected, and it was
not in fact until thirty-two years after his death that the Duc
d'Audiffret-Pasquier had his ancestor's work printed. Its
publication was awaited with considerable curiosity, all the
more so because a number of people had already had access to
the manuscript . . . and several extracts had appeared in such
journals as *La Revue des Deux Mondes* and *La Revue de Paris*,
before publication of the complete work, which was spread
over the years 1893–95. It consisted of six volumes: the first
being devoted to the years 1767–1811; the second to 1812–14;
the third to 1814–15; the fourth to 1815–20; the fifth to 1820–24;
and the sixth to 1824–30.[3]

Like all autobiography, the HISTOIRE DE MON TEMPS is not
free from prejudice, nor from considerable gaps. Its author
allowed himself to be influenced by his feelings of sympathy or
antipathy towards his contemporaries[4] and he did not always
avoid presenting the facts to his own advantage. But if we were
to confine ourselves to those memoirs that display complete
objectivity and veracity, there would be very few that could be
admitted as sources of historical research. On the other hand, it
is precisely by comparing documents, incomplete in themselves
and always tendentious, that we may hope to succeed in arriving
at the truth—in so far as the truth is obtainable when studying
the past. Of the almost infinite number of memoirs devoted to
the Revolution, the Empire and the two Restorations, those of
Chancellor Pasquier undoubtedly occupy an important place. In
our view, what especially distinguishes them is their two outstanding qualities: the wealth of information they contain, and the
care with which the author seeks to substantiate what he says.[5]

The HISTORY OF MY TIMES has not been republished since
1895.[6] To attempt to do so today would be a bold undertaking:

[3] Here the pages referred to in the Translator's Note are omitted.

[4] He did his best, however, to be fair, as may be seen from one of the documents
preserved in the Sassy archives. On the death of Talleyrand, Pasquier felt it
necessary to write a long note (unpublished) in which, in the light of the Prince
of Benevento's ambassadorship in London and the circumstances of his death,
he revised and modified some of the harsh judgements he had expressed about him.

[5] In the Sassy archives, the manuscript of the HISTOIRE DE MON TEMPS is
accompanied by five volumes of supporting evidence. Having dipped into these,
we feel justified in saying that these documents corroborate the text.

[6] An English translation of the first three volumes only of the HISTOIRE by
C. E. Roche, appeared concurrently with the original French edition.

where could one hope to find readers for these 3,000 octavo pages? Thus it has only been possible to envisage a volume of extracts. But how were these to be selected?

We have been guided in our choice by a twofold criterion. The first three volumes seem to us to be infinitely more readable than the three succeeding ones. In the first place because of the period they cover: no one ever grows tired of fresh evidence about the Revolution, the Empire and the beginnings of the Restoration, whereas the events of 1815–30 are by comparison with those of the twenty-five preceding years singularly lacking in colour. Moreover, Pasquier's part in the restoration of the Bourbons was of outstanding importance; so concerned was he with it that he devoted 765 pages, that is to say more than a quarter of the total, to the two years 1814 and 1815. Need we add that from 1816 onwards his narrative is intentionally heavy and verbose? Only the trials of Charles X's Ministers really arouse interest. Yet even so it is difficult to feel enthusiastic about the prolix passages in which the Chancellor is manifestly seeking to justify the balancing feats which enabled him to remain in office and led to his being nicknamed 'the inevitable'. From this point onwards it is the politician who is speaking. Fully to appreciate what he here says, it would be necessary to compare it with the four octavo volumes in which he published his speeches of this period—an arduous task, which, admittedly, we shrank from undertaking. . . .

The present volume therefore is devoted to the single period 1767 to 1815, but even within this limited framework the requirements of publishing demanded yet further cuts. We therefore decided on principle only to reprint those passages where his testimony was at first-hand. What a memoir-writer has himself seen and heard, however incomplete, is always more instructive than information, however circumstantial, that he has merely picked up as a result of his duties or his connections. On this basis our selection includes about one-quarter of the first three volumes. Naturally we have done our best to maintain the continuity of the narrative by means of summaries, which we have made as detailed as possible. We only hope that our readers will derive as much pleasure from these selections as we ourselves experienced when editing and annotating them.

But what about the man himself, it may be asked? We decided to allow him first to speak for himself, and only then

to express our own opinion, which will be found in the con-
cluding chapter. We should like to think, however, that the
publication of this volume may result in an adequate biography
of Pasquier being written, a task which curiously enough no
one has as yet undertaken.

I

The Ancien Régime
1767–1789

CHILDHOOD AND ADOLESCENCE – COUNSELLOR
IN THE PARLEMENT OF PARIS – DESCRIPTION
OF FRANCE IN 1789.

I was born in 1767,[1] in circumstances which seemed to presage
an agreeable existence and a great fortune that I never came into;
the way I was brought up during my earliest years was influenced
by the craze for the methods taught by Rousseau, which have
caused me considerable suffering. On the pretext of acclimatising
me to the inclemency of the weather, during two rigorous
winters (when I was four and five years old) I used to be taken
to the Tuileries gardens very lightly dressed, and was told that
if I wanted to get warm I must take exercise; I was told to run
about, but the cold robbed me of the strength to do so. The
result of this experiment has been that for the rest of my life I
have remained more susceptible to cold than anyone I have
ever met.

The powerful influence that the passionate eloquence of the
citizen of Geneva at the time exerted on people's imaginations,
especially those of women, was doubtless excusable. I have since
learnt that my mother[2] was unable to resist the very natural
desire to see the famous and extraordinary Jean-Jacques at
closer quarters, and that, in order to do so, she had availed herself of the usual pretext of taking him some music to copy. My
mother was a witty woman, and such was the charm of her
conversation that the would-be philosopher expressed a desire
to see her again. The banishment of Parlement, which occurred
in 1771, put an end to this relationship, however.

I was vaccinated at a time when very few people were. An

---

[1] In Paris, rue Bourg-L'Abbé. Another son and a daughter were to complete
the family.

[2] Anne-Thérèse-Nicole Gaultier-Despréaux, daughter of Jean-Louis Gaultier-
Despréaux, secretary to Louis XV and Farmer-General of Taxes.

English doctor called Horlock, whose arrival in Paris preceded that of the Suttons, had been called in for one of my mother's brothers who had caught smallpox; his life was despaired of; the doctor pulled him through. My mother, who was then pregnant, also caught this cruel disease, and her doctor, the famous Bouvard, declared that either mother or child must die.[3] Horlock, summoned once more, saved them both. On the strength of this success he proposed to vaccinate me. My father agreed on my behalf, but he could not obtain my mother's consent to the vaccination of my sister. Soon afterwards she caught the smallpox, was very ill and still bears the marks of it.

My mother's objection would be difficult to explain it if were not for the fact that, in those days, among very devout people, of whom she was one, there were many who considered that to inject human beings with a disease which they might never have caught was tempting Providence. An important section of the clergy was strongly of this opinion.

My education was to bear a twofold imprint: on the one hand, that of the old ideas and customs of a world that was about to disappear, and, on the other, of the irreligious and essentially innovating philosophical spirit which had been developing over the past fifty years. The latter had had little success within my immediate family circle, where the opposite tendency was deeply rooted, stemming from the ancient magistrature of which my grandfather, who died in 1783, was a faithful representative.[4]

A fellow pupil of Voltaire's, with whom he had studied classics in the sixth form under the most famous teacher at the great Jesuit college,[5] Father Porée,[6] he had never fallen victim to the allurements of the teachings of Voltaire and the encyclopaedists, whose influence could make no inroads against his sturdy commonsense and firmly grounded religious principles. His sincere piety was in no way exaggerated; he avoided all discussion

[3] Bouvard, who was regarded as an authority, remained obstinately opposed to the practice of vaccination.

[4] Shortly before his death Pasquier was visited by the father of the historian Denys Cochin, to whom he made some interesting revelations. 'We are both', said he, 'of old Parisian stock. My father was a close friend of your great-grandfather. They were on good terms with their parish priests, and venerated their bishops, but monks and that sort of thing counted for nothing with them . . . '

[5] The college of Clermont; now the famous Lycée Louis-le-Grand.

[6] 'Nothing will efface from my heart the memory of Father Porée, who was equally dear to all those who studied under him', said Voltaire.

of such matters and was content to bear witness to his faith by the regularity of his religious observances. I remember one instance of this, which I have often recalled since. He was nearly eighty, I twelve, and I was spending my holidays with him at Coulans, his country house. At that time he was paying particular attention to my education. Every Sunday we used to go to mass, which was said in the private chapel, and on one such occasion, when the person who should have been serving mass had failed to turn up, I saw my grandfather, after looking at me in a very significant way, get up from his place and go and kneel down in place of the absent server, who fortunately soon arrived and relieved him of this tiring position.

My earliest education, as regards the humanities, was not very happy. What I found most difficult about it to begin with was due to a peculiar characteristic of my memory; although in certain matters it was capable of extended application, and has served me very well in the career that I have followed, it has always resisted learning by rote. My dislike for this kind of learning began early, for my mother, in whom this faculty was highly developed, could not understand why in me it was so lacking; and, from earliest childhood, she therefore set me tasks which I was quite unable to carry out, with the result that I was often scolded and sometimes punished.

The education of children, which has nowadays become so affectionate, was in those days extremely strict; but with most parents the mistake was also made, as it is today, of not paying sufficient attention to the child's natural abilities, and of expecting the same response, the same application in every subject. It often happens that by demanding of children efforts they are incapable of making, aptitudes which would have repaid cultivation are neglected.

When I reached the age of seven I was handed over to tutors, of whom I had two in succession. The first tended to make the same mistake as my mother with regard to my memory. He was a scholarly man, very assiduous in his care of me but hard and sharp-tongued, and he tried to get more out of me than the frailty of my health and the degree of attention I was capable of permitted. He was replaced by a man who, in almost every respect, was the exact opposite. The experiment proved to be no more successful, neither of them fulfilled the hopes of my parents; but the truth of the matter is, private education rarely does succeed; and not the least of its drawbacks are the changes of authority to which the pupil is exposed. I may add that, in my opinion, with very few exceptions, this kind of education is full of dangers. More often than not it has the most unfortunate effects on the child's health or on its character. As regards health, the lack of exercise is not conducive to the development of physical energy and the child therefore gets bored, a condition that is difficult to put up with at any age.

When I was eleven years and four months old I was sent to Juilly. In those days one advanced rapidly in one's studies, from which it may reasonably be concluded that in general they were not very profound. The college of Juilly was run by the Oratorians, and was the best known of their establishments.

Father Petit, who was then the superior, well deserved the high reputation he enjoyed. He had several very clever assistants, among them Father Mandar, whose reputation as a preacher was sufficiently established for him to be one of those entitled to preach before the king. He was responsible for preparing students for their first communion, and I owe it to him that I performed this important act with the fullest assent of both heart and mind. The impression this occasion made upon me was as sweet as it was solemn, and I often look back to it with the greatest pleasure. As is well known, the Oratorians were closer to the Jansenists than to the Molinists, which is why my mother had decided to send me to a college directed by them; her extreme piety had attracted her to Jansenism, and she accepted their doctrines and observances. The most outstanding minds and intellects of this party used to meet at her house, and it was from their inspiration that she derived not only her own rules of conduct but also the sense of duty with which she sought to inspire her children. Father Mandar had certainly not made a scholar of me, but thanks to him I was a convert, full of faith and good resolutions.

I spent the two months of my holidays with my family. My mother questioned me about my religion and, discovering that I was profoundly ignorant about it, thought to overcome this by giving me a work of religious instruction from Naples, in three or four volumes, which I was expected to get through during the holidays. This work was enthusiastically accepted by everyone of any repute amongst the Jansenists. The study that I was obliged to devote to it utterly exhausted me; it had thrown me into such a state of mental confusion that only the peace and regularity of life at school, and above all the sweet simplicity of the Fathers' teaching, sufficed to restore my peace of mind. I cannot help thinking that those who maintain that public education nowadays is as religious as it used to be, either never saw for themselves what it used to be like in the period they are referring to, or else have retained a very imperfect memory of it. The religious corporations took greater pains in this respect than the secular colleges, but there was no great difference between them; and even where the ideas of the enlightenment prevailed, the external observances of religion were so much insisted upon that it was impossible to ignore them.

Among my fellow pupils were Molé,[7] D'Étampes, Mézy (who as long as he lived, remained my closest friend), and Arnault, who became a member of the Academy, a morose and peevish youth whose mind in those days was but little developed. No one was more astonished than I when, a few years later, after seeing a performance of *Marius at Minturnae*, I discovered that the author was my one-time school friend. His subsequent career is known to everybody.

Our holidays began on the same date that the Parlement went on vacation. My grandfather used to take me with him,[8] either to Coulans, or to Tubeuf, the home of his oldest friend, Madame Berryer.[9]

Great used to be the delight of the aging Counsellor of the Great Chamber when he got back to his home after long months of hard work. He would bid farewell to his dossiers as gaily as the school-boy did to his dictionaries. After the strenuous labours he faced with such courage, this peaceful, happy existence restored him to the tender pleasures of his family; country life, and his healthy enjoyment of it, reinvigorated his old age by reviving in him the emotions of his youth.

[7] The Chancellor's memory played him false. Molé—if he was referring to Louis-Philippe's future prime minister—was fourteen years younger than he.

[8] Family prophecies are not to be trusted. In a letter to his daughter in 1780 Pasquier's grandfather wrote: 'Étienne is a little too flighty, not sufficiently attentive: I doubt whether it will ever be possible to make him really serious. He will be a likeable fellow; he has a sense of what is right, is not lacking in intelligence and may turn out to be popular in society; but I fear, my dear daughter, that he will never achieve much more than this small success.'

[9] Mme Berryer's husband, who died in 1762, had been Lieutenant of Police, Minister of the Marine and Keeper of the Seals.

The Coulans property, which had been in my family for a long time, is situated three leagues from Le Mans, in a province which at that time still fell within the jurisdiction of the Parlement of Paris,[10] a fact which added considerably to the esteem in which its owners were held. The life led by Parlementaires whose estates were a long way from Paris, and above all a long way from Versailles, was very grand and ensured them the respect of the highest nobility.

The conveyancing of estates and division of inheritances gave rise to much litigation. The influence exerted by the Parlementaires was thus considerable, so that members of the many lower judicial tribunals were only too anxious to pay homage to them. Thus everything contributed to assuring them, if they proved themselves worthy of it, an honourable and enviable existence.

My ancestors had done everything to deserve such a position and, as a result, in the town of Le Mans and the surrounding countryside they had many friends belonging to the most distinguished society of the province. Though Le Mans was far from being an important town its social resources were considerable. Amongst the nobility, the magistrature, the upper bourgeoisie and the land-owners were men of ability, well educated and distinguished, and witty, agreeable women, fond of pleasure and capable of inspiring those around them with similar tastes. It was an easy-going, rather frivolous society, which was regarded by the higher clergy—and this throws considerable light on the morals of those times—with a good deal more than indulgence.

The bishopric of Le Mans was one of the most sought after. The stipend was considerable, the episcopal palace was very fine; and there was a charming country house, situated about a league from the town, that went with it. For many years past the see had been held by well-born prelates, sober men who scrupulously carried out the duties of their holy ministry. When it fell

---

[10] In the eighteenth century the Parlements (there were thirteen provincial ones in addition to that of Paris, but the latter's jurisdiction extended over a great part of the kingdom) were still exercising their original judicial function as the highest of the royal courts. But they were also playing an increasingly political role: as guardians of the fundamental laws of the country, they claimed the right to criticise and even reject laws promulgated by the King or his ministers, as well as an indefinite power of making police regulations. In effect they were aiming at nothing less than a veto on legislation and taxation. They were finally swept away by the Revolution. (Trs.)

vacant during the latter years of the reign of Louis XV, it had been bestowed upon the Abbé Grimaldi, a young ecclesiastic of good family, very attractive in appearance and with a mind as distinguished as his manners. Extremely easy to get along with, he was in addition deeply attached to those whom he honoured by admitting them to his friendship, and he proved this in respect of those whom he chose as members of the cathedral chapter. These were, for the most part, the impoverished younger sons of noble families, who only accepted the restrictions of ecclesiastical life as a means of securing a better position. He had become friendly with them during the years spent at the seminary of Saint-Sulphice, and had promised to send for them as soon as he became a bishop. Having once given this undertaking, he had not hesitated to carry it out, with the result that, when he arrived at Le Mans, he was accompanied by a troupe of Vicars-General, who before long had raised the see to a very different status than it had hitherto enjoyed.

They frequented every kind of social gathering, though choosing for preference those where it was possible to form the most agreeable connections. The Bishop regarded this giddy existence if not with complacency at least with considerable indulgence. In his diocese, pastoral visitations were rare, but long were the visits he paid to those châteaux where he found the society to his taste. Coulans was one of those where he was always glad to stay. His visits began during the period when M. de Maupeou had suppressed the Parlement. My mother's wit infinitely delighted him, and he was always prepared to listen with a good grace to the sermons she unsparingly inflicted upon him.

Monseigneur Grimaldi had been at great pains to improve his country house. He had laid out an English garden, which was certainly the first to be seen in the province, and had transformed the house into a charming dwelling. He left the diocese of Le Mans when he was appointed to the more important see of Noyon, but the Revolution landed him in England, where I believe he ended his days. There he showed himself to be not only punctilious but austere, and strongly disapproved of the priests and those of his fellow bishops who, in 1800, conceived it to be their duty not to refuse help to the government of France.

Le Mans was garrisoned by a regiment of Royal Dragoons, commanded by M. de la Châtre, and its officers were all men of the greatest distinction and brilliance, belonging to the best families; as they were highly patronised by the Court they were all extremely elegant.

M. de la Châtre owned a fine estate not far from Le Mans, and his château at Malicorne, where Mme de la Châtre came to do the honours on a number of occasions, was the centre of society for the whole province—and, one might add, in the words of Corneille, 'the abode of gallantry'. Mme de la Châtre's behaviour was not distinguished by austerity; very much in the fashion, she sought out anyone who could in any way enliven life at the château, and did her best to put up with her separation from one who had given proof of his passionate devotion to her. It is scarcely surprising that before long a succession of quarrels, duels and scandals broke out in this hitherto peaceful neighbourhood, several of which ended in tragedy.

We used to spend the last part of our holidays at Tubeuf, a fine big château, built of brick and surrounded by wide moats, standing in the middle of an extensive park, amongst centuries-old fir trees. Life there was simple, with none of the elegance that was already widespread. The furniture had been magnificent, but was no longer fashionable. I can still remember the armchairs and hangings of yellow satin in the drawing room that had been brought from China forty years previously, and which Mme Berryer had embroidered in silk. As was customary in the past, there were a great many servants; and two or three old footmen were always to be found in the ante-room to the state apartments, occupied in weaving tapestry.

Mme Berryer, the widow of M. Berryer, who had successively occupied a number of important positions (he had even been one of Louis XV's Ministers) was the mother of Mme de Lamoignon. She had an ample fortune, but the extreme delicacy of her health constrained her to follow the most severe regime, so that, though her household was run on a sumptuous scale, she herself lived in the most simple manner. Her life hung by a thread, yet, sustained by an unusual moral energy, she lived on into the early years of the present century. Endowed with a subtle and judicious mind, having spent her life amongst men involved in great affairs, and having in consequence seen and learnt a great deal, she possessed in the highest degree the art of conducting her salon, according everyone his due place while still maintaining her own authority.

8

This society, though certainly rather solemn, did not exclude intelligent and tasteful entertainment. Plays were performed there in a theatre set up in the orangery, and I remember, when I was eleven or twelve years old, taking part in one of these. It was a play which could not possibly have offended the most rigorous tastes, for it had been written by one of the numerous clergy who were under the jurisdiction of the manor of Tubeuf.

Few estates in France had so many benefices at their disposal as Tubeuf, eleven or twelve I believe, several of them richly endowed. The exercise of such an extensive right involved great responsibility, of which Mme Berryer was fully aware. She had therefore taken suitable precautions to lighten her burden by setting up a kind of council to advise her in her choice of candidates, as to whom, moreover, she always had a very good understanding with her bishop.

M. de Lamoignon's[11] large family (he had three sons and four daughters, of whom two at the time I am speaking of were already married) used to spend a few days at Tubeuf each September before returning to Basville (near Limours), where M. de Lamoignon was engaged in ruining himself.

Of his four daughters the third, Mlle Louise, was looked after by her grandmother, Mme Berryer. She was charming, and I still remember, despite the seventy years that have since elapsed, that sweet and candid creature, with whom I used to spend the greater part of the evenings, sitting beside the large harpsichord on which she was practising the exercises of Balbatre, at that time considered to be the outstanding music teacher. It was the education she obtained while she was under her grandmother's wing that instilled into her the self-assurance to which she owed the splendid match that she was soon to make. It was perfectly natural, no doubt, for a de Lamoignon to marry a Molé, but it would not have been easy for a young woman, brought up in the rowdy atmosphere of Basville, to adapt herself to the serious attitude to life that distinguished the Molé's house in Paris and their château at Champlatreux.

I lost my grandfather in the winter of 1783. He was suffering from no diagnosed illness and, on the day of his death, his friend Mme Berryer had left him at one o'clock in the morning, apparently quite unfatigued by their long conversation. Yet an hour later he was dead. God granted him a peaceful end, as

11 Keeper of the Seals in 1787.

9

compensation for all the labour and agitation of his long career. During the last years of Louis XV's reign Parlement had been involved in strenuous struggles which were brought to an end by its suppression under the Ministry of M. de Maupeou and the banishment of all its members.

Having left school I began to read for the bar, though not very assiduously. Like most young men of the time, riding, fencing and learning to dance, seemed to me to be the best use I could make of my time. Now and then Christian de Lamoignon, Monbreton and I would attend the lectures given by Sareste; but we did not lose much through failing to turn up, for the first book he gave us to read, and which he then used to expound to us, was Rousseau's *Social Contract*. This fact gives a good idea of the attitude that prevailed at the time: things had been very different in the days when those brilliant jurists who are the pride of the French bar and magistrature were being trained.[12]

How is it that such an inadequate education managed to produce men, who, in every profession, and especially in the judiciary, where a solid grounding is so imperative, were able to fill the most important positions with brilliant success and in particularly difficult times? The answer is very simple: practical life began much earlier than it does today; one started one's career at an earlier age; one entered the army at fifteen, the navy at fourteen; and yet French naval officers were generally considered to be the best educated in Europe. True, one had to be older to become an engineer, yet, at twenty, officers in the engineers were as well equipped theoretically as they were practically; and the position they occupied in the French army in 1792 proves the truth of this assertion.

One became a member of the judiciary at twenty; at twenty-five one was entitled to take part in discussion in Parlement. The rules that were observed by the Parlements were also applicable in the lower courts, and one knows how many of these there were; and it was the same in the Audit Office, the Board of Excise and so on. Throughout the administration properly so-called, that is to say in all the departments directly concerned

---

[12] Many positions in the judiciary could, in the eighteenth century, be bought. In some families, such as the Pasquiers, membership of Parlement was more or less hereditary: both the father and grandfather of Pasquier were Presidents of the Parlement of Paris. (Trs.)

with finance, no rule was laid down as to age, and generally speaking the candidates were extremely youthful. Since those who wished to enter the various professions were so young, it was of course impossible to subject them to the severe conditions of admission that we demand today of men who have often continued their studies to the age of twenty-one or twenty-three. Was this a good or a bad thing? As regards military service, whether in the army or navy, as I have already said, French officers were from the scientific point of view superior to those of any other nation. Nevertheless, they did not know a tenth part of what those who have passed through our military academies know today. There is good reason to suppose that Vauban himself would have been unable to pass the examination which any student aspiring to enter the Polytechnique has to take today.

Most people would agree that there are certain technical aspects of knowledge that can only be acquired at school. But this is not everything; other moral and physical qualities are necessary, and these have to be acquired elsewhere. Indeed, there are two kinds of education, one of which follows the other. The first is the product of classical or specialised studies; but, after that, comes the other, which depends upon the kind of society in which a young man lives when he leaves school, upon the examples, impressions and traditions that he there acquires. Today, this second education has lost most of its value and effectiveness. The young man who does not take part in social life until he is twenty-two or twenty-three is convinced that he has nothing more to learn; more often than not he has an overweening self-confidence and a profound contempt for those who do not share the ideas and opinions he has already formed.

Under the old regime it was quite otherwise. Though young people were admitted to society at a much earlier age, they entered it with considerable diffidence, conscious of their own inadequacy. Moreover, the world in which they had to make their way was a world of intelligent and distinguished people, and was firmly based upon an immutable hierarchy, hallowed by time, into which one was born and in which one had to live and die.

Consider, for instance, the society to which I was admitted at the age of seventeen, that of the magistrature, in which the Parlement of Paris occupied such an important position. Despite the influence that the outlook of the eighteenth century had already begun to exert, its way of life still preserved a certain gravity, combined in a good many families with a studied elegance, in all with a lively taste for the pleasures of the mind, and in some with an extensive knowledge of the most advanced sciences. Thus Parlement included such men as President Bochart de Saron, who devoted all his spare time, and not without considerable success, to astronomical research; or M. Dionis du Séjour, who, in his knowledge of the most advanced aspects of geometry, was not far behind d'Alembert. Poetry, too, had its addicts: M. Ferrand wrote tragedies, and M. de Favières amused himself by producing comic operas, though he did not actually put his name to them; *Paul et Virginie* was one of his works.

Thus, some thirty salons were open to me where I could count upon hearing agreeable and substantial conversation, which was all the more attractive since it was between people accustomed to meeting one another and exchanging ideas. Very large gatherings were unusual; as a rule they did not exceed more than thirty or forty people. Once admitted to these circles I was conscious of my ignorance, and was determined to overcome it. It was then that I acquired the taste for sustained and careful reading, which has never left me since.

I attended the lectures at the Lycée which had just been opened. The lecturers were M. de la Harpe, M. de Fourcroy, M. Garat and M. de Parcieux, most of them, that is to say, men of established reputation in science or literature. The cream of Paris society attended their courses with enthusiasm, for they derived from them not only basic personal education, but also the rudiments of conversation. Today, it would be difficult to conceive of such an intellectual movement.

Until 1788, politics played a very small part in it, but new works, plays, the most serious as well as quite frivolous books, were continually kept under review. They were the object of criticism and controversy to which the most active minds devoted all their resources. I can remember as if it were yesterday the day when *Le Voyage du jeune Anacharsis*[13] first appeared; for a whole winter it was to be the principal subject of discussion, and indeed it would have been hard to find a more agreeable one.

[13] Published in 1788 by the Abbé Barthélemy (1716–95), author of a number of learned works on antiquarian subjects, of which this was the most important. His *Mémoires* appeared posthumously in 1824.

For me this second, social, education, the importance of which I have already stressed, began as soon as I returned to my home. There, not a day passed when some discussion did not spring up, either during or after dinner, between my father and some of his friends or colleagues, with reference to the business that had been transacted during the morning at the Palais de Justice, either in the public hearings or in the Great Chamber. In the course of these conversations all the pros and cons were discussed, and the merits of the barristers, solicitors and judgements were canvassed. This training made a deep impression on one who was capable of appreciating its value, and who was determined one day to be able to play his part. Moreover, once one was admitted to the Parlement, though it was five years before one was entitled to speak and vote, it was of the greatest value to be able to be present during the debates, for it was this novitiate that completed the second education whose importance I am so concerned to demonstrate.

I was admitted as Counsellor to the Parlement of Paris in my twentieth year.[14] In 1787, almost every outstanding member of the peerage, almost all those in whom the glamour of this great honour was enhanced by that of a cultured and distinguished mind, came out openly in Parlement in favour of resistance. Nor shall I ever forget how powerfully the minds of the younger magistrates were influenced by the thought of following such distinguished guides. We suddenly found ourselves involved with these great names and lordly existences by the ties of party; and everyone knows how party spirit draws men together and even obliterates social distinctions. This alluring and unaccustomed intimacy easily turned our heads, and it did not need much to win us over: a friendly word, a readiness to display interest in our point of view, soon disposed of any difficulties, so that when we got home our minds were still alight with the memory of all that had happened during the meeting. There were about twenty of us who regularly used to dine together after these meetings, usually at the home of our colleague, de Trudaine, who was later beheaded.

Those who were more adroit than the others, or held more

[14] In January 1787, a few weeks before the opening of the Assembly of Notables summoned by Calonne (1734–1802) who, in 1783, had succeeded Turgot and Necker as Controller General of Finance.

advanced opinions, were on the look-out to exploit our enthusiasm. Thus it was at one of these dinners, at which M. d'Épréménil was present, that the Abbé Sabattier,[15] who was closely associated with the Duc d'Orléans, for the first time uttered the words 'States General'. At first they amazed us, but it was not long before everyone was using them. A few days later, when they were repeated in open session, they got a mixed reception, though there was perhaps no part of the chamber where they caused less astonishment than among the peers. The more sober minded members of Parlement, however, were disturbed by them, and I shall never forget what one of these elderly magistrates said to me on that occasion. Noticing my excitement as he happened to pass behind my seat, he stopped and said: 'Young man, a similar idea was often put forward in your grandfather's time. And this is what he always used to say: "Gentlemen, this is no child's play: the day the States General are convoked, that day France will have taken the first step towards a terrible revolution".'

This warning, and many others which were given us by men whose opinion carried some weight, caused a considerable number of us to hesitate. Most of us, however, were carried away by the mistaken advice of a talented man, who, on this occasion, made the first of a whole series of blunders. This was M. Ferrand. He was a good speaker and he was esteemed and influential; and it was he who usually drafted our remonstrances. He thought that if he could show how much the significance of Parlement would necessarily be diminished by the summoning of the States General, the demand for the latter would be rejected. But this idea, which might have made some impression on a few calm and sober minds, if he had taken them on one side and presented it to them skilfully, produced on the bulk of the Assembly a quite opposite effect to the one he had intended. For once it was clear that our own interests were at stake, we could imagine nothing more splendid than to sacrifice them to what we regarded as the public weal. We were so completely engrossed by our generous sentiments that nothing could hold us back. From that day I began to study the behaviour of large assemblies. I

---

[15] Sabatier, not Sabattier, de Cabre. It was in effect this Abbé, 'a witty buffoon of dubious reputation', who, on 9 July 1787, moved a resolution in the Parlement supported by twenty-five votes, in favour of a meeting of the States General. Cf. Jean Egret: *La Pré-Révolution*, Paris, 1962.

was struck by this particular feature, and I have remembered it more than once since then.

'Thus Parlement demanded the summoning of the States General, and declared itself to be disqualified from voting on taxation. . . . It was at this point that it became deeply involved in public activity and popular favour. . . . Almost all the best educated and most well informed young men in the capital used to surround the place where the meetings of the Chamber were held and applauded those magistrates whom they believed to be most strongly in favour of the views that were then popular.'

I cannot deny that many of us were very susceptible, more susceptible indeed than we should have been, to this applause; and that some of us even sought to encourage it, by passing on information that was, to say the least of it, extremely indiscreet. The result of this was that, while within the hall where the chambers were in session the freedom of speech was restrained within the limits of decency that no member of that gathering would have dared to overstep, it was a very different matter in the adjoining rooms, especially the one known as the 'salle des pas perdus'. There the speeches and resolutions were not merely audacious: they were seditious. However much I may have been carried away by the excitement of those stormy days, I could not help feeling uneasy about the consequences of the spectacle that met my eyes. Passages from Cardinal de Retz's memoirs kept recurring to my mind, and it stuck me forcibly that there was somewhat too close a resemblance between the way we were acting and the Fronde.

One day in particular, when I had been more than usually struck by this resemblance, I was on the point of referring to it in the course of a debate in the chamber just at that moment when, as the custom was, the usher called upon me to speak. My courage failed me, however, and I restricted myself as usual to agreeing with what one of the previous speakers had said. Had I yielded to the impulse I then felt, I should have created a considerable scandal, but as the result of my temerity I should have had the satisfaction, young as I was, of having shown a higher degree of foresight than a considerable number of people more experienced than myself.

However, it is only fair to my colleagues to add that there was not one of them, even amongst those who were most swept off their feet, who would not have been mortally afraid had they happened to remember the Fronde.

The fact is, they allowed themselves to be reassured by the purity of their intentions; moreover, they had that silly belief in progress that was to lead so many people astray; and then, it must be admitted, we were too easy-going, not nearly thoughtful enough. We had all the inexperience resulting from a long period of tranquility, all the heedlessness that springs from the continual pursuit of pleasure, from which even the gravest matters were powerless to distract us: if our mornings were spent at meetings of the chamber, our evenings were devoted to balls or to the opera. There the youngest of us used to meet the most serious minded, the most august and distinguished people. One evening I was accosted by a masked figure, an extremely witty individual, who amused himself by drawing a very piquant comparison between the pleasures of dancing and those of attending the chamber, where he had seen me in the morning. It turned out to be no less a person than Monsieur, later to become Louis XVIII. When in 1815 I had the honour of becoming one of his Ministers, he was pleased to remind me of this episode; yet another proof that His Majesty had one of the best memories of anyone in his kingdom.

The return of Necker and the approaching meeting of the States General led many of the members of the Parlement to ask themselves—rather late in the day—whether they had not gone too far. 'Parlement, having recovered its balance, had a presentiment of approaching revolution, and was anxious not to give the impression that it had in any way contributed to it. I remember quite distinctly our deliberations on that occasion, for they were of a completely different character; no more being carried away by events, no more enthusiasm, no more flights of eloquence. Instead, sober discussion; it seemed as though a dark veil had been drawn over the Assembly.'

I was present at the opening of the States General, and there, despite the majesty with which the royal authority was still surrounded, I watched the Ancien Régime drawing its last breath.

This regime, which came to an end in '89, ought, in my opinion, to be considered from two points of view: the situation in the country as a whole; and the relations between the government and the people. With regard to the first, I am firmly convinced that, at no time since the beginning of the monarchy, had France been happier than she was then. Since the collapse of Law's system the country had experienced no serious disaster. Cardinal de Fleury's long ministry, though certainly not glorious, had been both wise and circumspect, and had recouped the losses and reduced the expenditure incurred during the latter part of Louis XIV's reign. True, since then, one or two campaigns rashly undertaken and even more ineptly conducted had done much to compromise the honour and esteem in which the French army and government were held abroad. Yet though these wars seriously upset the country's finances, it is nevertheless fair to say that the ensuing state of confusion had only involved the fortunes of certain creditors and had not affected the springs of public prosperity; far from this, indeed, for what is known as public administration had made continual progress, and while there may have been no great ministers, the provinces had been governed by a succession of very enlightened and extremely skilful intendants. Communications had been greatly extended and everywhere made easier, and it should not be overlooked that this great boon was principally due to Louis XV's government. Its most important result had been a progressive improvement in agriculture.

Under Louis XVI a further impulse was given to this happy state of progress, which was not held up by the war at sea undertaken on behalf of American independence. Many cotton mills were built; and immense advances were made in the printing of textiles, as well as in the manufacture of leather and steel goods. Moreover, all this progress was considerably assisted by the development of the exact and natural sciences. Chemistry had already begun to show what a valuable contribution it could make to the development of the crafts; and Lavoisier, Berthollet, Fourcroy and their students were making giant strides. The Revolution killed Lavoisier, but those of his colleagues who survived him and rendered such great services to their country had, like him, been educated in the time of Louis XVI. This king had always shown great interest in their work; he also did everything he could to encourage agriculture. He introduced Merino sheep, that valuable breed which has done so much to enrich our farmers and wool merchants, and by establishing experimental farms he made an important contribution to both theory and practice. There was large-scale construction in the capital, and houses were going up in the villages. Streams of foreign visitors poured into Paris, which had attained a level of luxurious elegance never since surpassed.

I have seen the Empire in all its magnificence, and since the Restoration I have watched the almost daily creation of new fortunes, but to my eyes none of this could compare with the splendour of Paris in the years between the peace of 1783 and 1789. Fine houses were being built in the Marais district and in the Ile Saint-Louis; and what is the Faubourg Saint-Germain today compared with what it was then? And for sheer display, for those who can remember a military review or the Longchamp races, or even what the boulevards used to look like, everywhere packed with carriages, drawn by two, four, six horses and all vying with each other in magnificence, does not that leave far behind the stream of coaches and hired carriages, with here and there some elegant equipage, which today fills these same streets?

I am far from shutting my eyes to the real public prosperity that we enjoy today; I know what our campaigns have won; I am aware that what is based upon these solid foundations, even if more modest in appearance, is greatly to be preferred to a more magnificent exterior built upon less secure foundations. I am not one of those who decry the present day. Far from it, I agree that in many respects the results of the Revolution have been beneficial; for instance, the redistribution of land which, though so often criticised, should have the effect, provided it is kept within bounds, of increasing the wealth of the country by bringing affluence to a great many families who have hitherto not enjoyed it. And yet, at the same time, when I examine my mind and conscience as to what the France of 1789 would have been if the Revolution had not broken out, if the ten years of destruction that it engendered had not weighed so heavily on this lovely country, if San Domingo,[16] for example, had continued to pour out its treasures for her, if the progressive improvements referred to above had not been thwarted by great catastrophes, I am still of the opinion that, without revolution, France would at

---

[16] Ceded to France in 1697, by the time of the Revolution it had become one of the most prosperous of France's tropical colonies. It was granted independence on 1 January 1804, and took the name Haiti after a long drawn-out struggle in which the Negro leader, Toussaint l'Ouverture, played a major part. (Trs.)

the present time, have been even richer and more powerful than she is.

It was Rivarol, if I am not mistaken, who said about peoples in the condition I have just described: 'They catch the disease of happiness'. This could not have been better put, but he should have gone on to complete his picture by pointing out that this disease also attacks governments in a no less dangerous manner.

What, then, was the government of France in those days? It was no longer the ancient feudal monarchy, in which the throne, surrounded by its most powerful vassals, held itself utterly aloof from the rest of the nation, and in which the power that emanated from this throne imbued the common people, and even the intermediate classes, with what can only be called superstitious respect; in which the sovereign might well find himself faced with revolt by the most turbulent of his great vassals; in which such revolts, though they might develop into the Ligue or the Fronde, always ended up with treaties to the advantage of those who had inspired the greatest fear, treaties of which the whole expense was borne as a matter of course by the nation and the country.

Richelieu, and after him Louis XIV, had tamed these turbulent vassals and destroyed their feudal powers; the political structure created and maintained by the latter was replaced by one based on ostentation, by a theatrical monarchy, if one may use such a term, in which all greatness was concentrated in the king, who became the cynosure of all eyes. In creating it to fit himself, Louis XIV succeeded in giving it something of his own imposing appearance; despite the reverses at the end of his reign, despite the pettiness revealed in the last years of his life, so great had been his prestige at the beginning that it had certainly not been completely effaced at the time of his death.

During the Regency, and under Louis XV and Louis XVI, royal authority fell into such weak or incompetent hands, above all was subject to so much intrigue at court and even in the boudoir, that it was bound to result in an appreciable weakening in that public esteem which a government depends upon more under a monarchical system than under any other.

It was the administration that produced the country's prosperity, whereas the government, on the contrary, brought about the Revolution to which it was to succumb; yet this government was neither harsh nor provocative. Everything that was not governed by law was so, in fact, by usage and custom. The rights of property were fully respected, and for the vast majority of Frenchmen individual freedom was almost complete; apart, that is to say, from the one serious flaw that, despite continual representations from Parlement, the power of arrest, imprisonment and banishment could still be exercised by the king by means of *lettres de cachet*. During the latter years of Louis XV's reign, abuses of this power had been all the more frequent and repulsive in that it had been exercised not merely to ensure the triumph of this or that religious opinion, in themselves quite unworthy of attention, but even more often to pander to the malicious whims and vendettas of one or other of the king's mistresses, or perhaps even of the ministers who controlled this terrible weapon. Louis XV's death had put an end to this odious scandal. Under Louis XVI, thanks to the efforts of Malesherbes, political prisoners had been released from the jails; and during his reign, until 1787, *lettres de cachet* had been used with such moderation that they tended to be looked upon rather as a violation of principle and an offence against abstract justice than as doing any real harm to society. Moreover, when they were used, it was more often than not only at the request of heads of families in order to put an end to the misconduct of one of their members. For example, the famous Mirabeau was imprisoned at Vincennes at the request of his father.

I cannot, however, refrain from mentioning that, from 1785, there were revolting abuses of this power of arbitrary arrest and detention. M. de Beaumarchais, at a time when his *Figaro* was being triumphantly performed on the stage, was at loggerheads with the deputy chief of police over a preface that he wanted to include in the printed edition; and he was also accused of having written a very witty song in reply to a pastoral letter from the archbishop of Paris. He was arrested by a *lettre de cachet*, and taken to Saint-Lazare.

The Parlement of Paris saw two of its members arrested while it was in open session, and summarily committed to state prisons[17] while some deputies from Brittany, who had come to Paris to

[17] During the 'Royal Session' of 19 November 1787, a procedure halfway between an ordinary session and a *Lit de Justice*, Parlement was forced to register a decree calling for a loan of 420 millions and the summoning of the States General in 1792. On the following day the Duc d'Orléans, who was regarded as leader of the opposition, was exiled to Villers-Cotterets; and two counsellors, Freteau and Sabatier de Cabre, were taken to the fortress of Doullens.

present the demands of their order to the king, similarly found themselves shut up in the Bastille.

It should be recognised, however, that, apart from a few people whose activities were particularly annoying to the government, the rest of the citizens enjoyed complete freedom; they talked, wrote, and behaved with the greatest independence, and even defied authority with impunity. Though the press was not legally free, nevertheless it reported and printed everything with utter temerity, and was encouraged by the most serious-minded people; even by the magistrates who ought to have exercised restraint. They were to be found reading the most dangerous literature, the most prejudicial to all authority. Occasionally, in one of the Parlements, a few of the more zealous and conscientious members would raise some objection, but it would be treated with ridicule and more often than not have no effect. If anyone denies that this was liberty, it must at least be conceded that it was licence.

As to the daily influence of local authorities on the citizens, that exasperating influence from which we have all so often suffered during the last thirty years, it was barely noticeable, almost unknown. What remained of feudal power was now little more than a meaningless word, for it had been merged in that of the crown.

True, there were still financial dues belonging to the owners of feudal estates, but these were only a form of property like any other and could now be owned by commoners as well as nobles. Lords of the manor no longer exercised any personal control over their vassals, except in novels; and almost all that remained to them of their ancient feudal powers was a kind of obligatory paternalism.

As soon as Louis XVI succeeded to the throne he proceeded to get rid of such remnants of these powers as were exorbitant. Thus, between the nobility and the ordinary citizens, as between these citizens and the clergy, only one question still remained at issue: that of pecuniary privileges, and the advantage accruing to the two superior orders through this exemption from the taxation imposed upon the 'third estate'.

The influence of the clergy did not weigh much more heavily on ordinary individuals than that of the nobility; the concessions recently accorded to the Protestants as regards their civil status had encountered no opposition from the ecclesiastical authorities, which goes to show how tolerant they had become. The upper clergy shared in the so-called enlightenment of the century. As for the parish priests who were directly in touch with the common people, they behaved like fathers to them and often devoted the best part of their stipends to their relief.

Where, then, did this passion for reform come from, this insistence upon changing everything, that manifested itself at the end of the eighteenth century? It was due to a great stirring of ideas rather than to any real suffering; there had been so much writing and speechifying on political matters that everything was open to question. In particular, the power of the throne had been attacked, and Louis XVI's court had done little to restore the prestige of royalty, even as regards that outward splendour which is often enough to win obedience from the crowd.

Sceptical and corrupt, the court consisted of the descendants of the noblest families in France, but also of upstarts who had been promoted, not for services rendered, but through favouritism; the pretensions of the latter were in inverse proportion to their deserts, and their insolent arrogance made them hated. Idleness, and the need for money, had led to numerous scandals, which it is scarcely necessary for me to enlarge upon since the memoirs of the times are full of them. Unfortunately, in a country like France, such corruption is never restricted to the court; for a long time past relations between the court of Versailles and Paris had been so intimate that the example of the former was bound to exert a powerful influence on the latter.

How can I describe all the ruination that this public display of insolent luxury brought upon so many families? If I were to start repeating actual anecdotes it would sound as though I were writing a satire. Suffice it to say that, when I first entered society, I was introduced to the legitimate wives of my relations and family friends on much the same footing as to their mistresses, spending Monday evenings with the one and Tuesdays with the other; yet I was only eighteen years old, and came of a family of lawyers.

The spirit of irreligion, disputatious and philosophical, the inexplicable craze for every kind of chimerical utopia, the lowering of moral standards and, above all, the lack of respect for ancient institutions and old family traditions, all contributed to the development of those violent passions which were soon to sweep away for ever the old French society, the *Ancien Régime*.

The convocation of the States General was preceded by popular uprisings, caused unfortunately by the disputes in Parlement, first in Paris, then in other parts of the kingdom; and, for two years they were tolerated by the magistrates who should have put them down. One of the most serious was that which took place in the Faubourg Saint-Antoine, against a paper manufacturer called Réveillon, whose factory was burnt down (in April, 1789). This example of mob violence is worth considering, since it obviously served to suggest the means by which, a little later, the success of the insurrection of 14 July was achieved. I saw it at close quarters; it took Parisian society by surprise, for everyone was away enjoying the races at Vincennes. Immediately people heard what had happened, they all hurried back to Paris, though carefully avoiding the redoubtable Faubourg. But one of the young men I happened to be with insisted upon going that way, and three or four of us were determined not to let him go alone. We were on horseback, and we were lucky to escape from our foolhardy expedition, thanks to the fact that some of the most ragged of the insurgents took it into their heads to climb up behind us. It was entirely due to these strange companions that we managed to reach the boulevard in safety; and there they left us. This riot was obviously not spontaneous; the wretched creatures who took part in it had no idea either what they wanted or what they were doing, and it was clear that their anger had been instigated by others.

I happened to be in the street again at five'oclock that evening, when two or three companies of Swiss Guards and French Guards passed by on their way to the Faubourg; they had three or four cannon with them, and their matches were already alight. They soon put an end to the disorders. This was the first occasion up to then that the military, armed with artillery, had been employed in Paris, and the sight of them produced a tremendous effect; at the time it was scarcely possible to foresee how used to it we were to become. Clearly, at this stage, the French Guards were still loyal, but their loyalty served as a warning to the party working for the Revolution, who realised that the moment had come to undermine the morale of the troops, and everybody knows what this was to lead to.

Such then were the formidable preliminaries to the opening of the States General, and everything seemed to point to most serious difficulties in the immediate future. Indeed, how was it to be expected that men who had been incapable of conducting the country's affairs when they had all the resources of unchallenged authority behind them, would be either more fortunate or more skilful when confronted with an Assembly of twelve hundred members, in which the most conflicting interests and ambitions were soon to come to grips?

The only question upon which they were to find themselves in agreement was the necessity of overthrowing everything that existed. The first illusion to be destroyed was the extent of the influence exercised by Necker. I heard him deliver the voluminous report in which he sought to lay down rules of conduct for the States General and to outline the problems confronting them.[18] Scarcely was the session adjourned than the report was forgotten; no one even referred to it.

[18] He spoke for three hours. Jacques Necker (1732–1804), the Swiss banker who became Director General of Finance to Louis XVI, having been banished in 1787 and again in July 1789, was recalled amidst general acclamation after the fall of the Bastille but, proving unequal to dealing with the crisis, resigned in 1790. He retired to Coppet, his house near Geneva, later to become famous as the home of his daughter, Mme de Staël. (Trs.)

II

The Revolution

1789–1799

THE FALL OF THE BASTILLE AND THE OCTOBER
DAYS – THE EMIGRATION – LOUIS XVI'S WEAK-
NESS – THE FLIGHT TO VARENNES –IMPOTENCE
OF THE ROYALISTS – 10 AUGUST – EXECUTION
OF THE KING – PASQUIER'S MARRIAGE – HIS
FATHER'S EXECUTION – HIS OWN IMPRISON-
MENT – HIS RELEASE – LIFE IN THE COUNTRY
– THE 13 VENDÉMIAIRE – RETURN TO COULANS
AND THEN TO PARIS – ARRIVAL OF BONAPARTE

I was present at the taking of the Bastille;[1] what has been called
the *battle* was not serious; there was not the slightest attempt
at resistance. The fortress contained neither food supplies not
munitions; it was not even necessary to capture it.

The Guards regiment that was responsible for the attack
arrived from the direction of the Rue Saint-Antoine in front of
the main gate, which was protected by a drawbridge. A few
musket shots were fired, to which there was no response; then
four or five cannon shots. Some people maintain that one of
the cannon balls severed the chains of the drawbridge; I certainly
saw nothing of the kind, although I was standing very close to
the point of attack. What I did see quite clearly was the behaviour
of the soldiers, some of whom were pensioners, drawn up on
the platform of the central tower, raising the butts of their
muskets in the air and indicating, by all the means customary
on such occasions, their desire to surrender.

Everyone knows the consequences of this so-called victory,
from which the so-called victors derived so many rewards; the
truth is, this mighty battle did not for a moment frighten the
crowd of spectators who had hurriedly gathered to see the

[1] The most recent book on this question is Jean Mistler's *Le* 14 *Juillet*, Paris,
1963.

result. Amongst them were many very elegant women, who, in order to get there more easily, had left their carriages some distance away.

I was leaning against the end of the fence, on the side facing the Place de la Bastille, that enclosed the garden running along-side Beaumarchais' house, and on which, a few days later, he had the following notice put up: *'This little garden was planted in the first year of liberty'*. Standing beside me was Mlle Contat of the Comédie-Française;[2] we stayed to the end, and I then offered her my arm and took her to her carriage, which was in the Place Royale. As pretty as could be, Mlle Contat had, in addition to the charms of her person and her most remarkable talent, a brilliant wit. The only woman I have known whose shafts and unexpected sallies could rival hers was Mme de Staël.

Two days later, happening to be in the Rue de Richelieu, which was filled by a huge rabble, and not knowing what had attracted the crowd but anxious to escape from it, I almost tripped over the body of M. Foullon lying in the gutter, which I had not seen. The swarm of people had been dragging this corpse about for most of the day, and were now taking a moment's rest. Next day, in the Place de Grève, I watched the arrival of the cabriolet, the hood of which had been removed, containing the unfortunate Berthier, who ten minutes later had ceased to exist. And finally, when the king entered his capital, I followed him from the city gates until he was led into the Hôtel de Ville, protected by a dome of bayonets and drawn swords.

At the opening of the States General I chanced to be with a young man whose name has since become pretty well-known. As a result, we established relations which, later on, came to be of some importance. He was the son of a wealthy merchant from Bourdeaux, called Ducos.[3] In 1791 he became a member of the Legislative Assembly, and later on of the Convention.[4]

[2] Louise Contat, later Mme de Parny, became famous as a result of playing the part of Suzanna in the first performance of Beaumarchais' *Mariage de Figaro*. She was known for her wit. According to Charles de Rémusat, Pasquier 'rather used to imply that he had been Mlle Contat's lover'.

[3] Jean-Francois Ducos, future Deputy for Bordeaux, an ardent Girondin, was guillotined in 1793.

[4] After the National Assembly had adopted the new Constitution based upon the Declaration of the Rights of Man and of the Citizen, which swept away the Ancien Régime and proclaimed a constitutional monarchy, its place was taken

In 1789 he spent some months in Paris, after a long visit to Holland, during which he had taken the opportunity of observing the struggle that eventually led to the triumph of the Orangists over the Republicans. He was very devoted to the defeated party and its principles. I have known few men with such a brilliant mind and lively imagination, and, at the same time, such a friendly disposition.

As a result of this first meeting, and of the fact that we had one or two common acquaintances, we saw each other pretty often during the months between the opening of the Assembly and the 6 October.[5] The events that occurred during this period made much the same impression on both of us. The effect they had upon me was to make me what was then called an *aristocrat*, and, despite his earlier tendencies, they led him to almost the same conclusions; but he went to Bordeaux, where he again associated with men who revived his earlier outlook, so that by the time he got back to Paris he had become what was called a *patriot*.

The general impression that the horrors of the 6 October had left upon my mind was intensified as a result of my being called upon to carry out a very unpleasant duty. The day after the royal family had been dragged off to the Tuileries as prisoners, the Parlement was summoned, according to ancient custom, to wait upon the king and present him with a congratulatory address. Very few members of Parlement were then in Paris, and I happened to be one of the small number of those that the First President had managed to keep with him. The signs of violence that met our eyes, the confusion within the palace, the attendants' dismal air of consternation, the high-handed and triumphant attitude of those who, on the orders of M. de la Fayette, were acting as the palace guard and whose ranks we had to pass through, all this was but a feeble preparation for the heartrending sight that awaited us when we were introduced into the presence of our unhappy sovereigns. It was as though in the course of ten days they had lived through ten years.

by the short-lived Legislative Assembly (1.10.91–29.9.92). This body, however, having no mandate to alter the Constitution, which had become unworkable through the suspension of the king, dissolved itself, but before doing so convoked a National Convention (22.9.92–4.9.97), and substituted universal suffrage for the property qualification. (Trs.).

[5] On the night of 5–6 October, the Parisian *sans-culottes* marched to Versailles, and forced the king to return to Paris. (Trs.)

The king's face bore the stamp of resignation, as though he realised that his misfortunes were not yet at an end. In the queen's grief there was something more steadfast, and more than a hint of indignation. She was sitting with her son on her knees, and, despite the courage of which she had given so many heroic proofs during the past forty-eight hours, one could not help feeling that this son was a safeguard to whom she looked for protection. When she received us it was easy to see from her eyes that she could tell from the expression in our own how deeply the sad felicitations we were there to offer contrasted with what we felt in our hearts, and what it cost us to have to utter the banal phrases, consecrated by the usage of happier days, without being able to say anything else.

The emotion that the scene aroused in me was as profound as it was lasting: all that inclined me intellectually and attracted me emotionally in favour of a wise liberty, subject to the rule of law, faded away before the indignation I experienced in the presence of this pitiful spectacle. Every day, indeed, one saw fresh disasters, new instances of theft and crime; my feelings were deeply hurt, none of the things that I was accustomed to venerate were respected; I was neither sufficiently heedless to try to forget what I saw, nor stoical enough to look upon it as a necessary condition of the high destiny that awaited a regenerated France.

Despite my royalist opinions, a certain pliancy that has always been a part of my character and all too often deserved the reproaches of my friends and relations, enabled me to remain on fairly good terms with a number of people who held quite different opinions. I used to meet a good many of them at a club, known as the Valois,[6] which was perhaps the only one where identity of political outlook was not a strict condition of membership. It was thanks to this that I was rather more inclined to see both sides of the question, that I continually read journals representing all political views, and in this way acquired, during this period, certain lessons in political tolerance, so that eventually I came to realise that it was possible for an intelligent man, provided he had an upright heart and

---

[6] The Valois Club, opened even before the meeting of the States General, was more a fashionable meeting-place than a political club. La Fayette, Talleyrand, Siéyès, Biron, Chamfort and Condorcet all belonged to it.

honest character, to hold different political opinions from myself, without necessarily being a criminal fit for the gallows. It was in those days, too, that I came to hate those coarse, and even offensive, pleasantries, which all too frequently were the delight of many of the other *aristocrats*. I was often able to point out how unfair they were, and I was always aware of the harm they did.

I must also admit that, while remaining fully convinced of the justice of our cause, I could not help recognising that our opponents were better behaved than we were, and cleverer. Many of us took the view (a mistake that I myself did not share) that before things could get better they must first get much worse. This false idea influenced the greater part of the right wing in the Constituent Assembly. I frequently attended its sessions and all too often was able to observe this deplorable fact. Everything, or almost everything, that was done at that time by the party opposed to the Revolution was done on impulse, nothing was properly thought out.

Who, for example, had seriously considered the question of the emigration? Many people have wondered how such an extraordinary decision was ever arrived at: how it could ever have entered the heads of men endowed with ordinary common-sense that there was any advantage to be gained from forsaking all the positions where they could still exercise authority; from abandoning to their enemies the regiments under their command and the government offices they still controlled; from completely surrendering to the arguments of their political opponents the peasants, over whom it was still possible, in many provinces, to exert a useful influence, and amongst whom they still had many friends; and all this in the hope that they would one day be able to return, and win back at the sword's point positions, some of which at least could have been retained without fighting.

Presumably they would have claimed that the peasants had already begun to burn down the châteaux, that the soldiers were mutinying against their officers. But this was not true as regards what has been called the first emigration, at the very least it was as yet by no means general; and, in any case, is danger a good reason for abandoning an important position? And is it not a fact, moreover, that this danger, which to begin with had been serious, had considerably diminished just at the

time when the emigration was attaining its greatest impetus?
What are we to say to all this? Simply this: that the voluntary
emigration of practically the whole nobility of France, of many
of the magistrates, who ought never to resort to arms, in
addition to a large number of women and children, that this
decision, without precedent in the history of our country, was
neither conceived of nor debated as a political measure, but
simply happened by chance; to begin with, some of them
merely followed the royal Princes, who had been forced by
14 July to seek safety outside France; and these then called
upon the others to join them.

To begin with, it was merely a question of a pleasant journey
abroad. Once one was outside France, one could say what one
pleased, and hold any political views without let or hindrance;
there was nothing to prevent one from anathematising the
Revolution, for almost everywhere one met people who were
saying the same thing. At first, only the wealthiest were prepared
to incur the expenses of the journey, and the presence of one or
two brilliant and gracious ladies of the court added to the
attraction of staying in one of several foreign towns situated
near the frontier. Little by little, however, these small groups
increased in size, and some people began to think of making
use of them. A number of men belonging to the entourage of
the Comte d'Artois, who were strongly influenced by M. de
Calonne, conceived the notion that here was an opportunity of
creating for their prince a French kingdom outside France,[7]
which, though it might not provide him with any territory,
would at least supply him with subjects; and that in this way
he would acquire some importance in the eyes of the foreign
powers, which would induce them to support his cause.

The women made a great deal of duty and honour, threatening
to overwhelm those who hung back with ridicule; they even
went as far as derisively sending them *distaffs*, and in general
behaved as though they were disciples of St Bernard preaching
a new crusade, the only difference being that the crusaders of

[7] Calonne never had the idea of 'creating (for the Comte d'Artois) a French
kingdom outside France'. What he was in favour of was the formation of a purely
French army, the arrival of which on national territory would, according to him,
ensure the success of the counter-revolution. In his view the foreign troops
would then be reduced to the role of 'auxiliaries'. Of course neither the Emperor
nor the King of Prussia supported this thesis, which led to the disgrace of the
one-time Comptroller-General of Finances just before the battle of Valmy (1792).

St Bernard were setting out to conquer a foreign country, not to reconquer their own.

Thus, in the years '89, '90 and '91, emigration was for some a question of escaping from danger; for a very small number, a genuine enthusiasm; for many a point of honour, to be accepted without argument; for the great majority, the fashionable thing to do; while for all or nearly all of them it meant hope sustained by the craziest correspondence and the intrigues of a few ambitious men bent upon making their fortunes. Such were the motives that led to this mass emigration, so confident to begin with, so much to be pitied later on, most of whom bore with courage and resignation their misfortunes in foreign lands, although these misfortunes nonetheless continued to weigh heavily upon France and are still a source of uneasiness whose effects she is bound to feel for a long time.

The king blamed his brothers[8] for leaving France and taking with them so many people on whom he should have been able to rely for support. He felt that their behaviour could only increase the suspicions of his enemies and, in consequence, the very pressing dangers that threatened him. There is not the slightest doubt that the emigration was repugnant both to his sense of duty and to his reason. But did he have the strength of mind to express his opposition to it clearly?

The unfortunate facility with which he changed his plans, the contradiction that so often existed between his words and his deeds, were never more glaringly revealed than in the wretched incident of his flight to Varennes [20.6.92]. When he left Paris he had declared that he was not free and could no longer tolerate such an illegal and humiliating position; yet, two months later, he assented to the Constitution without having the courage to insist that, even so, his assent would only be valid provided that at least the semblance of freedom was restored to him. He was unable to take advantage of a situation which would have put his enemies in a most embarrassing position.

During the twenty-four hours after the royal family's departure I saw the effect that this unexpected news produced in Paris. At first no one doubted that the venture would be successful.

---

[8] The Comte de Provence, later restored to the throne as Louis XVIII (1814-24); and the Comte d'Artois, usually known as 'Monsieur', who succeeded him as Charles X and was deposed by the Revolution of 1830. (Trs.)

As the king had a twelve hour start, it was to be assumed that, whatever route he chose to take, measures would have been taken to ensure the safety of his journey; whether, as was generally believed, he intended to cross the frontier, or whether he meant to take up residence in some important town inside the country. On either hypothesis, the people of Paris considered that their position was very critical, since they had always regarded the king's presence in their midst as a guarantee against the danger of revenge by which they were threatened.

In addition to this, almost the whole of the National Guard felt a genuine devotion to the king and his family, having often during the last two years been privileged to see them at close quarters, a privilege still much appreciated by the Parisian middle class. This created considerable difficulties for the men of the Revolution, and they were none too sure of which party to support or whom they could rely upon. The army, too, was a further source of uneasiness for them. With soldiers it takes so little to change their outlook; seeing the king in their midst they might easily become royalists again, and even very ardent royalists.

That day I happened to be dining with the President of the Assembly, M. de Beauharnais, MM. de Barnave, Menou, Lameth and also M. de Saint-Fargeau.[9] They had all come in search of relaxation to a small room adjoining the club referred to above, which was reserved for the use of members and where meals were served by a man called Robert. These gentlemen, having just left the Assembly, wanted to be able to breathe freely, to lay aside for a while the formal role that they had to sustain so long as Parlement was in session; and they felt completely at ease with me and the two or three other members of the club with whom I was dining. Their conversation showed all the signs of utter dejection; they had no idea of where to turn next, and it was all too clear that they were entirely ignorant of which way the king had gone; and I am therefore convinced that M. de La Fayette, with whom they

[9] Louis-Michel Lepeletier, Comte de Saint-Fargeau, was President in the Parlement of Paris in 1789. Elected as the representative of the nobility to the States General, he supported the most advanced ideas and was elected Deputy for the Yonne during the Convention. His forcefulness in demanding the execution of the king probably had some influence on the vote. The day before the execution he was assassinated by a one-time member of the king's bodyguard. The Convention awarded him the honour of being buried in the Pantheon.

1 The riot in Faubourg Saint-Antoine, 28 April 1789

2 Louise Contat   *Anonymous drawing*

were all on intimate terms, knew nothing about it either, and that all the assumptions that have since been built up around this question are without the least foundation.

The only one of these gentlemen whose behaviour surprised me was M. de Saint-Fargeau, *Président à mortier* of the Parlement of Paris, and a Deputy; for it was on this occasion that he first gave vent to the violent feelings of hatred with which his heart was overflowing. Outwardly cold, he had all the overweening arrogance that was typical of his family. He had contributed little to the debates in the chamber, and although he was a very talented speaker I do not remember having ever heard him utter three consecutive sentences. As a Deputy to the States General he had, so long as the three orders remained separate, continued to support the majority of the nobility; that is to say, he had opposed joint meetings of the three orders, the one step essential for the further development of the Revolution. Gradually, however, though still without declaring himself publicly, he had gone over to the majority in the Constituent Assembly, that is to say, to the party which was working for the Revolution, and regularly voted with it. Apart from this silent acquiescence, however, he refused to become involved, and spent most of his evenings at the club, never opening his mouth on any political question but spending all his time playing billiards, at which he lost a great deal of money without turning a hair.

Now, for the first time, he broke silence and, while M. de Beauharnais and M. Menou appeared to be reproaching themselves for not having brought sufficient pressure to bear upon the king and for having in some respects let him down, we heard him, to our great surprise, launch into the most vehement invective against the king and queen. In vain his colleagues sought to calm him, to make him understand that this was a time for wisdom and moderation. But all their efforts were without effect, and we saw him get up from the table and leave the room, apparently in a violent rage. This was the man who later on not only voted for the execution of Louis XVI, but also, through the zeal with which he persuaded others to vote for it, did more than anyone else to ensure that the sentence was carried out. The day after the scene I have just described he recovered his usual phlegm, and appeared to be concerned with nothing in the world but his game of billiards. He remained the same until 10 August 1792. From that time onwards I never met him again.

The suppression of Parlement confronted its members with a serious problem: 'Ought we to break up in silence? . . . At first it was simply a question of some kind of formal farewell from the ancient magistrature of France to the French people. . . . However, as draft succeeded draft, the character of the declaration was modified. Some of us came to the conclusion that a protest would be suitable; was, indeed, essential. . . .' But once the wording of this protest had been agreed, 'we had to decide what was to be done with it'. Pasquier and his father were in favour of making it public. The great majority of their colleagues, however, were of the opposite opinion, and it was decided that it should be kept secret. M. de Rosambo, the son-in-law of Malesherbes, 'was made responsible for its safety'.

This was Pasquier's one positive action in the months following the king's return. A conversation with the Girondins, particularly Vergniaud, to whom his friend Ducos had introduced him, convinced him that 'we were destined to experience dangers of a quite different kind from those we had had to put up with for the past three years'.

Events were to justify his fears.

It was expected that 14 July, the time when the Federation was annually celebrated, would be a day of crises, but this proved to be a mistake; there were still some preparations to be made, and the catastrophe was adjourned.

I was present at this Federation.[10] Quite by chance, as soon as I arrived, I happened to meet the beautiful Mme de Fontenay, later to become famous as Mme Tallien. At that time she shared all my fears with regard to the present, all my anxieties about the future. I have often recalled this meeting and the friendly footing we then found ourselves on, for very shortly afterwards we were destined to take quite different roads; hers was to lead her through the dungeons of the Terror, and by way of affairs with Tallien, Barras and Ouvrard to her eventual marriage with the Prince de Chimay. Whatever may be said about her

[10] The original 'Federations', in which the National Guards of neighbouring districts had met to swear mutual friendship and obedience to the decrees of the Assembly, had originally developed spontaneously in 1789. In the following year the Assembly decreed a general Federation of the whole of France to be celebrated annually in the Champs-de-Mars on 14 July. (Trs.)

private life, no one who had an opportunity of knowing her well would dream of denying her, in addition to the homage due to her beauty, a sincere tribute of esteem for her kindness of heart and the happiness she continually found in helping others under the most difficult and dangerous circumstances.

Such, then, was the company in which, for the last time, I saw Louis XVI, standing before the altar of his country and swearing loyalty to the Constitution. I can still see Panis and Sergent[11] wearing their tricolour sashes as they rode on horseback across the Champ-de-Mars. They were more powerful than their sovereign, and it was only for them that the crowd of *sans-culottes*, with 'Long live Pétion!' scrawled across their hats, were prepared to make way respectfully.

The Federation, as well as the king, swore to observe the Constitution, yet only three days later a group of them appeared at the bar of the Assembly, boldly demanding the suspension of executive authority as represented in the king's person. They also demanded the arraignment of La Fayette, the punishment of the Directorate of the Department of the Seine and the restoration of the judiciary. To all these demands the President, M. de Vaublanc, merely replied that they must not despair of the public welfare.

Similar measures were repeated during the next few days, and in the end it became so clear that the factionalists had won the day, that the members of the Directory of the Department of the Seine, the only administrative authority in the capital that was not under their control, felt obliged to resign. M. Roederer, the attorney-general, remained at his post.

At this time, massacres took place in several towns in Provence, particularly at Arles, and the leaders went unpunished. They were a warning that that famous battalion, the *Marseillais*, which was to play such a decisive part on 10 August, was about to arrive in Paris. Never perhaps has any party embarked upon a policy of savage destruction so openly and audaciously.

[11] Étienne Jean Panis was one of the leaders of the uprisings in Paris on 20 June and 10 August, 1792. The first of these had led to the invasion of the Tuileries by the people; the second, under the leadership of Robespierre and Danton, paved the way for the execution of Louis XVI. Panis also took part in the September massacres of the same year. Antoine François Sergent-Marceau was Secretary to the left-wing Jacobin Society which, after the setting up of the Republic in 1792, included in its title the words: 'Friends of Liberty and Equality'. Pétion was the republican Mayor of Paris, in succession to Bailly. (Trs.)

No more theories, no more idle talk, but everything straight to the point. They were impatient to get on with the job; they said so frankly; and action followed hard upon the heels of threats.

And what about those who should have been keeping them in check? How did they deal with all this bold activity? What kind of resistance did they put up? Alas, they continued to live in a state of complete illusion. During these last months I saw our poor queen at the Opéra, at the Comédie Italienne, hailed by the acclamations of a fashionable crowd, vying with one another to offer her consolation. I heard their rapturous applause when Meunier and Mme Dugazon sang the duet from the opera *Unforeseen Events*, which ends with the words: 'Oh, how I love my master! Oh, how I love my mistress!' And when they got back to the Tuileries they hastened to assure her that what she had just been listening to was a true expression of her subjects' feelings.

The more serious-minded and intelligent of them lost precious time in obscure and futile intrigues, seeking to win over some of the Deputies by bribery. Because they had unexpectedly managed to escape on 20 June, they seemed to think that provided they remained on their guard they had practically nothing further to fear. Many of them, moreover, were mad enough to think that they only had a difficult period to get through, and expected the help promised by the Duke of Brunswick to arrive shortly: all that was needed, they said, was a little patience!

At the same time, however, they continued to make courageous and devoted preparations in the event of an attack upon the palace. They had at their disposal part of the regiment of Swiss Guards and one or two battalions of the National Guard, whose loyalty was doubtful. In addition to these obvious means of defence, they could count upon the zeal of a considerable body of devoted men, who had been allowed to enter the palace and who were firmly resolved to sacrifice their lives to protect the royal family.

I myself, as well as the Prince de Saint-Mauris, intended to take our place amongst these latter and, on the morning of 9 August we had written to M. de Champcenetz[12] to ask him

---

[12] The Chevalier de Champcenetz was famous for his collaboration on the *Actes des Apôtres*, a royalist journal, in which the well-known royalist writer, Rivarol, played a major part. He was guillotined on 17 July 1794.

for passes. They did not arrive that evening, and during the night of 9–10 August we made several futile attempts to enter the palace, which by then was already threatened. I note this fact, not for its intrinsic importance, but because of two events connected with it, one of which proved to be fatal, while the other turned out most happily. The pass I had asked for on the ninth, reached me by post two days later when everything was over. What could have made it so late, unless it had been intercepted? And, in that case, why was I not arrested? It was a stroke of luck that I have never been able to explain. It was the Prince de Saint-Mauris, however, who met his fate. His initiative was no more successful than mine, but with this difference: not only did his pass never reach him, but he never heard another word about it. Nevertheless he later lost his head on the scaffold, having been found guilty of taking part in the defence of the Tuileries.

Both of us saw everything that happened. We were present in the Tuileries gardens when the king passed through, yielding to the advice to present himself at the Legislative Assembly and place himself under its protection. Cannon balls were already falling in the gardens as we left them. The struggle did not last long, but it was enough to destroy the oldest and most powerful dynasty in Europe.

As was only to be expected, this event led to the most horrible confusion, the complete collapse of society, which could no longer ensure safety for anyone. No one could feel sure that he would still be alive next day. My own safety was seriously threatened by an imprudence in my dress. On the morning of the 11th, I was foolish enough to leave the house wearing my hair plaited and held up by a comb. I had quite forgotten that this was a distinctive feature of the Swiss Guards' uniform. The result was that I was immediately attacked by a crowd of two or three hundred furious people on the Boulevard de la Madelaine, who flung themselves upon me and, without my being able to get them to listen to me, began dragging me away to the Place Vendôme, where they were hanging from the lamp posts any of the Swiss Guards or other fugitives from the palace that they could find.

I was saved by a young drummer lad from the district who recognised me. It had usually been his job to notify me when it was my turn to go on guard, and since I never used to perform my military duties, I used to pay him very handsomely for taking the trouble to find a substitute for me. He rushed into the midst of the angry mob, managed to obtain silence by beating his drum, then yelled at the top of his voice that I was not a Swiss and gave them my name and address. Thanks to his testimony I was led home in triumph, and as a mark of my gratitude to him I undertook to pay for his equipment so that he could join a company of volunteers.

'The best thing to be done was to escape as quickly as possible from the scene of so much horror.' Thanks to Ducos' help, Pasquier and his family were able to find asylum at Abbeville. Nevertheless they were back in Paris by November. 'I would like it to be known that, as far as lay within our power, both my father and myself contribu°ed to the defence of our unhappy king. . . . Throughout all the debates my father took his place on the tribune reserved for the lawyers defending the king, taking notes and helping them in their task. During this whole period I never left the public seats and corridors of the hall, making enquiries, following up the smallest clues and taking the results to my father, who passed them on to these gentlemen.'

It remains to be said that I was present on 21 January.[13] I was staying in a house that looked out on to the boulevard, at the corner of the new church of the Madeleine. Since early morning my father and I had been sitting opposite one another, sunk in grief and without the strength to utter a word. We knew that the procession was approaching, following the boulevard.

[13] The Duc de Broglie, at that time a young auditor to the Council of State, recalls in his *Mémoires* how, in 1810, Pasquier described to him the execution of Louis XVI. Broadly speaking, what is said here conforms with the account in the Duke's *Mémoires*, although the latter were written twenty years later. 'I watched the fatal cart slowly advancing, I heard the shouts of the mob which was accompanying it. There was a widely spread rumour that before the execution took place an attempt would be made to free the august victim. I did not believe it, but at all events . . . I joined the crowd. Once I was caught up in the stream of people I found it impossible to free myself from it. At first I was swept along, then almost carried, quite close to the scaffold that had been set up at the end of the Champs-Élysées. I could not hear either the words spoken by the King nor what he said to the Abbé Edgeworth; but gazing at the crowd, which was shouting ferociously, it struck me that their faces showed more terror than anger. When the executioner held up the bleeding head for them to see, the whole crowd, which covered the open space between the river and the Garde-Meuble, cried out as one man: "Long live the Nation!" and then dispersed as hurriedly as possible. A few minutes later there was nobody left save the executioner and his assistants.'

Suddenly we heard a loud noise. I rushed out of the house, urged on by the thought that perhaps an attempt was being made to free the king. How could I help hoping for this until the very last moment? I got there; all I could hear was the yelling of the infuriated creatures surrounding the carriage; I found myself hemmed in by the crowd that was following behind, which swept me along as far as the square, setting me down almost opposite the scaffold. Thus it was impossible to avoid the horrifying spectacle. No sooner had the crime been consummated than someone standing at the foot of the scaffold shouted *'Long Live the People!'* and the cry was taken up on every side, and swept through the whole of that vast crowd. The shouting was followed by a deep, dejected silence. Shame, horror, fear were already hovering above the immense open space. I crossed it a second time, borne along by the same wave that had carried me thither. The crowd was walking slowly, scarcely daring to look at one another. The rest of the day was spent in a state of profound stupor, which brooded over the entire city. Twice I had to leave the house, and twice I found the streets silent and almost deserted. The assassins had lost their customary insolence; confronted by the public grief, they were speechless. For the rest of the day they continued to respect it; but the truce was of short duration, and the assassination of M. de Saint-Fargeau, bringing home to them the danger that threatened them personally, soon revived their usual ferocity.

Ten years were to elapse, which Pasquier might have summed up in the words of Sieyès: 'I managed to keep alive.' The greater part of the time he spent in hiding, then a short period in prison, and for the remainder he lived inactively either in Paris or the provinces. Nothing seemed to foreshadow the brilliant destiny that was awaiting him.

'From January (1793) *to May I dragged out a painful existence in Paris'. Returning to Abbeville a few days before* 31 *May, he found a 'fairly safe' refuge there, which he was forced to leave, however, by the arrival of two representatives of the Convention, 'who had been entrusted with the task of ridding the departments that comprised the ancient province of Picardy of the disaffection that was entrenched there'. He returned to the neighbourhood of Paris, and chose the little village of Champagny-sur-Marne as a temporary resting place. Here life was*

complicated by an event which, in retrospect, seems to have bewildered him: he became engaged to Mlle de Saint-Roman, the widow of the Comte de Rochefort. 'When one remembers the events of that time, when one recalls the kind of life we led, the dangers that unceasingly surrounded us and everything that might so easily have broken our hearts and destroyed our spirit, it is difficult to understand how it was possible to think of anything else, how one could have dared to get married.' His boldness, however, was crowned with success, despite the fact that in connection with this event Pasquier found it necessary to return to Paris. The civil ceremony took place at the Hôtel de Ville, 'the church's blessing was bestowed (at Passy, in the house of M. and Mme Pasquier) by the Abbé Salamon . . . who had secretly been invested by the court of Rome with the rank of Nuncio'. Then 'I remained at Champagny with my wife, concealing our modest happiness as best we could'.

In January 1794, the secret protest of the Parlement of Paris fell into the hands of the Committee of Public Safety. Orders were given to arrest the secretaries, of whom Pasquier's father was one. His reaction was unexpected. 'Scarcely had he arrived at the prison to which he had been allocated, than he experienced a feeling of relief which, better than any words of mine could do, expresses the horror of the life to which we had been condemned for the past year.' 'The effect these impressions made on his mind was so powerful that, after a few days, having found a means of getting a letter to me, he urged me to consider the position I was in, and to ask myself whether the life I was leading. . . . was not a hundred times worse than his. . . .' In short, he invited his son to join him in prison, and promised to reserve a room for him. . . . The future Chancellor was not to be tempted, however. 'I resisted, and shortly afterwards left the village of Champagny. With my wife I found another refuge, at Montgé, ten leagues from Paris, near Juilly . . .'

A few weeks of peace, then the first warning. Every three months Pasquier had to apply for a certificate of residence, which spared his father the additional danger of being accused of having an emigré son. To obtain one of these, he had to go to Paris. There he experienced nothing but difficulties. The first time he was arrested, he was set free thanks to the intervention of a member of the Convention, Levasseur, whom his family had known before the Revolution when he was practising as a surgeon at Le Mans. But this man had had the unhappy idea of vouching for the favourable opinion that his friend, the Martyr of Liberty [i.e. Lepeletier de Saint-Fargeau: see footnote 9 to this chapter] had expressed about the young Pasquier. The member of the Revolu-

tionary Committee responsible for his arrest, decided to check the truth of this with the 'martyr's' brother. Pasquier trembled, for 'no one was more hostile to me than he'. Luck favoured him, however. The 'very well-spoken woman' who kept house for 'citizen Félix' and looked after his niece, the daughter of the assassinated Fargeau, had also met Pasquier's father and grandfather. She obtained the testimonial he required and he was able to return to Montgé, though in a pretty sorry state! 'I ought here to give some idea of the get-up to which I was reduced, consisting of what was known as a carmagnole, *that is to say a short jacket and trousers of the same material. The material my suit was made of was of the poorest quality, a kind of coarse flannel, or duffle, dark brown in colour and of a very rough texture. As I had spent the last three or four days chasing about the streets in mud and rain, and as moreover I had not had time to pay the slightest attention to my toilet, I was covered in mud up to the knees.' This get-up at least had the advantage that it in no way suggested that he was an 'aristocrat'. But he had also taken a further precaution. When he presented himself at the city gate he was wearing a 'superb policeman's headgear, its soft crown forming a red cap, and its blue brim decorated on one side with a portrait of Marat and on the other with that of the martyr of liberty'.*

'I need scarcely say how happy I was to get back to Montgé, the peacefulness of which contrasted so sharply with the emotional atmosphere of Paris.' Alas! during the Easter holiday, news reached him of his father's execution. 'This was followed by two months of horrible strain. . . . In June I discovered that my hiding-place had been denounced by a servant, who had been dismissed by me eighteen months previously.' The same night Pasquier and his wife left for Picardy. 'For nearly a month I wandered about between Amiens and the frontier, looking for a chance to emigrate; it was the only way I could still hope to escape the dangers that surrounded me.' But all his attempts proved abortive; and, in the end, members of the Revolutionary Committee arrested him, as well as Mme Pasquier, at Amiens. 'They put us in two separate post-chaises and took us back to Paris, each of us having one of these odious individuals sitting beside us. The one to whose lot I fell was a little bandy-legged fellow whose body was as malformed as his soul was perverse.' Providentially they did not reach the Saint-Lazare prison until 8 Thermidor. But despite the execution of Robespierre on 9 Thermidor [27.7.94], it was nearly a month before they were allowed to leave it.[14]

[14] During his imprisonment 'citizen Pasquier' addressed a rather pitiable petition to his accusers. In it, indeed, he unashamedly disavowed his old friends.

Once again they were free. But what were they to do? 'The ending of the Terror . . . did not result in the restoration of my property, which had been confiscated as a result of my father's sentence. As regards my wife's fortune, things were little better, and the depreciation in the price of *assignats made the little that remained to us almost worthless. In this situation, to remain in Paris was out of the question. I found a small house at Croissy, near Saint-Germain, and there we made our home'. There, too, his sister joined them, and was to remain with them permanently.*

The next two years were spent in complete retirement, occasionally interrupted by 'good neighbourly relations . . . with Mme de Beauharnais[15] *. . . whose prodigious good fortune we were far from foreseeing'. 'The 13 Vendémiaire*[16] *upset our peaceful existence. What a day! It was in Paris that the principal movement manifested itself, but the whole of France responded. The Revolution was attacked in its holy of holies . . .' Pasquier was in Paris, hovering between hope and despair. 'It is impossible to say which was the more amazing, the blindness, the negligence or the ineptitude which allowed such an opportunity to go by. By five o'clock in the evening it had been lost; a few cannon shots fired at the steps of Saint-Roch had sufficed to decide the issue. I left at six o'clock, and was able to give my friends at Saint-Germain the first news of the disaster . . .'*

The early days of the Directory[17] *were nevertheless a tranquil period for*

'It is well-known', said this document, 'that he [Pasquier] shared none of the opinions of the former Parlement, that he never signed any protest or decree opposing the Revolution, and that the only connection that he had had with it was through citizen Michel Lepeletier, the "martyr of Liberty" ', i.e. the Comte de Fargeau (*see above*, f.n. 9).

[15] The future Empress, whose first husband, M. de Beauharnais, had been president of the Legislative Assembly at the time of the King's flight to Varennes, had a house next door to the Pasquiers', and 'used to come there once a week to entertain Barras'.

[16] On this day, 5.10.95, a rising against the Convention by the Paris *Sections*, backed by some thirty thousand National Guards, which would have favoured the Royalist cause, was put down by Barras with the assistance of General Bonaparte. (Trs.)

[17] Shortly before its close in October 1795, the Convention sought, under a new Constitution, to set up a regular government. It established a Directory of five members and a Legislative Body composed of two Councils, the Ancients and the Five Hundred, elected on a property suffrage. Two years later, alarmed by the counter-revolutionary majority elected to the two Councils in May, Barras and the two other prominent members of the Directory appealed to the army. By the coup d'état of 18 Fructidor (4.9.97), the elections in forty-nine Departments were quashed by Bonaparte's lieutenant, Augereau. (Trs.)

Pasquier. His house at Coulans, near Le Mans, was restored to him. He set up house there a month before 18 Fructidor. Did he then give vent to his secret feelings? 'Everywhere, even in the park and courtyard, they pointed out to me places where the peasants of the Vendée had been buried, those admirable examples of courage, loyalty and resignation whom history will surely remember'. *When, in its dying agony, the Directory had recourse to a forced loan, accompanied by the arrest of hostages, the future Chancellor felt himself to be in danger, and decided to return to Paris.* 'The more closely one was in touch with the government of the Directory, the better one realised the secret of its weakness.'

'One evening at the theatre, I happened to be sitting next to a box occupied by two very pretty women, both of whom were unknown to me. In the middle of the performance they received a message. I saw a considerable commotion and signs of delight. They disappeared and I soon learnt that they were sisters of Bonaparte, who, as a courier announced, had just disembarked.' *Pasquier and his friends were not over-pleased.* 'We had no great confidence in the views and intentions of the conqueror of Italy, and this was hardly surprising. We had seen him for the first time on 13 Vendémiaire; it was mainly to him that we owed 18 Fructidor and the government which resulted from it.'

Magic of genius! Only eight months later the writer of these words was seeing things in a very different light. 'I saw Bonaparte's return to Paris after the battle of Marengo [June, 1800]; I was in the Tuileries an hour after his arrival, at the very moment when he appeared at the window of his study in response to the acclamations of the crowd. It was one of those fine days at the end of spring. Enthusiasm was at its height, and it was fully deserved.' *After the peace of Amiens [March, 1802], Pasquier returned once more to the Sarthe.* 'The situation had entirely changed, and life there had become as tranquil and happy as it had previously been troubled and painful.' *His inactivity began to weigh upon him and, like many of his friends, he wondered whether the moment had not arrived for him to offer his services to the Consular Government.*

III

The Consulate and the Beginnings of the Empire

1799–1810

REVIVAL OF SOCIETY LIFE – GENERAL PACIFI-
CATION – PASQUIER AND HIS FRIENDS CON-
SIDER OFFERING THEIR SERVICES TO THE
GOVERNMENT – EXECUTION OF THE DUKE OF
ENGHIEN CALLS A HALT TO THIS PROJECT –
AFTER AUSTERLITZ PASQUIER NEVERTHELESS
DECIDES TO ENTER THE ADMINISTRATION –
MAÎTRE DES REQUÊTES IN THE COUNCIL OF
STATE – PORTRAITS OF LEBRUN, CAMBACÉRÈS,
FOUCHÉ, AND TALLEYRAND – DISCUSSION OF
THE DECREE ON JEWS – MISSION OF THE
RHINELAND – ATTORNEY GENERAL TO THE
COUNCIL OF SEALS AND TITLES – EARLY
DOUBTS AS TO THE SOUNDNESS OF THE
IMPERIAL RÉGIME – NAPOLEON HURRIEDLY
LEAVES SPAIN – SCENE WITH TALLEYRAND –
THE DIVORCE – APPOINTED COUNCILLOR OF
STATE

Until the crime of Vincennes,[1] many of us were beginning to
think that it was time for us to emerge from the obscurity and
idleness to which we had been condemned for the past fifteen
years; we realised the danger of allowing power to remain in
unworthy hands. The government had the wisdom and skill to
encourage this point of view.

[1] More than twenty-five pages are devoted to the affair of the Duc d'Enghien,
brother-in-law of the Duc d'Orléans (Philippe Egalité) and the last representative
of the Condé family. Wrongly suspected by Napoleon of being concerned in a
plot against the French revolutionary government, he was arrested, tried by
court martial, and secretly shot at Vincennes (1804). Interesting as Pasquier's
account is, it is here omitted in accordance with the principle that only events in
which Pasquier participated at first-hand should be included.

In the Departments the Prefects had, in general, come to terms with the principal landowners; under the new electoral system, some of the most honourable men had been elected as district chairmen, whatever their antecedents; and, finally, a number of concessions, of little importance in themselves, but sufficient to indicate that the government had different aims from those which had so long predominated, were a powerful inducement to us to adopt the new ways. It was some time before we made up our minds, but we did so in the end.

As chairman of my own district I became a member of the Electoral Assembly at Le Mans, and there I was appointed candidate to the Legislative Body.[2] This was in the autumn prior to the conspiracy. I had therefore gone to Paris, if not fully determined, at least strongly tempted, to get appointed by the Senate as a member of the Legislative Body. I could easily have done this, for I had the support of a number of people, including that of Tronchet, who had been one of Louis XVI's defence counsel. The president of the Legislative Body was M. de Fontanes.[3]

We used to meet one another at various salons where the remnants of French society were once again beginning to associate. For a long time the house of M. de l'Étang, whose fortune had survived the inroads of the Revolution, had been the only one where, even during the worst days, the survivors of the learned and literary world had been able to meet the few foreigners who had had the courage to visit our distracted country. Mme de Pastoret[4] presided over her uncle's salon. She

[2] By the *coup d'état* of 18 Brumaire (9.9.99) Napoleon had taken the decisive step in destroying the Republic. The five-man Directory was replaced by three Consuls, Napoleon himself, Cambacérès and Le Brun, while the Council of Ancients and the popularly elected Council of Five Hundred were gradually replaced by an appointed Senate and the Legislative Body, whose responsibility to a restricted electorate was continually diminished. By the time Napoleon assumed the title of Emperor, by the Senatus Consultum of May 18, 1804, both these bodies had ceased to exercise any effective authority, and Napoleon's power was supreme. (Trs.)

[3] Fontanes, who owed his fortune to his liaison with Eliza Baciocchi, became Chancellor of the University in 1808. Noted for his excessive adulation of the Emperor, at the time of the Restoration in 1814 he did his best to conceal it. Thus, in the address to the army which he drew up on behalf of the Provisional Government, he spoke of Napoleon as: 'this man who is not even a Frenchman...'

[4] The Marquis de Pastoret, at first attracted by revolutionary ideas, had been a Deputy to the Legislative Assembly, where he moved the decree by which the church of Sainte-Geneviève, later the Panthéon, was consecrated 'to the great

had considerable natural intelligence, in spite of a very neglected education, and had enjoyed great success in the rather advanced social circles of her husband and uncle. MM. de Talleyrand, de Montesquieu and de Pange were amongst her most assiduous visitors; she used to say whatever came into her head with such originality that anything was forgiven her. As a faithful disciple of Rousseau, she had for a long time accepted the principles proclaimed by the philosophical school; later, having been admitted to the society of the Duchesse d'Angoulême, the examples of lofty virtue that she there encountered inspired her with feelings of piety which she was to retain until her death.

During the period when I was received by her, her husband, one of the *fructidorisés* deputies, was living abroad. It was at her house that I met M. Cuvier and M. de Humboldt (the latter, just returned from America, used to astonish people by the range of his knowledge and his inexhaustible fluency which, though doubtless to be admired, soon became rather tiring); M. Suard, a very worthy representative of the ancient spirit of the Académie Française; M. de Vaisnes, one of the survivors of the Duc de Choiseul's circle at Chanteloup; as well as Mme de Staël, Mme Cottin,[5] Saint-Lambert and Mme d'Houdetot, Mme de la Briche, and her son-in-law, M. Molé. The latter was then only twenty years old, yet his lofty spirit, which was in complete harmony with his handsome and noble features, was already attracting attention.

The return of the emigrés, interrupted for a time by the 18 Fructidor, had started once again, thanks to the sense of security inspired by the Consular Government. I was able to renew my acquaintance with many society women whom I had known before 1792: the Duchesse de Montmorency, Mme de Caumont, Mme de Contades and the Princesse de Vaudémont, a Montmorency by birth. The Princesse had married a Prince of the house of Lorraine, and was thus related to almost all the ruling families in Europe; passionately fond of society, and easy-going in her choice of people, she was convinced that her noble origins entitled her to indulge her every fantasy. Her salon

men' of the Revolution. He had emigrated in 1793, but returned to France in 1795, and became a member of Napoleon's Senate.

[5] A somewhat forgotten novelist (1770–1807), in whose works, according to the counter-revolutionary writer Michaud, 'one finds throughout a true portrayal of the tenderest and most virtuous characteristics of mankind'.

brought together men of all parties: M. Fouché and M. de Talleyrand, who ensured her political safety, M. de la Valette, aide-de-camp to the Emperor,[6] as well as the most intransigent royalists.

For thirty-five years she was on intimate terms with every distinguished foreigner and all the members of the diplomatic corps; no secret was unknown to her, yet she never betrayed a confidence and never deserted a friend. Her weaknesses, the irregularity of her private life, were those of her times, and did no harm to anyone but herself.

I had occasion to meet Mme de Beaumont when I sold her the lease of the flat I occupied in the rue de Luxembourg. Such were the charms of her person and the superiority of her mind that I quickly became devoted to her. She was the daughter of M. de Montmorin, one of Louis XVI's last ministers. Under the regime of the Terror she had suffered severely: her father, brothers and sisters had all been executed, and she alone of her family survived, living in a cottage near Montbard. When she returned to Paris in the hope of restoring some remnants of her fortune, she soon became the centre of a select social circle. As its most distinguished member I may mention Mme de Vintimille, one of the best informed and wittiest people I have ever met, a woman of the most distinguished and reliable judgement. Her friendship is one of those I most pride myself upon, and none played a greater part in my life. Mme de Saussure often came with Mme de Staël, whose life she wrote with remarkable skill and genuine affection. M. de Fontanes was another of the most frequent visitors, as well as M. Joubert, who lived with Mme de Beaumont in the most touching and devoted intimacy; he was a superior man, broad-minded, with great natural originality yet not the slightest trace of affectation, reserved and never seeking to push himself forward. I should also mention MM. Guéneau de Mussy, Chênedollé and Molé among those who used to visit the rue de Luxembourg almost every evening from seven to eleven. And finally, M. de Chateaubriand, who was to play so great a part in Mme de Beaumont's life.

---

[6] Obviously Pasquier should have written 'aide-de-camp to the First Consul'. La Valette later became Postmaster General. At the beginning of the Second Restoration, having been condemned to death for high treason, he made a famous escape thanks to his wife.

What constituted the great attraction of these gatherings was the attitude of forbearance, the complete freedom, that obtained there; the pleasure of meeting one another made everything run smoothly. We readily forgave one another slight differences, even considerable divergences, of opinion, which we should never have put up with before 1791; all quarrels were forgotten, and there was none of that spite and hostility that were to become so prevalent again under the Empire and the Restoration.

In those days we were spared such scourges, and lived quite unconstrainedly, able to discuss everything under the sun, with no other restraint than the respect that we felt for one another. There was hardly a question that was not mooted in that little circle. We discussed politics at home and abroad, in the past and in the present, the nature and value of different constitutions, the religious needs of the new society; we argued about classical literature and the great masters of the century of Louis XIV, as well as about the literary revival that seemed to be foreshadowed by *Atala* and *Le Génie du Christianisme;* and great was the rivalry between the admirers of Mlle George and those of Mlle Duchesnois.

Though all of us had in one way or another been victims of the Revolution, and though we all regarded it with sincere disapproval, nevertheless, though still attached to the royalist cause, we were beginning to feel that the time was approaching when the disgust and even the aversion that the Revolution had inspired ought to yield to the necessity of aiding and supporting any government that showed itself to be animated by a sincere desire to restore order in France and to encourage a return to those principles which alone enable society to exist.

Could we refuse credit to the Consular Government for its good intentions? We were all more or less prepared to take advantage of the opportunities we should be offered to emerge from our isolation. M. de Chateaubriand accepted the position of First Secretary of the Legation in Cardinal Fesch's embassy in Rome. Mme de Beaumont intended to join him there after a short visit to Mont-Dore, where she hoped the waters might cure the chest complaint from which she was suffering; but she died there a few months later. M. de Fontanes had drawn the First Consul's attention to the merits of M. Molé, and I, for

3 The execution of Louis XVI, 21 January 1793

4 Alexander I, Emperor of All the Russians
Portrait in the Musée de Versailles

my part, had almost made up my mind to follow his advice and take advantage of the interest that both he and M. de Cambacérès had shown in me.

The death of the Duc d'Enghien, however, changed all this.[7]

Yet how to resist indefinitely the intoxication of success? For Pasquier, Austerlitz completed the evolution that Marengo had begun. His administrative career began with his appointment as a member of the Council of State: he was then approaching his forties.

The desire to end my long idleness, which I had first experienced two years earlier but had then been thwarted by that terrible event, now returned to me. Yet I still felt considerable hesitation. I dreaded the objections I should have to put up with from the society I was living in, which included many intolerant people who would find it hard to forgive the step I was proposing to take.[8] Yet there were very strong reasons to be set against their criticism! Were we to forget one of the harshest lessons the Revolution had taught us? Had it not proved that it was only commonsense to overcome our aversion, and to devote all our energies to preventing a repetition of the calamities we had already endured? Was not the best way, perhaps the only one, of achieving this aim, to rally round the government those men whose support would enable it to resist revolutionary ideas? Since the government was prepared for such a reconciliation was it wise to reject its advances? Why should one resist the desire not to waste one's life in complete inactivity, of which we had already seen so many examples?

I went to see M. de Cambacérès again, he undertook to present my request, and I was appointed *Maître des requêtes* to the Council of State when it was first instituted.[9] From that

[7] Chateaubriand, having resigned his position as Minister, was visited next day by the future Chancellor. 'M. Pasquier', he says in his *Mémoires d'outre-tombe,* 'embraced me . . . saying that he was happy to have such a friend as me. He remained for a considerable time in a state of honourable indecision, withdrawn from place or power'.

[8] Forty-six years later Pasquier was still haunted by this question. In a letter to Montalembert in 1852 he said: 'You cannot imagine how worried I was when I took this decision, although I have never repented of doing so. It meant breaking so many ties, even within my own family circle, and I was overwhelmed with every kind of reproach'.

[9] The Council of State, initiated during the Consulate, continued as an important part of the governmental apparatus throughout the Empire, although in an

day a new way of life had begun for me, and, though I had not changed my principles, I inevitably began to see things in a different light. In this respect I have nothing to hide, and in all that follows I shall be as truthful about myself as about others. I may say, however, that once I entered the service of the imperial government, a decision I had only arrived at after mature consideration and because it seemed to me to be reasonable, and of use both to my country and myself, I served that government honestly, with complete loyalty and without any ulterior motive.

The cause of the Bourbons was an unhappy one, but it was the one to which I had first pledged myself; I was attracted to it by my birth, my convictions, the sacrifices I had made, and it was impossible for me to feel anything but the deepest sympathy for it. But I believed that if this cause were again to triumph it could only do so in the very distant future, and as a result of events that it was quite impossible to foresee. Thus the interests of my country seemed clearly to demand that all the means at one's disposal should be employed in ameliorating the existing state of affairs by one's support, and by bringing it into line as far as possible with the principles of sound reason and eternal justice.

Such was the aim I set myself when I became a member of the Emperor's Council of State, and I hope I never knowingly departed from it.

His duties brought Pasquier into touch with a considerable part of the leading personnel. Four men, according to him, 'had free access to the Emperor' and 'exerted some influence on his deliberations', Lebrun, Cambacérès, Talleyrand and Fouché.[10] *The portraits he draws of all*

almost completely advisory capacity. Ministers and Grand Dignitaries were *ipso facto* members, but the bulk of its membership was recruited from administrative and technical experts. Its importance may be judged by the fact that the Emperor himself frequently presided. The *maîtres de requêtes*, a title inherited from the defunct Parlement, constituted a lower grade of membership; if they proved their ability to Napoleon's satisfaction they were promoted Councillors of State. (Trs.)

[10] Since the names of all four men recur frequently in this and the following chapters, a few brief biographical details may be of interest. (1) C. F. Lebrun (1739–1824), financial advisor to Chancellor Maupeou, whose downfall he shared in 1774, after the Revolution became a liberal member of the Constituent Assembly. Following the *coup d'état* of 18 Brumaire, he was appointed Third Consul and played an active part in the financial and administrative reorganisation of the

four of them are regarded as classics, despite the prejudices that certain of their characteristics aroused in him.

The *Arch-Treasurer, Lebrun, 'mild, humane, opposed to all violence, had groaned beneath the evils that followed in the wake of the Revolution . . . ' Yet he 'was devoted to all the philosophical principles of the XVIII century . . . and no one pursued more fervently than he the dream of perfect equality . . . Titles and honorific distinctions seemed to him to be the merest baubles, and he could not refrain from shrugging his shoulders whenever he saw the slightest importance attached to them . . . '*

This meant that *'it would have been difficult to find two men more unlike one another' than Cambacérès and he . . . 'Never has anyone taken such delight in titles, orders and ribands as the Arch-Chancellor. He was enchanted by official display; and in the salons, even in public, he used to bedizen himself as happily as a child with his orders, which were sometimes made of gold, sometimes of pearls, sometimes of diamonds.' 'Despite these puerilities, however, he was certainly the best*

country. After a short period as Arch-Treasurer of the Empire, he reluctantly accepted the title of Duc du Plaisance (Piacenza). Subsequently reconciled to both the First and Second Restorations. (2) J. J. R. Cambacérès (1753–1824), a Deputy to the Convention, where he expressed moderate views and was mainly concerned with the codification of revolutionary legislation, was later one of the candidates for the Directory. He was not elected, but in 1799 was appointed the second of the three Consuls, and did much to ensure to Napoleon the Consulship for life (1802). Arch-Chancellor of the Empire, and President of the Senate in perpetuity, he was created Duc de Parme in 1808, and remained one of Napoleon's most trusted advisors. Having again taken office during the Hundred Days, he played little part in public life after the Restoration. (3) Joseph Fouché (1763–1820), educated for the church, in 1792 was elected Deputy to the National Convention and soon became notorious as one of the fiercest of the Jacobins; yet two years later he was to be one of those responsible for overthrowing Robespierre. Under the Directory, in touch with the communist Baboeuf and then offering his services to the royalists, in 1799 he became Minister of Police for the first time, and supported the *coup d'état* of 18 Brumaire. He was dismissed from office in 1802, only to be recalled two years later, subsequently becoming Duc d'Otrante and Minister of the Interior. The main stages in his later career are described by Pasquier. (4) C. M. de Talleyrand-Périgord (1754–1838). Prior to his appearance in these *Memoirs*, the liberal free-thinking nobleman, whom Louis XVI had reluctantly made a bishop on the eve of the Revolution, associated himself with the left-wing of the National Assembly, and in 1791 entered the sphere of diplomacy. Under the Directory he became Foreign Minister for the first time in July 1797, to which post, after a brief resignation, he was restored by Napoleon in 1799; and later created Prince of Benevento. After the famous scene in 1809, described later in this chapter, he sent in his resignation, which was refused. He played a major part in the Restoration and at the Congress of Vienna; and filled his last diplomatic post, under Louis-Philippe, as French ambassador in London. (Trs.)

mind in the Imperial Council. As a lawyer his knowledge was all the more profound in that, although very extensive, he did not allow it to dominate him exclusively, and it was always controlled by that exquisite sensibility and superior reasoning power which alone make a legislator.'

He was haunted by his past, especially by his extremely complex attitude towards the trial of Louis XVI. *'Bonaparte, it must be admitted, had appointed him as a concession to the Revolutionary party, to the most deeply compromised, the most odious men. Yet, despite such auspices, he was soon to prove, of all the First Consul's advisors, one of the most zealous partisans for a return to the ideas of order and the monarchical principle. . . . In his social relations M. de Cambacérès showed himself to be kindly and helpful insofar as his natural timidity permitted. He was faithful to his friends, quick to overlook an injury but never forgetful of services rendered, and in this respect was greatly superior to his colleague Lebrun who, essentially individualistic and egotistical, hardly spared a thought for anyone but himself and his family.'*

Of Fouché, Pasquier writes with far more acerbity. *'Devoid of any solid education, incapable of consistent thought or sustained application, he would have been quite unsuitable for any position except that of Minister of Police, which relies much more on gossip than on consistent office work. . . . In this respect, Fouché's antecedents gave him all kinds of advantages. I have already said that he had seen everything and known everybody, to which I must add that he had no serious belief in anything whatsoever. Without the slightest affection for anyone, false and perfidious to an extent that has perhaps never been equalled, capable of sacrificing to the least personal interest people who, only the day before, regarded themselves as his friends, possessing to a supreme degree if not the cleverness, at least the impudence, of a born liar, with a frivolous, superficial mind but a happy gift for repartee, and always maintaining the outward appearance of imperturbable sangfroid, it cost him nothing to betray anyone who had any dealings with him, beginning with Bonaparte, although during his first period of office he served him with a fidelity that had every appearance of devotion.'*

Talleyrand is treated even more mercilessly by the future Chancellor. *'It is not easy to draw M. de Talleyrand's portrait. . . . The more one studies his character, the less one understands it. The fact is, it is almost impossible to discover any consistency in his behaviour. In certain respects eminently gifted, it is hard to tell what quality of soul or heart it is possible to accord him. Capable of immoderate desire rather than of violent passion, susceptible to every new impression, he shrank from no means of satisfying his desires and indulging his tastes. There has perhaps never been a man so utterly devoid of delicacy of feeling, so incapable of consistently pursuing a moral ideal; and certainly no one has ever been so completely regardless of public opinion. He continually defied it both in his public and in his private life, in his moral behaviour as well as in his political conduct . . .'*

' . . . I said just now that he was lacking in delicacy of feeling; he had not enough even to make him resent an insult for more than a very short time. . . . His moral personality seemed to be enclosed in a hard, polished skin, which scorn and injury simply skimmed without penetrating it. There was no affront that he was not ready to overlook, provided he could see the slightest advantage in being friendly with the man who should have been the object of his resentment. . . .'

'One cannot help wondering how such a man was able, for so many years, to play such an important part. The reason is that he was lucky enough to appear at precisely the right moment, when everything was in chaos and the whole of society completely disorganised. At any other time, his intelligence, brilliant as it may have been, would probably have won for him no more than the ephemeral success provided by drawing-room life; it would certainly never have put him in the position to manage public affairs in an order of society where solid and conscientious talents, where respect for himself and for the public, would have been the necessary conditions for any great political achievement . . .'

Following these bravura passages, Pasquier goes on to describe his own role in the Council of State.

The first occasion on which the Emperor indicated the confidence he was disposed to accord to his *Maîtres des requêtes* was a discussion relating to the Jews,[11] and the manner in which they conducted themselves in those provinces where they were most numerous. They were accused, not without grounds, of having for several years, especially in Alsace, pushed usury to such a point that, if they had still been in a position to demand the repayment of all their debts, they would have been the owners of most of the land in that province. They had pursued their discreditable and traditional occupation especially among the farming community, and they had been

[11] At that time there were some 77,000 Jews in the Empire, 46,500 of whom lived in the old French kingdom. The latter's right to citizenship had been recognised on 27 September, 1791, subject to their taking the civil oath.

singularly favoured, not only by the difficult times experienced by the small landowners, but above all by the extraordinarily heavy financial burden that a state of continual warfare had imposed upon the Departments along the frontier of the Rhine.

An imperial decree, dated 30 May, 1806, had already suspended for a year the effect of prosecutions brought by these pitiless creditors; but this provisional measure had only been adopted in order to allow time and opportunity for an enquiry into the whole legal position. It was an arbitrary measure because, without any of the interested parties having been heard, all title deeds were regarded as being equally suspect, irrespective of their nature and without any attempt to distinguish between the equitable and inequitable ones, solely on the grounds that they belonged to a particular class of French citizen; for the right to citizenship could not be denied to the Jews. They were entitled to it by legislation that was adopted after the Revolution, and they accepted all the responsibilities involved, including that of military service. True, they did their best to avoid conscription by taking advantage of the fact that, for a long time, no register of their birth had been regularly kept; most of them had managed to avoid making the prescribed declaration to the municipal authorities. In addition to this, the fact that surnames were not used by them was a marvellous excuse when it came to recruiting for the army. But these difficulties had been overcome by the time the Emperor decided to suspend payment of the money owing to them.

In the Council of State this measure led to a lively controversy; the department of the Ministry of the Interior responsible for drafting the decree had expressed considerable dissatisfaction with it, particularly the chairman, M. Regnault de Saint-Jean-d'Angély,[12] who had opposed the proposal as contrary to the principle of civil law and as impairing religious freedom. And, indeed, was it not a manifest violation of this freedom if a citizen, merely because he professed the Jewish faith, could be deprived of certain of the benefits of common law? For M.

---

[12] Regnault de Saint-Jean-d'Angély—who in 1814 was to manifest an ardent though belated zeal for the royalist cause—was highly esteemed by Napoleon. Chaptal gives an amusing explanation of the imperial favour: 'I have seen him (the Emperor) display a great predeliction for Regnault de Saint-Jean-d'Angély because he used to answer all his questions boldly, and would not have been the least embarrassed if he had asked him how many million flies were to be found in Europe in August.'

Regnault, protecting the Jews was not only an act of justice towards them, but also a means of guarding against the pretensions of Catholic priests, whom he especially distrusted.

It so happened that, from a very different point of view, a young auditor, attached to the same Department and responsible for much of the preparatory work, had not hesitated to come out very strongly in favour of the proposed measures against the Jews. The Emperor was not unaware of this, and it had appreciably increased the good opinion that he had expressed with regard to this auditor, none other than M. Molé. The day the debate in the Council began, he paid him the almost unheard of compliment of inviting him to open the discussion, and gave orders for his report to be published. The stay of proceedings was later drawn up in conformity with the views he had put forward, but it was further decreed that an Assembly of Jews living on French territory should be summoned to meet in Paris on 15 July.

The members of this Assembly, to the number laid down in a table annexed to the decree, were to be appointed by the Prefects, and chosen from amongst the rabbis, landowners and other Jews most distinguished for their enlightened outlook and probity. The Emperor was to acquaint the Assembly with his intentions through a Commission especially appointed for the purpose. The members of this Commission would at the same time be responsible for noting any views that might be expressed as to the most expedient way of reviving the practice of the useful arts and crafts among the Jews, thus offering them an opportunity of earning a living by honest industry instead of the discreditable pursuits to which so many of them had devoted themselves, from father to son, for centuries past.

When, later on, the question of appointing the members of this Commission came up, the Emperor's first thought was of M. Molé. This mark of confidence was naturally due to the part that he had already played in the matter; and, indeed, in addition to what I noted above about his report to the Council, the Emperor had also instructed him to prepare a work entitled: *An Enquiry into the Political and Religious Status of the Jews from Moses to the Present Day*. We had not had to wait long for this essay, and it had been printed in full in *Le Moniteur*, where it filled eighteen columns. It amounted to an impeachment of the Jewish people, for it proposed to establish that usury, far from being the result of the misfortunes sustained by the Jewish race, as had too often been assumed, was not only tolerated, but even decreed, by the law of Moses and by the principal scholars who had interpreted it; that the essential purpose of this pre-scription by the Hebrew law-giver had been to effect the complete separation of his people from all other nations; and that, in consequence, the vice of usury must be regarded as inherent in the nature of every true Jew, and so deeply rooted that no power on earth would ever succeed in extirpating it.

The two other members of the Commission were chosen from the *Maîtres des requêtes:* M. Portalis,[13] son of the Minister of Public Worship, was the second, and myself the third. When we came to consider our instructions, we felt convinced (I am speaking for M. Portalis and myself) that they failed to express the Emperor's thoughts on the subject adequately, and that these had escaped M. Molé[14] and the Council of State; that he clearly intended that, from what had at first been regarded merely as a compulsory measure, there should now emerge a great political act. Indeed, according to the documents sub-mitted to us, what was involved was nothing less than to ascertain from the Jews themselves whether their religion did in fact permit them to accept the status of citizen in the one country that was prepared to welcome them as such; whether their religion contained any prescriptions which would make complete submission to the laws impossible, or at least very difficult, for them; and whether it would eventually be possible to use, for the benefit of society as a whole, the fortune, industry and talents of a people who, hitherto, had remained in a state of manifest hostility.

Looking at things from this point of view, it was necessary to get the Jews to undertake a serious examination, firstly to discover what they believed to be permissible, and secondly to find out what they believed to be forbidden. Was it a fact that

[13] The son of Jean-Marie Portalis (1746–1807), who played a major part in the drafting of the Code Civil and in preparing the Concordat during the Consulate.

[14] Molé was only twenty-five years of age (*see also* footnote 12, Ch. VII). In his *Mémoires* he makes the following comment on his two colleagues: 'One of them, Portalis, consoled himself by attributing the imperial favour that I seemed to enjoy to the name I had inherited; the other, full of ambition and self-esteem, awaited uncomplainingly the chance of making himself known to his master, and already saw himself as a Councillor of State.'

the law of Moses allowed Jews to practise usury with anyone who did not profess their faith? Could they forego this right in those countries where usury was forbidden by law? Could their doctors and rabbis guarantee obedience on this point? Was military service compatible with several of their religious observances, like that of the Sabbath, for example, or of certain fasts and the prohibition of certain kinds of foods? Could one feel satisfied that they would honestly consent to take their place in the French army, whenever they were called upon to do so by law?

These two difficulties were the principal ones that had to be resolved, and they give some idea of how much the Emperor hoped to derive from an Assembly which would be without precedent in the annals of the world since the dispersion of the tribes after the capture of Jerusalem and the destruction of the temple by Titus. This Assembly, which took place almost unnoticed, was in reality a noble conception, and if its results did not adequately correspond to the idea that had inspired it, if it left behind but small trace of its existence, this must be mainly attributed to the rapid succession of events which absorbed public attention. And yet it was a most interesting experience to listen to these discussions between men ardently devoted to a religion of whose true spirit so little is known, inspired by feelings so different from those of the men responsible for conducting the affairs of Christian peoples. They had been asked to examine seriously how far they were capable of surmounting their most deeply rooted habits, of taking their place in the modern world and participating, without betraying their conscience, in the benefits of European civilisation.

I therefore undertook with the greatest enthusiasm the quite unexpected responsibilities that had been entrusted to me. Even now, as I write these lines, the memory of taking this first step towards an understanding of major human affairs is still full of interest for me. In undertaking this enterprise, Napoleon was certainly inspired by a conqueror's policy. By trying to discover, with the assistance of all that was most enlightened in the Jewish race, how best to help them emerge from the abject condition in which they had languished for so many centuries, he probably considered that he would in this way be associating all the members of this race with his own fortunes, so that in every country through which they were scattered he would find allies prepared to support his plans. He was about to embark upon a new invasion of Germany, which would take him across Poland and into the neighbouring countries, where business was at that time carried on almost exclusively through the agency of the Jews; it was therefore natural to suppose that no allies could be more useful than they, and consequently, more essential to win over.

This certainly was his attitude towards the question at the time when he issued the imperial decree which, in the course of the year 1808,[15] provided legal status for the religious organisation of the Jews and the exercise of their civil and political rights throughout the whole extent of the empire. But before long the victorious general came to believe that, standing at the head of the French army and nation, he needed no other ally than his sword, and that this would enable him to dispose of the fate of Europe from the banks of the Neva to the columns of Hercules. The question of the Jews, therefore, lost interest for him.

M. Molé, as the first member of the Commission to be appointed, was elected chairman without a vote. The speech he delivered at the opening of the Assembly on 29 July was very hostile to the Jews and certainly gave them no cause to feel any confidence in the government's intentions. The choice of members of the Assembly, of whom there were 112, had been entrusted, as I have said, to the Prefects of those Departments in which the number of Jews were sufficient to make them of some real importance. First among these were the Departments of the East, of the Midi, especially that of which Avignon was the capital, then the department of the Seine, and after that of the Gironde. As was to be expected, the Prefects had chosen the Israelites held in the highest esteem, and also those they assumed to be the most accommodating. It was chiefly amongst those from Bourdeaux that it was hoped to find both the most enlightened and those whose influence could be used with the greatest safety. These Jews, usually known as 'Portuguese

---

[15] Three decrees adopted on 17 March drew up rules for opening synagogues, appointed consistory courts to draw up the order of worship, made it obligatory for Jews to choose their first name from the list drawn up for Christians, forebade them to adopt any surname 'taken from the Old Testament or from the name of a town', and imposed many restrictions on the recovery of debts by Jews. Generally speaking, the State recognised the Jewish religion, but made no contribution to the payment of the rabbis.

Jews', were reputed to be descended from the large Jewish colony established for centuries near the mouth of the Tagus.

One of the most outstanding personalities was M. Furtado, a highly esteemed merchant from the Gironde; he was chosen to preside over the Assembly. It soon became clear that the Portuguese Jews were suspect in the eyes of all their co-religionists, who regarded them as apostates. The chairman, Furtado, was especially open to suspicion. They seemed to think that he only maintained his religious beliefs from that feeling of human respect, which prevents people from forsaking the faith into which they are born except in those cases where they are carried away by the strongest of convictions. Now this was not M. Furtado's outlook; the basis of his opinions was a philosophical scepticism. The rabbis from Alsace and those from the ancient county of Avignon, who were held to be the most learned, said of their president that it was easy to see he had only studied the Bible in the writings of Voltaire. In a gathering of men inspired by the deepest religious conviction his influence was negligible. It was generally supposed that they were solely concerned with their financial interests, only supporting their religion by force of habit, and, above all, because it offered a sop to their conscience for living at the expense of those countries that were prepared to admit them and put up with them. We found ourselves confronted by men very superior to the rabble with whom they were generally confused. Educated with the utmost care in the principles of their religion, their attachment to it was strengthened by the censure that it attracted; no aspect of human knowledge was foreign to their highly cultivated minds. It was thus no longer permissible to disregard the existence of a Jewish nation, only the dregs of which had hitherto been seen, when, thanks to the care that had been taken in choosing the members of the Assembly, they spoke a language that deserved to be heard.

The questions posed by the Emperor were considered with the most careful deliberation. Their slowness could not fail to displease him, and it was the occasion of very lively remonstrances on the part of M. Molé. This was going directly against the aim that we should have set ourselves. One fact, which concerned the latter personally, served to increase the horror which his manner of speaking inspired in those it was his mission to win over. It was pretty generally regarded as a fact that his great-grandmother, the daughter of Samuel Bernard, a well-known financier at the end of Louis XIV's reign, was a Jewess by birth, and there could be little doubt that the great fortune which his family enjoyed came almost entirely from this marriage. As a matter of fact, however, he himself claimed that Samuel Bernard's Jewish origin was a pure fiction, based on the choice of a Christian name more usually found among Jews than among Christians.

After several weeks, we were still more or less where we started from. Apart from the difficulties of the question, and though on almost every point they appreciated the justice of the proposals that were put to them, the most enlightened and influential members of the Assembly told us that the declarations they were being asked to make were not only embarrassing for them, since they involved delicate questions of conscience, but that from what they could see they would also be completely useless; that they were in no position to command obedience from their co-religionists; and, since they had been selected by the government, it was impossible to regard them as being representative of the Jewish nation with the right to act in their name. Several times they had referred to the ancient gathering of rabbis known as the Grand Sanhedrin. This Council, they said, would alone have had the right to pronounce on such matters in the days when the Jewish people existed as a nation, and it would still be the only one qualified to discuss them.

When the members of the Commission reported these comments to the Emperor, he immediately seized upon the idea, and it soon became known that he was very much inclined to authorise the convocation of a Grand Sanhedrin in Paris, constituted as far as possible according to the rules and forms laid down by the Mosaic law. What he had in mind was that all the synagogues throughout his vast territories, and even in Europe, should be invited to send either learned men qualified to take part in this Sanhedrin, or deputies who could join the already existing Assembly, whose labours would run parallel to those of the learned gathering; in this way, he said, they would be satisfied that they were ensuring the most legal representation of both the Jewish religion and the Jewish nation; it would be seen as a resurrection of their nation; and its members certainly would not fail to recognise how important it was for them to prove themselves worthy of so great a boon.

Conferences were arranged to prepare the questions to be submitted to the Grand Sanhedrin, and their meetings were long and frequent. In them, a huge number of questions was raised, religious, historical and political, on which many of the rabbis displayed very extensive learning, and, sometimes even, on matters touching their faith, an eloquence full of fire and inspiration. The attitude displayed by the members of the Commission remained the same as previously: M. Molé continuing to threaten; M. Portalis and I striving to win over, by more conciliatory methods, those whom our impetuous colleague incessantly exasperated. M. Portalis shone in these discussions, displaying that wise erudition, supported by the best authorities and full of good faith, of which he has since given such ample proof. The impression this made on those he was concerned to convince was all the greater, in that his position as son of the Minister of Public Worship added weight to his words; while the Commission was, in general, considerably impressed by my obvious desire to ensure that our debates achieved a genuinely useful result.

On one occasion their gratitude to me was so marked that I find it hard to forget it. It was after one of those conferences in which M. Molé had been even more bitter than usual, and I had done my best to dispel the harmful effect of some of the things he had said. Next day several of them sought me out and, not knowing how to express their thanks, ended by assuring me that, before six months were out, even their brothers in China would know that all Jews should be grateful to me for what I was striving to do for them and for my admirable attitude towards them.

These words have always struck me as being most remarkable, in that they show the extent to which these men, scattered at such great distances over the surface of the world, living in such different climates and in the midst of such dissimilar societies, maintain relations with one another, identify themselves with each other's interests and are animated by the same outlook. In truth, if one compares the results of all the legislative systems, ancient and modern, with those of the Mosaic law, one is struck with amazement when one realises how great must have been the strength of the political and religious bonds with which Moses succeeded in uniting his people, since even their dispersion twenty centuries ago has not succeeded in breaking them.

It was especially in the discussions relating to usury that uniformity of Jewish beliefs was most strikingly manifested. On this issue the views of the doctors and rabbis were never for a moment in doubt: contrary to the opinion put forward in M. Molé's memoir, they were all agreed in regarding the supposition that usury practised upon foreign peoples was authorised by the law of Moses as an undeserved insult.

'Usury', they say, 'arose amongst us as a result of our unfortunate position in the world, of the necessity to which we have been reduced, since the dispersion, of having almost always had to struggle to save the remnants of a fortune that others have ceaselessly striven to despoil us of. In this state of continual warfare against society, we naturally sought to save whatever we could obtain from our persecutors and to profit from all the advantages offered us by the needs of those amongst whom we lived, but our political and religious law has nothing whatever to do with this result. Far from it, indeed, for the only point of view it expresses on this question was dictated by the feeling of brotherhood which it was constantly striving to create amongst us. To establish the opposite opinion, men have abused the meaning of a word which they have not properly understood, and to which they have given an interpretation all the more false in that it presupposes the existence of a fact, an idea, that was unknown at the time when this law was given to us. That is to say, what has since been called *legal interest* on money was not known, and therefore the word *usury* was not to be found in the language, since there would have been nothing for it to express. All interest derived from the loan of money was equally legal, at whatever rate it was charged; this rate depended entirely on the wishes of the contracting parties. That is why, in the Hebrew tongue, only one word exists signifying *interest*, and none signifying *usury*.

'What did the law of Moses do? It forbade the Jews to charge any interest on money lent amongst themselves, and only allowed them to charge it on money lent to foreigners. It was impossible for the law to distinguish between interest that was usurious and interest that was not, because, at that time, this distinction was not recognised. Thus it is not true that it ever allowed usury towards foreigners, while prohibiting it as between Jew and Jew. Men have applied to usury what was only true as regards interest, and they have quite indefensibly used the word *usury* to translate what simply means *interest*. Such is the law as it remains today, and which is, or should be, binding on Jews between themselves. A conscientious Jew should charge no interest on money he lends to another Jew, and this is what the strict interpreters of the law still teach.

'The commercial operations to which the Jews have been obliged to devote themselves from one end of the world to the other, have made the strict application of this precept difficult, and doubtless laxity, which in this respect the doctors have been unable to prevent, has led the majority of Israelites to assume that, since the law had prescribed a distinction between the way one dealt with a brother and a stranger, this distinction was that between interest and usury. A belief so convenient to their greed was easily accepted, and has become no less easily in-grained; but as it is contrary both to the spirit and the word of the law, it will always be the duty of the rabbis to fight against it when they are challenged on the subject.'

In the light of all the information we had been given it was impossible for us not to recognise that the Jews, however grasping in the trade they pursue, always display the most exemplary charity to one another; that one would hardly ever find them asking for help from anyone but their co-religionists; and that, provided it was not a business deal, that is to say, as regards all loans from one Jew to another, or when it was a question of meeting the urgent needs of one of their number, it was almost unheard of for the loan to bear interest. Finally, they assured us in a manner that made any doubt impossible that, when a Jew without personal resources had some pressing business to conclude in a place far away from where he lived, he could call upon the rabbi or a leading figure in the Jewish community he belonged to, and, having explained his require-ments, would be given a certificate that would enable him to travel across Europe, even to the most remote part of Asia, and be welcomed and succoured by the Jews he encountered at various points on his journey, all of whom would treat him, not as a poor man appealing to them to help him out of pity, but as a brother with whom they would share what they possessed.

Our ideas were equally clarified as regards the nature and extent of the powers of the rabbis. Since we had been insisting strongly on the extent of these powers and on the use we were urging them to make of them, on the supposition that, since they were given by God himself to the servants of the temple, they must have considerable authority over the minds of a people whose government in many respects might be regarded as a theocracy, they assured us that this was not so, and that it was important for them to clear up the mistake. They established in a positive manner and according to the most unexceptionable authorities, that any direct descent from the tribe of Levi had been entirely lost since the last diaspora; that since that time there had been no priesthood among them, since the priesthood was hereditary within that tribe; and that therefore all priestly power had been abolished among them. It is certainly one of the most extraordinary facts in the history of this people, so faithful to their traditions, so attached to their civil and religious customs, that such a precious line of descent should have so completely died out, especially as it must have been the object of the strictest precautions, since, only through its preservation, was it still possible for them to carry out, at any period whatsoever, the most sacred ceremonies of the Jewish religion.

Supposing, indeed, that the temple of Jerusalem were to be rebuilt, which must always remain the hope of every good Israelite, the sanctuary of this temple would remain empty, and the sacrifice could not be performed there, unless by a miracle the God who gave them their holy law upon Mount Sinai were to reveal to them the true descendants of this tribe.

If there are no longer any Levites, priests or pontifs, what then are the rabbis? Nothing more than learned men accepted by their co-religionists to recite the prayers and perform certain religious and occasionally judicial formalities, for which, in Judea itself at the time when the law was most scrupulously observed, the older members of each family had been considered to be competent. Seen from this point of view, it is easy to understand why the influence of these rabbis, based solely on esteem, could only achieve anything as a result of the confidence they inspired, and why it was therefore impossible for those taking part in our Assembly to claim any formal authority for imposing their opinions. Thus this situation fully explains the circumspect attitude they felt bound to maintain, which at first we had not at all understood.

This authority of their learned men, the only one that has existed amongst the Jews since the diaspora, the sole bond that has kept them united in their faith, is a phenomenon that deserves the closest attention. It was from this authority that the supplement to the law of Moses, known as the *Talmud*, was derived; a somewhat incoherent collection, consisting of interpretations, often very far-fetched, of the sacred text. It has caused numerous controversies and still gives rise to many disputes, and it is to these that they attribute in large measure the relaxation of Jewish morality. On the whole, the rabbis did not think much of the *Talmudists;* while recognising the merit of some of them, they appeared to regard them in the main as extremely dangerous.

Eventually we obtained from the Assembly satisfactory replies to all the questions we had put to them. On 18 September, the members of the Imperial Commission announced that His Imperial Majesty, anxious that these findings should have the greatest authority possible in the eyes of Jews of every country and every century, had decided to summon a Grand Sanhedrin, whose function it would be to formulate as doctrine the findings so far arising from the provisional Assembly, and any others which might result from the continuation of its labours.

This communication was received with enthusiasm and, in the days that followed, all the measures necessary for carrying out the Emperor's latest wish were discussed, adopted and executed with the utmost goodwill and energy. In conformity with ancient usage the number of members of the Grand Sanhedrin was fixed at 71, not counting its leader. All the rabbis already taking part in the Assembly, of whom there were 17, were summoned to take part in it. The synagogues of the French Empire and the kingdom of Italy were asked to send 29 others, while a further 25 members, to be drawn from amongst the ordinary Israelites, were chosen by secret ballot from the Assembly itself. Letters and all necessary instructions were at once sent to the French and Italian synagogues.

At the same time the Assembly addressed a proclamation to all their co-religionists in Europe, informing them of the wonderful news that a Grand Sanhedrin had been summoned, and urging them to hold meetings in order to send to Paris men distinguished for their wisdom and their love of truth and justice. The effect of this proclamation fell very far short of what had been expected, and, indeed, was practically nil in those countries that were not part of the French Empire or kingdom of Italy.

It remained to persuade the Assembly to recognise the need for some kind of organisation for the observance of its faith, and to win it over to support the setting up of such an organisation. Now this was an undertaking that the Assembly would certainly be reluctant to give, since it could not possibly fail to realise that there was none for which it would be more difficult to ensure the backing of its co-religionists. Was it not apparent, indeed, that the government could scarcely fail to take advantage of this opportunity of intervening, to a greater or lesser extent, in the inner life of the synagogues, and of assuming the right to supervise the behaviour of the rabbis? Now, in the eyes of the latter, this almost amounted to laying hands on the sacred Ark.

Despite all these difficulties, however, which were certainly enhanced by the unhelpful attitude of our chairman, a solution had to be found. M. Portalis and I therefore decided on an approach which was eventually crowned with complete success. Choosing a day when we knew M. Molé would be absent from Paris, we took advantage of the fact to invite the greatest possible number of influential men to M. Portalis's house, and there, after a meeting that lasted for six hours, we succeeded, by dint of sound argument and smooth words, in getting them to adopt as good a settlement as could be wished.

A few days later it was endorsed by the full Assembly. At the same time a decision was taken to beg His Imperial Majesty to give his blessing to the settlement and to agree to the rabbis being paid. In addition, we asked, what could only be most acceptable to him, that he would deign to make known to the local authorities throughout the Empire and the kingdom of Italy that it was his wish that they should act in concert with the consistory courts to overcome the aversion which the Israelite youth appeared to have for the noble profession of arms, and in this way to ensure their complete obedience to the conscription laws.

The opening of the Grand Sanhedrin could not take place until 9 February 1807; the most distinguished of the newly-elected members almost all came from the kingdom of Italy, particularly from the provinces which had previously formed part of the ancient Venetian states. By 9 March a writ had been published by which the doctors of the law and notables of Israel then assembled gave notice that they had constituted themselves as a Grand Sanhedrin, in order to find ways and means of promulgating religious regulations in conformity with the principles of their sacred law, which might serve as an example for the rule of conduct of all Israelites. It went on to say that 'this law contained both *religious* and *political* aspects; that whereas the former were absolute the latter, which had been designed for the government of the people of Israel in Palestine, could no longer be applicable since the Jewish people no longer formed a nation. Thus the polygamy permitted by the law of Moses, being merely optional and no longer customary in the West, was to be regarded as prohibited: in France the civil marriage should be performed before the religious ceremony; annulment or divorce could take place save in accordance with the forms laid down by the civil law; and marriages between Jews and Christians should be regarded as valid. Since the law of Moses ordained that the members of any nation who recognised God as creator of the world should be treated as brothers, all Jews should regard it as an essentially religious duty, inherent in their belief, habitually and regularly to perform the acts of justice and charity prescribed by the scriptures towards all such people.

'Any Jew admitted to legal citizenship should obey the laws of the country and, in all transactions, conform with the decrees of the customary legal code. When called upon for military service he was, for the duration of that service, exempted from any religious observance that could not be reconciled with the law. The Jews should, for preference, enter the industries and professions and acquire real estate, this being the best way of devoting themselves to their country and deserving public approbation.

'In conformity with the law of Moses, usury was indiscriminately forbidden, not only between Jew and Jew, but between Jews and fellow citizens of another religion and also as regards foreigners belonging to all other nations, this practise being an iniquitous abomination in the eyes of the Lord.'

It would have been difficult for any jurist and moralist whatsoever to expound this last prescription more carefully and forcefully. This decree, having been conceived so emphatically, was unanimously adopted. The general Assembly insisted on adding to it an address to the Emperor and a resolution, both of which were intended to fill out and confirm its effect. It led naturally to a wish being expressed that His Majesty, reassured by the happy results that were bound to ensue from all the decisions that had just been reached in so impressive a manner would, in his great wisdom, deign to consider whether it would not be advisable to set a limit on the suspension of mortgages in those Departments affected by the decree of 30 May, and whether this limit should not coincide with the expiration of the stay of execution that had been prescribed by this decree.

In this way the Assembly was expressing its desire that the Emperor would be pleased to take the most effective measures to ensure that, in future, some Jews, as a result of such mortgages as they might be in a position to get accepted, should not bring about the same kind of ruin of men's fortunes as had already been the subject of complaint, and for which, all too often, all their co-religionists had to bear the shame and punishment. Never had greater efforts been made, with such frank and sincere intentions, to achieve a reform that had so long been desired by all enlightened minds; but at the same time never had a similar opportunity been offered to the Jewish race since the diaspora; and many centuries may elapse before such favourable circumstances occur again.

Deflected by political considerations from a matter that had for so long occupied his attention, the Emperor failed to take advantage of the overtures that were made to him. The repayment of Jewish creditors was again suspended, beyond the period laid down in the decree of 30 May 1806; and the fact that the only notification of this was in an ordinary ministerial circular caused great discouragement to the Jewish population.

In obedience to the orders we had received, the Grand Sanhedrin was dissolved on 6 April 1807, and its proposals were submitted to the Council of State for discussion. The Emperor's attitude towards the Jews had meanwhile been unfavourably modified, probably as a result of the impression produced upon him by the Jewish populations of Germany and Poland. M. Molé's plan was to triumph, despite the efforts of M. Portalis and myself. Nevertheless, we did manage to obtain sanction, without any changes being made, for the regulations that we had had such difficulty in getting adopted for the organisation of the Jewish faith and their internal administration throughout the French Empire and the kingdom of Italy.

The arrangements for regulating the effects of the suspension of payment came eventually, after a long delay, from the Emperor's headquarters; they were of such severity that I have no fear in saying they transgressed all the rules of equity.

This seems to be the only question where Pasquier played an important part. Moreover, Napoleon had certain reservations about him. 'I appeared to him from the start as a man that might be of some use to him, but who would never be as completely devoted to him as he would have liked. With M. Molé it was a very different matter: he was not only wealthier than I, but had become a member of the Council at the age of twenty-five.'[16] *'It was not until the third year that I was appointed to a position which, since it kept me in Paris, was agreeable enough, though it could have been of little importance in the eyes of the Emperor because it called for no ability and carried no real influence. It was the position of* Procureur général *to the* Conseil des Sceaux et Titres.'*

A mission to the Rhineland in 1808, however, interrupted the monotony of legal committee work, in which Pasquier had specialised and where he more and more frequently spoke.[17]

It was with complete confidence that the Emperor returned to France in order to take command of the army which had left Germany and was about to set out for the banks of the Ebro. On its way across France this army had met with a succession of triumphs that did much to raise the morale of the soldiers. One particular incident made me realise that, in this respect, the Departments were not to be outdone by the capital. On his way to Erfurt, the Emperor wanted to take a new road between Metz and Mayence, which he had ordered to be opened a few months previously. Contrary to his expectation this road was far from being completed, and it was only with the greatest difficulty he was able to proceed at all. In his impatience he jumped to the conclusion that the administration was responsible, or at least that it had been guilty of considerable negligence; he therefore ordered the Archchancellor to despatch a *Maître de requêtes* immediately in order to survey the work that had been done, to draw up a detailed report and, finally, to check up on

[16] This opinion is confirmed by a remark of the Emperor's quoted by Mme de Rémusat: 'I exploit one of them [Pasquier], but I am creating the other [Molé].'

[17] He had been in the habit of reading his speeches. Regnault de Saint-Jean-d'Anglély urged him to speak freely. 'I took his advice and thus acquired the small talent to which I owe my political existence.'

the cost. The choice having fallen upon me, I had to set off, much against my will, for at the time I was far from well, and in addition I was very busy acquainting myself with my duties as *Procureur général* to the *Conseil des Sceaux et Titres*.[18]

However, I obeyed with my usual alacrity and, beginning the enquiry in the neighbourhood of Kaiserslautern, I continued it as far as Mayence. It soon became clear that the road was execrable; my carriage was flung into a ravine at least a hundred feet deep; it was completely smashed up and I owed my life simply to the fact that I had got out of it a few minutes previously. At the same time, however, I arrived at the conclusion that neither the administration nor the contractors were to blame, that they simply had not had time, and that the only mistake they had made was to allow the Emperor to take this road instead of having the courage to tell him that it was not yet fit for use. All this, moreover, thanks to the good offices of the Minister of the Interior and the Director of Roads and Bridges, was already known to him even before my mission was completed, which was therefore quite useless, apart from the pleasure I had derived from travelling through lovely country and getting to know the banks of the Rhine. Everywhere I encountered regiments from the different branches of the service who had just crossed the river, and everywhere I witnessed the enthusiasm with which the people rushed to meet them. Triumphal arches, festivities and dances awaited them on all sides.

The army corps commanded by Marshal Victor was amongst those who crossed the Rhine, and it had entered Mayence the same day that I arrived from the opposite direction. It was well known that this corps, the most badly disciplined in the whole army, was completely out of hand, and it had been preceded by rumours of the disturbances it had caused in the German provinces it passed through. It was therefore awaited with an anxiety that proved to be all too well justified, for within an hour of its arrival in the town two men had already been killed.

[18] In 1806, by a series of decrees, Napoleon was busily creating a new nobility: in all, 31 dukes, 388 counts, 1,090 barons and about 1,500 knights. In order to ensure the splendour of these new titles he granted generous endowments to their holders. The Department of Seals and Titles to which Pasquier was appointed as legal advisor, was responsible for making these arrangements.

I happened to be with the Prefect when the news was brought to him. He was a certain Jean Bon Saint-André, one-time member of the Committee of Public Safety, who, in those days, had more than once given proof of his terrible energy. During the few years he had been Prefect, he had become noted for the zeal and vigour with which he protected those living within his jurisdiction, many of whom had suffered grievously at the hands of the soldiers continually passing through the town. M. Jean Bon was no sooner informed of the crimes committed by the soldiers than he wrote Marshal Victor a letter, which he gave me to read, and in which he demanded prompt and exemplary justice. Receiving no reply, he went to the house where the Marshal was billeted, but the latter was either out or else hiding.

The Prefect spent the rest of the morning sending messages and visiting the barracks, but with no better success: 'It's no use, I'm not going to let him escape me', he told me, 'and you will be my witness.' And indeed, having followed him to the theatre, he insisted upon my accompanying him to the Marshal's box, where, in front of his staff, he gave him one of the roughest dressings-down you could hope to hear! 'This is not enemy country you are in', he told him. 'Even if it were, the behaviour of your soldiers would still be preposterous, and your weakness in permitting it equally inexcusable. I am going to dispatch a courier to the Emperor this very evening, with a report of what has occurred.' The manner and tone of voice with which these words were spoken proved to me that M. Jean Bon had not forgotten the part he had once played as representative of the people with the armies of the Republic. The Marshal's attitude was very like that of a general of 1793, confronted by one of the proconsuls of those days. He stammered a few words, promised that justice would be done and earnestly begged that the courier should not be sent. The Prefect promised nothing, and what he did I do not know: but the next day I was assured that several soldiers had been arrested, and there was no more talk in the Department of scenes of this kind.[19]

[19] Beugnot quotes another example of the energy and freedom of speech of this former member of the Committee of Public Safety. One day in 1813, says he, Jean Bon Saint-André, who, 'wearing the simplest possible Prefect's uniform . . . and otherwise dressed in black, including his cravat', used to make the 'gilded' chamberlains and imperial aides-de-camp smile, let himself go in an outburst that must surely have made him many friends. 'Fortune is by nature capricious', he exclaimed. 'She has raised France to a very high position; sooner or later she

On my return to Paris I devoted myself to my new post with the *Conseil des Sceaux et Titres*. It was an extremely bold conception to give France a new nobility, and to dare to confront it with that other nobility which, although legally annulled, was still alive in everyone's memory. The basis upon which this new order could be created was already there. Mankind has always been ready to reward military glory with titles of honour, and those who win battles have never had any difficulty in rising to the highest rank in society; it is from them that the most illustrious families have always stemmed, from the royal family downwards. But titles are nothing without wealth, and the most illustrious fame cannot long withstand poverty. The granting of new rights of entail was seriously hampered by the need to comply with the laws of inheritance; and, moreover, the number of considerable fortunes was too restricted for the exercise of this right to be available to many people.

The Extraordinary Domain which the Emperor kept at his own disposal, and which, in addition to the estates reserved to himself in the conquered provinces, included money derived from levies upon enemy countries, served as the basis for the endowments which the Emperor distributed with such munificence to all those whom he wished to reward, firstly in his army, from Marshals down to ordinary officers, then in the various branches of the administration and the court. All these endowments, granted in entail by the *Conseil des Sceaux*, carried with them titles, and reverted to the crown in the event of the male line dying out.

The Emperor's purpose was not only to create a new nobility, but to fuse it with the old, and to this end he bestowed on all the bearers of ancient names who had supported his government new titles, which differed from those they had borne before the Revolution, and which, however much it went against the grain, they were obliged to accept.

Amongst those who were upset in this way, there was much talk of Mme de Montmorency, a lady-in-waiting to the Empress, though, on the surface, her ambition appeared to be quite modest. She had been made a countess, whereas she wished to

may well bring her down again, as low as she was in 1793. Then we shall see whether such painless measures suffice to save her, and what all these gentlemen will do about it, with their embroidered jackets and feathered hats, and above all, their white silk stockings.'

be only a baroness, because this was the title she had borne in 1789 and was the one that had always been preferred by the eldest sons of the family of Montmorency, jealous of preserving the title of *first baron in Christendom*, which had belonged to them from time immemorial. Napoleon firmly rejected her demand, and referring to a certain flightiness in her youth, told her: 'You are not a good enough Christian for me to endorse such a claim.'

To sum up, despite all the wrangling, inevitable at the start of an institution that was bound to affect so many interests, and which could only satisfy some people by upsetting others, and despite the quite ridiculous airs adopted by some of the newly ennobled, even those of highest rank, it was not long before the new nobility was established in France, while it was even more readily accepted abroad, where it was accompanied by all the prestige of military fame.

In France, the soldiers especially attached great importance to this new type of reward, and were deeply impressed by it. Many of them, it is true, did not fully appreciate its significance, and I had a considerable number of petitions through my hands, demanding promotion to the nobility in much the same way as they might have demanded it in a regiment. Yet there can be no doubt that this creation of a new nobility accustomed France once again to the acceptance of hereditary distinctions, and that this essentially monarchial institution enormously facilitated the resumption of their titles by the old nobility at the time of the Restoration. Everyone was delighted that, included in the Charter, was this conciliatory article: 'The titles of the old nobility will be restored; those of the new will be retained.'

This happy alliance removed all obstacles, and here once again was an example of the way in which Bonaparte's omnipotence had opened up the road that the Bourbons were to follow, but which they would have had difficulty in adopting on their own. The great service that Napoleon's nobility thus rendered to the Restoration did not prevent their existence being severely weakened by the abolition of endowments, thus depriving them of the benefits of wealth which, today more than ever, is indispensable for the maintenance of social distinctions.

Here I should say something about the rather special character of the *Conseil des Sceaux et Titres*. Its president, M. de Cambacérès, attached the greatest importance to all the titles it created, because no one was so full of wordly vanity, so that in this respect everything seemed to him to be of importance. Three senators and two members of the Council of State were associated with him in this work. Among the Senators was M. Garnier,[20] a one-time attorney, a great enthusiast for the teachings of the economists and a witty, talented man, but one whose ideas had previously been much more opposed to than favourable to all aristocratic institutions. I am convinced that this was the real reason why he had been chosen and that the Emperor hoped, through him, to initiate the education of the recalcitrants. And, in fact, before long the title of count with which he was invested gave him the greatest pleasure. The second Senator was M. de Saint-Martin, a well-born Piedmontese and very proud of his birth, though in his own country he was considered to be rather revolutionary. He, too, had to re-educate himself, but in a quite opposite direction from M. Garnier. The third, M. Colchen, was simply there to make up the numbers.

M. d'Hauterive, Councillor of State, one-time Oratorian and a very experienced diplomat, seemed as well suited as anyone could be to the new duties that were entrusted to him; all he brought to them was a kind of witty naïvety which invariably enabled him to see the bright side of things and to give the most specious explanations of them, though it did not always allow him to appraise them correctly. His colleague, M. Portalis, endowed with a more positive and a much wider intelligence, was, in truth, the only member of the Council, apart from the President, who was capable of understanding the new institution, and who, while fully aware of its weak aspects, realised from the very start the advantages that could be derived from it. He, therefore, jointly with myself, was entrusted by M. de Cambacérès with the preparation of all the regulations that were necessary to enable the Council to go ahead with the granting of titles, and especially with the establishing of entails. Now once these regulations had been drawn up and adopted, carrying them out could scarcely present any serious difficulties.

We also had to suggest what form the various coats of arms should take. I only mention this because it was the occasion for a display of petty-mindedness quite remarkable in such a man

[20] In 1809 Comte Germain Garnier became President of the Senate. He was the author of several works of political economy and, in particular, translated Adam Smith's famous book, *The Wealth of Nations*, into French.

as Napoleon. He would never agree that the coats of arms should be surmounted by different kinds of coronet, which, according to the generally accepted custom throughout Europe, indicated the rank of the bearer. He seemed to regard the use of these insignia as a usurpation of his rights; and his susceptibility on this point was quite invincible. Instead of coronets, therefore, we had to invent a variety of plumes, consisting of from one to seven feathers in accordance with the precise rank. This did not at all please the Archchancellor, who felt that nothing could possibly look so well on the door of his carriage as a coronet. I was created a Baron, and I saw no reason to complain, though no one seemed to realise that my family had borne this title before the Revolution.

Napoleon's popularity and authority appeared to be indisputable. A few lucid minds, however, were beginning to worry about the future. 'I am convinced', Pasquier wrote in 1829, 'that the battle of Eylau had led M. de Talleyrand to reflect very seriously upon the weakness of a regime based solely on a life that was so often risked in the most dangerous enterprises.'

The Emperor's departure for Spain at the end of 1808 accentuated the Prince of Benevento's apprehensions.

Scarcely had Napoleon crossed the Pyrenees and set out on the road to Madrid, than M. de Talleyrand began to manifest his bitter dissatisfaction. I found it impossible to doubt this when I saw him again, on my return from Mayence, at the house where we usually met.[21] He began making the most sinister predictions, and he was one of those who appeared to believe that the Emperor would be in personal danger from the vengeance of the Spaniards. It was then that I heard him for the first time openly criticise the conduct of affairs at Bayonne. Nevertheless, what is quite remarkable, he was not condemning the invasion of Spain, but only the way in which it had been carried out. 'To want to expel the Bourbons', he said, 'was natural enough, even perhaps essential, if the Napoleonic dynasty is to be firmly

[21] At the house of Mme de Rémusat, who in 1802 had been appointed one of four ladies-in-waiting to Josephine, wife of the First Consul. The *Mémoires* of Queen Hortense, Mme de Rémusat, Mme de Chastenay, Beugnot, Thibaudeau and Metternich, as well as Arnaud de Montor's book on *Hauterive*, all bear out the account that follows.

established. But what was the use of resorting to all this scheming, contrivance and perfidy? Why not simply have declared war, for which there were plenty of motives? In such a war the Spanish people would have remained neutral. Intoxicated as they then were by Napoleon's fame, they would have watched without the slightest regret the collapse of an exhausted dynasty, and, after a few engagements involving the regular army, the entire Peninsula would have joyfully accepted the accession to power of a family which, in France, had already so gloriously superseded that which had given Philip V to Spain. In this way the entire heritage bequeathed by Louis XIV might have easily been restored once more.'

This was certainly a very plausible proposition, and it would have been very difficult to deny its soundness; but, precisely for that reason, it was bound to strike Napoleon as the sharpest possible criticism of his behaviour, by, of all people, one of his oldest ministers, a leading dignitary of his Empire. Had M. de Talleyrand been content to expound his views only at Mme de Rémusat's, to the small number of people who used to forgather there, the danger of his indiscretion would not have been so great; but he was too excited and self-confident to limit the expression of his ideas to such a narrow circle. He was in touch with too many people of every kind, many of whom he had every reason to distrust. What he was thinking soon began to get about, and from that moment it ceased to be a secret for the considerable body of people in Paris who are always in touch with the latest gossip. What had thus become more or less public property in the capital could scarcely help reaching the ears of the Emperor; thus, even before he got to Madrid, he was warned, and, in addition, only a few days later he learnt of an incident that must have led him to reflect very seriously on what might be hatching in France during his absence.

The long and persistent breach which had existed for so many years between M. de Talleyrand and the Minister of Police, M. Fouché, was suddenly healed. Both men, apparently, had come to see things from the same point of view and, having lost all confidence in Napoleon's fortunes, were beginning to say to themselves that, in the event of his death, they alone would be in a position to dispose of the Empire and, in consequence, ought to settle the succession according to their own interests. But, in order to achieve this aim, they had to come to an understanding, agree on their course of action and abandon a hostility which was now out of place. Both had made advances, and their final reconciliation had been brought about, if I am not mistaken, through the intervention of M. d'Hauterive, head of the Archives Division at the Foreign Office, in his capacity as an old Oratorian who had always been on good terms with M. Fouché. M. d'Hauterive had certainly not grasped the significance of what he was doing, and had simply yielded to the temptation, which he was never able to forego, of having a finger in every pie. He imagined he was working wonders by furthering a reconciliation, which, it seemed to him, would ensure the peace of the world and also be very acceptable to the Emperor.

What was most astonishing about this unexpected agreement was that two such prudent people should have considered it opportune to make such a stir about it. Either they must have believed that their partnership made them extremely powerful or they were convinced that the Emperor's cause was in any case lost. I still vividly remember a brilliant reception given by M. de Talleyrand, and the effect produced by M. Fouché's entrance, his first appearance in that salon. People could scarcely believe their eyes; and they were even more astounded when in their determination to appear on good terms, these two men spent the rest of the evening walking from room to room arm-in-arm. One of those who always kept an eye on anything happening in Paris that might interest Napoleon, and who maintained a regular correspondence with him, was one of his old aides-de-camp, M. de la Valette, who had married his niece, Mlle de Beauharnais, and had since been put in charge of the postal service. A very witty man and unusually sagacious, M. de la Valette was deeply attached to his benefactor and one-time commander, but he was all the better able to estimate his position because, despite his admiration for his talents, he had few illusions about his weaknesses.

Now at this time he regarded the Emperor's position as being very critical, and must therefore have thought it very important, when he saw what was going on between two men whom he looked upon as capable of anything, especially when one of them was M. de Talleyrand, who, despite his great reputation, had never inspired him with the least esteem or confidence, while the other, M. Fouché, had always been the object of his very decided aversion. He therefore wrote to the Emperor and told him what he thought of a friendship that could only have come about for political purposes inimical to his interests; and it was not long before the fears he expressed were confirmed by an incident which throws the clearest possible light on the mysterious aspects of this intrigue and clearly reveals its purpose.

I have never had any actual proof of this, but what I learnt later from the lips of M. de la Valette and the Duc de Rovigo leaves no room for doubt in my mind. In the event of Napoleon's death it would be essential at the earliest opportunity, and whatever might be decided later, to have someone to put in his place. The new friends therefore thought of Murat, who had just been made King of Naples, but whose crazy vanity was by no means satisfied with this promotion since he had been counting on the Spanish throne, which he believed himself to be the only man fit to occupy and to which he thought he had a right in view of the energy he had displayed at Madrid during the conference of Bayonne. In this respect, we must remember the revolt that he had suppressed in such a terrible way, and which had done so much to bring about the insurrection that broke out throughout the whole Peninsula.

M. Fouché had always been on a very intimate footing with him, and used to boast of his influence over him. M. de Talleyrand looked upon him as being even easier to overthrow than to set up, and was in any case quite convinced that his presence would not worry them for long. As for Mme Murat, the Emperor's sister, her ambition was so overweening that she could be persuaded to accept anything, as she has since abundantly proved. They did not hesitate to inform the new King of Naples that he must hold himself ready to come to France, at the first signal, to seek the high destiny that awaited him. Either their letter or their messenger was intercepted in Italy by Prince Eugène, who had doubtless been warned by M. de la Valette to be on the look-out and maintain the strictest surveillance. The Prince lost no time in sending details of his discovery to Spain, and this certainly helped to hasten the Emperor's return. Indeed, it could not escape notice that the speed with which he travelled was even greater than usual, and this despite the difficulties of the journey; he was obliged to travel several stages on horseback.[22]

[22] General Thiébault has left a picturesque account of one such stage: 'I was approaching the last stopping place before Burgos . . . I was travelling in my

When he first arrived in Paris, everybody supposed that he had been recalled by the state of affairs in Austria. It was not until five or six days later that he gave vent to his anger at the intrigues of M. de Talleyrand and M. Fouché. Apparently he was anxious to verify the facts for himself; moreover, he was careful to conceal his wrath from the second of the two men, paying little attention to him and concentrating his attack on the first. It is always difficult to make changes at the Ministry of Police, because anyone who has occupied the position for long inevitably holds many threads in his hand. Napoleon therefore decided that M. Fouché should not be replaced until all necessary precautions had been taken to ensure that there was nothing to fear from his resentment. Besides, he foresaw the necessity of a new campaign in Germany, and he did not want to disorganise any part of his internal administration just as he was about to embark on it. He doubtless thought that, once this new danger had been overcome, there would be nothing to prevent him from carrying out all the acts of justice amongst his entourage that appeared to be advisable.

As to M. de Talleyrand, who at the time had no special duties and thus took no active part either in the administration or the government, he had no hesitation in loosing upon him the full weight of his anger. The first warning appeared in *Le Moniteur* of the 30th: an announcement that the office of Archchamberlain was to be taken over by M. de Montesquieu, and had therefore been withdrawn from M. de Talleyrand who had occupied it since the setting up of the Imperial Court. Although this change was attributed to the fact that, since his promotion to the position of Vice-Grand Elector, he had only been carrying out the duties of the Archchamberlain provisionally, his disgrace was none the less manifest since no one was fooled by such an implausible pretext. Moreover, it almost immediately became known that this decision had been preceded by the most violent scene in the throne room, in which, in the presence of several

barouche, drawn by three magnificent horses . . . when my valet came up and told me: "I think that must be the Emperor". I immediately opened the door and got out, whereupon I heard someone shouting: "Who's in that carriage?" Scarcely had Jacques had time to answer, "General Thiébault", when I was passed by Savary at full gallop and the Emperor, who was furiously whipping the hind quarters of his aide-de-camp's horse and spurring on his own, as he made that incredible journey, in which he covered the distance between Valladolid and Burgos in three hours and a half . . . '

high-ranking officers and almost all his ministers, the Emperor had treated M. de Talleyrand as the scum of the earth, heaping every kind of reproach and insult upon him. I heard about this the same evening from Mme de Rémusat, who had received an account of all he had been through from M. de Talleyrand himself. I was also to hear, many years later, a similar description of this terrible scene, though with more details, from M. Decrès, one of the Ministers who had witnessed it; and since it was he who at the time behaved most generously towards M. de Talleyrand, and subsequently did the least to turn his back upon him, his account deserves the fullest credence. What had especially struck him, and what he still could not get over even despite the considerable lapse of time, was the apparent insensibility of the victim, who for nearly half an hour, without moving a muscle or attempting to reply, endured a stream of invective such as had probably never before been heard in such a place by people in their position.

'You are a thief, a coward, a faithless wretch who doesn't even believe in God! Throughout your life you have failed in all your duties, you have cheated and betrayed everyone. For you, nothing is sacred; why, you'd sell your own father. Though I've heaped riches upon you, there's nothing you are incapable of doing against me. Thus, for the last ten months, because you imagined that one way and another things were going badly for me in Spain, you've had the effrontery to tell anyone that was ready to listen to you that you have always disapproved of what I was attempting to do there, whereas it was you who put the idea into my head in the first place, and have persistently urged it upon me. And that man, that *wretched creature* [he was here referring to the Duc d'Enghien], who was it who told me where he was living, and provoked me to deal so severely with him? And what are you up to now? What is it you want? What are you hoping for? You daren't even say! If you got what you deserved I should smash you like a wine-glass. And I could do it; but I despise you so much I can't be bothered to!'[23]

Despite his apparent self-effacement, Pasquier's position in the Council of State continued to grow stronger in the years 1809 and 1810. The

[23] Pasquier softens his description of the scene. The famous apostrophe with which Napoleon used to conclude his outbursts of invective is well-known: 'Why, you are nothing but a silk stocking full of piss!'

seizure of the Roman States by France had shocked him profoundly. 'This spoliation was hateful; it was simply a case of the strong oppressing the weak. It had a quality of ingratitude that revolted even those most disposed to approve and admire everything he did, though in justice to the Council of State I should mention that it was visibly affected by it.' But once again military success came to the Emperor's help. 'The repercussions of this utterly unforeseen act of violence, throughout the whole of Europe, were, fortunately for Napoleon, modified by the victory of Wagram.'

The scene was darkened by yet another shadow: the divorce. 'Never perhaps was there an occasion when members of his court were so embarrassed . . . They had to approve their master's decision . . . But Josephine retained a considerable position . . . I shall never forget the last evening that the forsaken Empress presided over her court . . . For several minutes I was standing quite close to her, and I could not help being struck by the perfect propriety of her bearing . . . Only women have the gift of carrying off the difficulties of such a situation, but I doubt if it would have been possible to find another capable of carrying it off so gracefully and with such perfect decorum; Napoleon was more out of countenance than his victim.'

On 8 February 1810 Pasquier was 'at last' appointed Councillor of State. To this mark of imperial favour another was soon added. On 16 May the Emperor chose him to be chairman of a Commission that had been set up to study the financial and economic problems of Holland.[24] He must have had specialised knowledge of the affairs of that country, for already, in 1809, it had been rumoured that he had been selected as tutor to Napoleon-Louis, the eldest son of the king of Holland, Napoleon's brother, Louis.[25]

[24] The Allies' continental blockade created considerable difficulties for Holland, difficulties which Napoleon sought to resolve by annexing the country after the abdication of his brother, King Louis, on 1 July 1810.

[25] Police Bulletin No. 1156 of 15 March: 'As tutor to the Crown Prince of Holland, the Grand Duke of Berg, there is talk of Molé, Fontanes or Pasquier.'

IV

The Height of Imperial Power
1810–1812

PASQUIER, PREFECT OF POLICE – COOL RELA-
TIONS WITH SAVARY – SETTING UP OF THE
POLICE COMMITTEE – VISITS TO PRISONS AND
HOSPITALS – CONVERSATIONS WITH THE
EMPEROR: VARIED CHARACTER OF HIS
QUESTIONS – PARIS STREETS OBSTRUCTED BY
BUILDING MATERIAL – GROWING OPPOSITION
OF THE CLERGY – PORTALIS DISGRACED
DESPITE PASQUIER'S EFFORTS – PROBLEMS OF
OBSCENE LITERATURE AND PROSTITUTES –
REGULATIONS FOR DOMESTIC SERVANTS –
REORGANISATION OF THE FIRE BRIGADE
– ECONOMIC CRISIS – STABILISATION OF FOOD
PRICES – DISCUSSION WITH NAPOLEON ON THE
EVE OF HIS DEPARTURE FOR RUSSIA

At this time I enjoyed real standing in the Council of State.
Without any of those personal responsibilities that are always so
difficult to bear, I had plenty to do,[1] all of which gave me
pleasure. In general, the work of the Council had considerable
attraction for me, and that year [1810] it was of great importance;
apart from the laws and decrees I have already mentioned, we
had to prepare a draft law on mining, and this led to excellent
and very instructive discussions;[2] then there was the organisation

[1] Especially after the setting up of the Committee for Disputed Claims, the
reorganisation of indirect taxation, and 'that mass of regulations of the public
services which reorganised almost everything that the Revolution had destroyed'.
Pasquier goes on to say: 'In justice to Napoleon, it should be recognised that he
allowed complete freedom of discussion, that we could say what we liked, that
he listened to everything patiently and with close attention, without appearing to
be upset if anything was said to displease him, even upon matters which most
immediately involved his absolute authority.'

[2] Which were to lead to the famous law of 25 April 1810.

of the imperial courts of justice; and, on top of this, the questions that arose every day on all kinds of matters.

Thus I was as satisfied with my life as one can hope to be. I had no ambition; and judging by the pains the Emperor was at to dismiss me from the position of chief attorney to the *Conseil des Sceaux et Titres* in order to give it to M. Dudon, I gathered that he still did not like me. At the same time, however, I came to the conclusion that I was to be left in peace as a member of the Council and should not be sent away on one of those remote missions that were so frequent at the time, and which I certainly should not have cared for. It suited me better to remain in the honourable position that I had attained and, as I was attached to the Committee of Internal Affairs, the only thing I should have liked would have been the chairmanship of this Committee, if M. Regnault were to give it up either because he found it too much for him or as a result of promotion. He himself had often given me to understand that he considered me to be the best suited to take his place. This was the pleasant position I found myself in, when suddenly it changed, quite unexpectedly and not at all in the way I had hoped.

I have already noted how badly the Duc de Rovigo's[3] appointment as Minister of Police had been received, especially in Paris. The Prefect of Police was M. Dubois, who had filled this position since the beginning of the Consular government; he was a man of small intelligence, in no way malicious but without any definite principles on anything at all. Absolute power could scarcely have found a more docile and devoted instrument. Solely concerned with retaining his position and increasing his fortune, he had few scruples as to the methods he chose to achieve these two aims. Having completed his education by working as an attorney, his manners were common, not to say coarse, and his social connections displayed the same bad taste

[3] The title granted to General Savary in 1807. Having served with distinction throughout the revolutionary wars, and shown great daring in the pursuit of the Prussians after the battle of Jena (1807), he was given command of a corps. After the disgrace of Fouché he was appointed Minister of Police in 1810, and transformed this office into a veritable inquisition. It is probably apocryphal that Napoleon said of him: 'I like him; he would kill his own father if I bade him'; but certainly few of his generals remained more faithful to him. One of the last to desert him at the time of his first abdication, he wished to accompany the Emperor to Saint Helena, but was not allowed to. Restored to favour by the July revolution of 1830, he was for a period in command of the French army in Algeria, and died in 1834. (Trs.)

that distinguished him personally. He had recently married the daughter of a housemaid, with whom he was known to have been carrying on a most scandalous intimacy for many years. This marriage increased the disrepute in which he was held, and it was difficult to undertand how such a man had managed to retain a position of such importance for so long. It was, however, to be explained by the hostility that existed between him and M. Fouché. The Emperor, who always distrusted the latter, found it useful and convenient to keep the man who would be most delighted to catch him out in a position where it was always easy to keep an eye on the Minister. When M. Fouché was dismissed, M. Dubois doubtless regarded it as a blessing, though it turned out to be the cause of his own downfall. For as soon as Napoleon was satisfied that, in the Duc de Rovigo, he had found a Minister upon whose loyalty he could rely, there ceased to be any point in having a Prefect to spy upon him; and from then on he became much more aware of all the drawbacks attaching to M. Dubois. He even reckoned that his removal would be regarded by the people of Paris as a well-earned reward, which would compensate for the fear caused by the Duc de Rovigo.

In the middle of all this there was the fire at the Austrian Ambassador's ball.[4] On this occasion the Emperor had been dissatisfied both with the fire service and with the failure of the Prefect of Police to put in an appearance. M. Dubois' dismissal was therefore decided upon, but a successor had to be found. Practically all the members of the Council whose capacity for action would have enabled them to cope with the difficulties of the position, already had duties that it would be difficult to withdraw them from. What was required was a man who understood the way the people of Paris lived, and whose name was held in esteem by them.

The Emperor was anxious that the new Prefect of Police should be acceptable to the city of Paris. He spent a long time looking for the right man, and I am quite sure that to begin with my name had not entered his mind. I believe that it was M.

---

[4] The fire that broke out at the ball given by the Prince of Schwarzenberg in honour of Napoleon and Marie-Louise in 1810 resulted in four deaths, one of them being the Ambassador's sister-in-law, and many injuries. It was an unpleasant reminder of the 136 victims at the festivities held in Paris to celebrate the marriage of the future Louis XVI and Marie-Antoinette.

Maret,[5] though at the time I had had no relations whatever with him, who helped to persuade him to accept it. M. de Cambacérès (at least so he assured me) was only informed at the last moment that I was under consideration, while I myself had not the slightest suspicion.

The Court was at Fontainebleau. I went there on Sunday, 14 October [1810]. I was walking up and down the gallery, waiting for the Emperor to pass by on his way to mass, when M. de Sémonville said to me:[6] 'You've been made Prefect of Police!' At first I merely laughed, then, as I realised that strictly speaking it was not impossible, I found myself trembling. A moment later M. de Cambacérès, who was in attendance upon the Emperor, warned me that he had something to tell me after mass and, in the course of a very short conversation that I then had with him, he informed me that I was to be summoned to the Emperor's study to take the oath as Prefect of Police. I replied that it was impossible for me to accept such duties, that I was in no way suited for them and should be completely out of place. Whereupon he gave me to understand that to refuse such an appointment would be bound to arouse the Emperor's justified suspicion that I was not prepared to serve him zealously and felt little devotion to him personally. He pointed out that if, in fact, I was not suited to this post, the Emperor would soon realise it, would nevertheless be grateful to me for my obedience, and would find me some other employment better adapted to my tastes. Furthermore, he maintained, I should not be too concerned as to the nature of the services that would be demanded of

5 H. B. Maret (1763–1839), more usually referred to in the following pages by the title of Duc de Bassano, which he received in 1809, became one of the First Consul's secretaries immediately after the 18 Brumaire. Though he held a number of ministerial appointments, his most important function was that of private secretary to Napoleon, whom he served with unwavering devotion, accompanying him on most of his campaigns including the disastrous invasion of Russia. He remained with Napoleon to the end, and in 1815 was exiled for five years before being allowed to return to France. He was to remain consistently friendly to Pasquier. (Trs.)

6 The Marquis de Sémonville, well-known for his fondness for intrigue, was a favourite butt for Talleyrand's wit. When someone said to him that Sémonville was putting on weight, he replied: 'I can't understand it.'—'What, Your Highness?' —'I don't understand whose interest Sémonville hopes to serve by getting fat.' And, on another occasion, with regard to the Chamber of Peers, of which Sémonville was the Grand Referendary: 'At least in the Upper Chamber, Your Highness, they have a conscience.'—'Yes, you are right, all too many. Why, Sémonville himself has two.'

me; anything that involved the Emperor's intimate and personal confidence, which it was not necessary for me to aspire to, would always be a matter for the Duc de Rovigo.

In the end, he was so persuasive that I entered the study without having definitely decided to refuse. I had to make up my mind in the course of the discussion. After the Restoration it was publicly stated in certain pamphlets, the titles of which escape me, that Napoleon, wishing to test me, had asked me, after informing me of my appointment, what I should do in the event of a Prince of the house of Bourbon being discovered in Paris, and whether I should arrest him; a question to which I should have unhesitatingly replied that I would carry out my duty. M. de Las Cases, improving upon this invention, has given a fairly long account of the scene in the second volume of his *Mémorial de Sainte-Hélène*. He there makes the Emperor ask me, not only whether I would order the arrest of the Comte de Lille were he to be discovered in Paris, but also, in the event of my being a member of a Commission charged with trying him, whether I would be prepared to condemn him. According to him, I replied equally affirmatively on both points—and in what terms! He failed to realise that this odious invention was almost as disparaging of his hero as it was insulting to me. Never was an allegation more devoid of foundation, and I take this occasion to deny it formally.[7]

When I entered his study Napoleon was alone, and our whole conversation took place without witness. Not only did he submit me to no such test, but he avoided saying anything that might have caused me to entertain such an idea. He was at pains to avoid anything that might have upset me. I pointed out that since I was completely unacquainted with the men of the Revolution and their intrigues, I was very little suited to an office which required close familiarity with such matters. He replied, as M. de Cambacérès had already done, that these were the Duc de Rovigo's concern, and that what he asked of me, indeed expected of me, was to restore the Prefecture of Police to its position as a branch of the *magistrature*, as it had been in the time of the

[7] Nevertheless Molé maintains that in 1815 Napoleon reported to him, in almost identical terms, what Las Cases was to repeat later in the *Mémorial*. He adds that Pasquier, when he told him about this conversation, did not deny the fact, but insisted that the question had been put to him not by the Emperor but by Cambacérès. Moreover, according to Molé, he agreed that he had answered in the affirmative.

Sartines and the Lenoirs. 'You have been a magistrate', he added, 'and it is as such that I have chosen you. The man you will be replacing will have left you plenty to do in this respect, plenty of things to be put right. I want you to clean up the police for me. I am not talking about all the financial muck that M. Dubois is mixed up in; it would be insulting you to dream of cautioning you against such a danger. But when the chief has shown so little delicacy, one is bound to assume that his subordinates will have got into the habit of not being too particular, and you will have to go into things very closely with them. For the rest, I have complete confidence in you, and I am sure that you will prove to be worthy of it.'

It was difficult to resist such words, spoken by such a man, and an hour later I had taken the oath. Napoleon was particularly insistent that it was as a *magistrate* that he had chosen me, and that he intended the Prefecture of Police to become a genuine branch of the magistrature, for in the course of the day he told many people so, amongst others M. Mollien and M. Daru, who more than once repeated to me what he had said.

So there I was, Prefect of Police.[8] No one was more astonished by this great change than I; indeed, I was more than astonished, I was dismayed. My mind was filled with the most disturbing thoughts. However, I was also given considerable encouragement, for everybody was delighted that the police had been taken out of the hands of the man whom I was replacing. They might well have doubts as to my ability, but they did me the justice to raise none as regards my intentions, and of all the consolations that could have been offered me there was none I valued so highly.

I was not, of course, unaware that it would mean breaking with my old social connections. Friends, whose feelings and opinions I had shared, would not forgive me for becoming so closely involved in an order of things which they did not fully accept. In the life of a public man there are few incidents more painful than those that lead to changes of this kind in his personal relationships. Still, I did not have too much to complain about; I succeeded in retaining pretty well all those friendships that

---

[8] With a salary of 30,000 francs (equivalent today to about 90,000 francs), to which must be added an allowance of 10,000 francs as Councillor of State; which was increased in 1812 by a supplement of 12,000 francs a year, made up out of the revenues from the Extraordinary Domain in the Ilyrian provinces.

meant most to me. It was especially on my wife's account that I dreaded the resentment, the hostility, of society; I was rather worried about the effect that this new situation, so remote from her experience, might have upon her. Thanks to her superior understanding she quickly showed herself to be above all secondary considerations; she was determined to see only the good that she herself would be able to do; and the world, which is not always either unjust or ungrateful, soon did her justice and gave her the position she was entitled to.

His new post seemed to Pasquier all the more difficult in that he was not acquainted with his immediate superior, Savary, Duc de Rovigo, who had succeeded Fouché some months earlier. 'I had no liking for him, and he had as little for me.' He might, it is true, have derived some satisfaction from the fact that Cardinal Maury, appointed Archbishop of Paris on the same day that he became Prefect of Police, professed to see some similarity between his own position and Pasquier's: 'He kept saying to me: "The Emperor has satisfied two of the chief requirements of the capital. With a sound police force and a sound clergy, he can always be sure that public order will be maintained, for an Archbishop is also a Prefect of Police".'

'. . . Happily, with one exception, Inspector-General Veyrat[9] and his son, two of the worst types I've ever come across . . . the organisation of the Prefecture of Police was in good shape, because it had originated in 1789 when, during the mayoralty of Bailly, the police had been linked with the municipal council, and it had preserved the procedures and good traditions of those days'. In addition, there was a Committee consisting of the Minister of Police, two Councillors of State, MM. Réal and Petit de la Lozère, a Maître des requêtes, M. Anglès, and the secretary-general of the Ministry M. Saulnier, which used to meet once or twice a week, and which ensured the coordination of the Paris Police force with those in the rest of the Empire. 'All arrests ordered by any one of them had to be confirmed before being carried out by the Minister, who thus became responsible for them.'

The existence of the Police Committee, which I have just explained, could, without the slightest doubt, be a useful guarantee against those abuses of authority that are so easily committed

---

[9] According to Pasquier, Veyrat was 'in close touch with Constantin, the Emperor's valet, through whom he transmitted a daily bulletin intended as a check on the bulletin submitted by the Prefect.'

when one controls such a redoubtable force as that which was entrusted to us; and, thanks to the attitude displayed by most members of the Committee they were often able to prevent, or if that was impossible, to minimise, any unnecessary harshness.

There was another part of the powers assigned to me, which did not derive from the Ministry of Police, in respect of which I came immediately under the direction and orders of the Ministry of the Interior.[10] This was the municipal police properly so-called, which included the lighting and cleansing of the town, supplying the markets, collecting the bread tax, as well as the responsibility for making or enforcing that swarm of regulations that is required if the inhabitants of a great capital are to be in a position to satisfy their needs and pleasures. This part of my duties, though involving great attention to detail and in itself taking up a great part of my time, was nevertheless the one that most pleased me; it gave me an opportunity to do a great deal that was useful, without demanding any of that severity which is always so painful to exercise. It required firmness, however, for there were many abuses I had to put an end to. It was here especially that all that dirty business was carried on which had sullied the reputation of my predecessor's administration.

Another task, which from the outset demanded my close attention, was the prisons. I was responsible for them as regards everything concerning security and the maintenance of order. Thus the porters and jailers were under my orders, whereas, by a curious distribution of powers, everything concerning their material needs, food and clothing for prisoners and the upkeep of the buildings, fell within the jurisdiction of the Prefect of the Seine; hence the continual wrangling between the two Departments, the everlasting complaints and quarrels, that were as detrimental to the authorities as they were to the prisoners. As soon as I arrived at the Prefecture of Police I discovered that, on this subject, relations with the Prefect of the Seine had reached a state of deplorable bitterness. My first care was to restore things to a better footing, convinced as I was that a good understanding between two branches of the administration that have to work together is the first condition for success. Besides, in certain respects, M. Frochot was an excellent man; he welcomed my advances with enthusiasm, and from then on we were always on the best of terms.

[10] A position then occupied by Montalivet.

Right from the start I was determined to visit the prisons myself; it was a painful duty and they made a deep impression on me, especially the one at Bicêtre.

During a visit to Saint-Lazare, a penal prison for women under sentence, in which some splendid workshops had been established, I was continually accompanied, in addition to the porter, by a little man who performed the duties of clerk of the works, and who seemed to be able to answer any questions I asked. He followed close at my heels, and appeared to want to attract my attention. I was just about to leave when, unable to contain himself any longer, he addressed me in these words: 'Your honour does not recognise me. Yet it was I who had the honour of signing you in here in 1794.' I had in fact been detained in this prison at the time when the Terror was piling up its victims and I was one of those who seemed doomed to certain death. Indeed, it was only the excution of Robespierre that had saved me. It was certainly a singular fate that had brought me back, equipped with such vast powers, to a place where I had once been so cruelly oppressed; and this little fellow, who over the same period of time, had experienced so many different regimes, was almost proud of having done so; and, in order to draw attention to himself, was not afraid to recall the position of trust that he had enjoyed under the Terror. Fundamentally, what was he but what we usually regard as a good employee, a man who never looked beyond what he considered to be his duty, and who had been solely engaged in carrying out honestly the job that provided him with a living? Are we not making a mistake, if we presume to demand of the general run of mankind that they should do anything more than this?

For anyone who had merely glimpsed the prisons of Paris before the Revolution, it was impossible not to recognise what a remarkable improvement there had been in conditions since then, especially from the point of view of health. Yet nevertheless how much still remained to be done! And what an immense difference there was, for example, between what had been achieved for the hospitals and what had been done for the prisons! What was this distinction to be attributed to if not to the advantage the hospitals enjoyed in being administered on a charitable basis, entirely dependent upon benefactions and solely inspired by the passion for doing good? But would it be impossible to extend to the prisons all the advantages of such a free, charitable administration? I did not think so. Certainly, the need for security, which had to be vigorously maintained, would not make it possible to allow an administration of this kind the same latitude that had been accorded to it in the hospitals; but it would be quite easy for it to play a part, and that would already be of considerable importance.

After the prisons I had to visit the hospitals. They were not under my immediate supervision, but nevertheless my administration normally had a number of points of contact with them, and for this reason I felt obliged to have a thorough knowledge of them. Moreover, as Prefect of Police I was a member of the General Council for hospitals, and I was determined to carry out my duties on this Council as assiduously as possible.

My predecessor had always been unwilling to attend, because he would have had to accept the chairmanship of the Prefect of the Seine, which he considered to be beneath his dignity. I disregarded this point of etiquette, which struck me as being all the more out of place in that it was a question of a charitable enterprise in which I should be associating with the most honourable men. They were most grateful that I was so eager to help them in the good work they were trying to do, and were in fact doing; for it was thanks to them that the hospitals of Paris were, without doubt, the best run of any in Europe.

The part that I was able to take in their work, and the services that I was in a position to render them, contributed much to the friendly attitude that people displayed towards me, of which the Parisian bourgeoisie gave me proof on more than one occasion. This class, if I may be allowed to say so in passing, is one of the most estimable that one can hope to meet with in any capital of the world. I have always found it to be devoted to public order, extremely conscientious and ready for every sacrifice demanded by the public good. Its morals are generally sound; and one peculiarity which often amazed me was the perfect innocence of many of its young girls, who lived, and were sometimes brought up, alongside the haunts of prostitutes.

The Duc de Rovigo was not at all pleased about my appointment; and it was not long before I had plenty of evidence of his malicious attitude towards me. Every day I used to get notes, passed on by his Department, and always containing admonitions or complaints about something that had been done by one or other member of my administration. He welcomed these complaints, and indeed encouraged them, pretending that he was mixed up in all sorts of business and responsible for it. Strengthened by the Emperor's lack of confidence in M. Dubois, he had taken advantage of it to arrogate to himself the right to make all important appointments to the outside staff of the Prefecture. Since these employees did not, therefore, owe their position to the Minister to whom they were responsible, they naturally felt less consideration for him. Determined not to put up with this, I should have been obliged to offer my resignation, had it not been that the Duc de Rovigo himself became convinced, by a fortunate conjunction of circumstances, that this right of appointment had, as far as he was concerned, been reduced to a mere formality, and that, apart from one or two cases where the decision was difficult, the officers proposed by myself always had to be accepted. The Duke was surrounded by subordinates always ready to flatter him, and they had no great difficulty in turning his head for, although naturally intelligent, he was entirely lacking in education. Every morning he used to invite the editors of certain newspapers who were in his pay to lunch with him, and it was then all these unjustified and unreasonable complaints about my Department were put forward. On one or two occasions I was present at these luncheons. They were only too anxious I should be invited because they would have been delighted to trip me up and get me to convict myself out of my own mouth. But I found these gatherings so disgusting that in order to avoid attending them I soon fell back upon the all to wellfounded excuse that I was too busy.

In the whole of this malevolent group the most dangerous of my enemies was a certain Desmarets.[11] He seemed to have assumed a special responsibility for keeping me under observation, spying upon me and catching me out. His reports were calculated to strengthen the Duc de Rovigo's prejudices against me. Fortunately for me, I found justice and protection at the hands of M. Maret, Duc de Bassano. As I mentioned earlier he had some hand in my appointment; I had called upon him immediately he returned to Fontainebleau, and he had insisted upon my

---

[11] Desmarets was head of the Sûreté Générale de l'État, the secret police. It was his Department—in fact a certain Jean-Marie François, a former royalist lawyer—which prepared the famous bulletins for Fouché, and later for Savary. Cf. Ernest d'Hauterive: *La Police Secrète du Premier Empire* (1808–09), published by Jean Grassion, Paris, 1963.

visiting him frequently. He had no liking for the Duc de Rovigo, then rather looked down upon by his colleagues; he had a very low opinion of his abilities, and was anxious, moreover, lest this newcomer to the government should make too rapid an advance in the Emperor's confidence, a confidence which he himself preferred to enjoy exclusively. His wife, who had considerable influence over him, detested the Duchesse de Rovigo. Thus from that side, everything was in my favour.

M. de Sémonville, my old comrade in the Parlement and a close friend of M. Maret, also helped to establish me in his estimation, and I soon found myself waiting upon the Secretary of State from ten o'clock to midnight almost every evening, sometimes staying till one o'clock in the morning. There, in the course of chatting and playing billiards with the Minister,[12] I had the opportunity of telling him everything that I thought might usefully be conveyed to the Emperor, and that seemed likely to offset the mischief-making to which I was submitted.

I used to seek the Archchancellor's advice upon all matters where he was willing to give it, for in this respect he was prudent enough to insist upon considerable circumspection. This was characteristic of the extreme concern about their positions that was felt even by those who held the highest posts in Napoleon's entourage. The first time I met M. de Cambacérès again after my appointment to the Prefecture of Police, he hastened to warn me that henceforward I must expect to see him less frequently than in the past. 'Since I may well be the depository of very important secrets, that must be kept between the Emperor and myself,' said he, 'it would not be proper for me to maintain too intimate relations with anybody, as this might occasion uneasiness about my discretion.' There was never much danger of this because, very fortunately for me, what he had said to me at Fontainebleau turned out to be correct, and Napoleon's confidences to me never put me in a difficult or embarrassing position. However, as Prefect of Police, I was, whenever I wished to be, entitled to be present at the audience that he used to give when he was getting up, and there I used to meet those who enjoyed his closest intimacy—his marshals, the generals commanding his

[12] The future Marshal de Castellane, who spent several evenings at the Duc de Bassano's in March 1811, notes that: 'His Excellency played billiards with Baron Pasquier who was much better than he was. The latter used to boast that he allowed the Duke to win a game from time to time, one out of three for example, simply to please him.'

bodyguard, his aides-de-camp, and those who had just returned from an important mission or who were about to take up some high command and had come to receive their final orders.

Before this audience, which was known as 'le grand lever', there was another, 'le petit lever', to which only the members of his personal staff were admitted, the chief of whom was the Marshal of the Palace, Duroc. The Abbé de Pradt, who was the Archbishop of Malines, was, as his Almoner, also entitled to attend this 'petit lever', which he often used to do. We nearly always knew when he was there because his conversations with the Emperor lasted so long; it was with him that Napoleon most frequently used to thrash out the affairs of the clergy.

These gatherings at the 'grand lever' were often very curious. Everyone paid the utmost attention to the master's slightest word; as a rule he spoke to everyone, putting some question relating to his duties to each individual in turn. As a rule, it was easier to tell whether he was satisfied from his expression and a certain affability in his manner than from anything he actually said. If he was annoyed, however, he expressed himself curtly, even roughly. If one had anything to tell him of a private nature, one had to ask the Chamberlain on duty for an interview, and this was rarely refused. I seldom availed myself of this privilege, and never, I think, during the first year.

The few words that I did exchange during this period with Napoleon were restricted to questions about some of the details of my administration, questions that I knew I must always be able to answer exactly. He had, for instance, a mania for asking such questions as, How many wine-barges are there on the river? How many sacks of wheat in the market?, etc. etc. And you always had to give him the precise number, he was never satisfied with an approximation. Unfortunately, I had precisely the kind of memory least adapted to supplying him with this kind of information, and the difficulty of giving accurate answers decided me to keep a little notebook, which I often carried with me, containing the principal and most curious statistical details of my administration.[13] I showed this to the Ministers of the

[13] Pasquier was not the only one to have had this idea. If Las Cases *Memorial* is to be believed, Napoleon said that Mollien 'had organised the Treasury on the lines of an ordinary bank: so much so that in one small notebook I constantly had in front of me a complete account of my business affairs; receipts, expenditure, arrears and resources'. In addition, Colbert used to do the same for Louis XIV,

Interior and of the Police and to the Prefect of the Department. They were all struck by its usefulness; the Prefect decided to prepare a similar one for his own administration, and this was the origin of that statistical work on the Department of the Seine which M. de Chabrol brought to such perfection, and which is today accepted as authoritative by anyone concerned with statistics about the country's economy.[14]

It was the custom for the Prefect of Police to send the Emperor every evening a bulletin drawing attention to anything that had occurred during the day and required attention: the number of arrests that had been made during the previous twenty-four hours and the reasons for them; the state of supplies in the market and so on. In the same envelope one could include any special notes that one felt it might be useful for him to see, and this was a valuable means of arousing his interest. My predecessor had made considerable use of it; I did so only on fairly rare occasions, being quite willing to forego this method of drawing attention to myself in the eyes of the Minister of Police, who, like me, also used to send a bulletin every evening. One result of the care I took to limit the use of my privilege in this way was that I never became on intimate, let alone familiar, terms with the Emperor, and that he therefore never showed me any of the marked favours which he showered upon men whom he regarded as being devoted to him heart and soul. At the same time, I never had to put up with any of those rebuffs, those extremely offensive snubs, with which he was equally free. I always kept my distance and, if the esteem which I believe he felt for me was of no great benefit to me, at the same time I was spared the unpleasantness of being browbeaten by him.

Scarcely had I entered upon my new duties when I was put to a fairly severe test. I had to ensure as quickly as possible the carrying out of a decree insisting that the streets, squares and boulevards of Paris should be cleared of all the building materials that were cluttering them up as a result of the number of monuments of every kind that were being constructed from one end of the capital to the other. The amount of material that was lying about had become almost unbearable, and it had been the

to whom he would submit an agenda which 'His Majesty could carry in his pocket, and from which he could always tell the state of his finances'.

[14] Pasquier is referring to the *Recueil de tableaux dressés et réunis d'après les ordres de M. le Comte de Chabrol*, four volumes, quarto, Paris, 1821–29.

occasion for a pretty sharp comment from the king of Wurtemburg. Asked by the Emperor what he thought of Paris, which he had just been examining with the greatest interest, he said: 'Well, for a town that the architects have obviously just taken by storm, I think it's quite good!'

This pleasantry had not fallen on deaf ears, and orders were immediately given for the town to be cleared up. It was pretty generally accepted that the decree would not be carried out. The architects especially, even the Emperor's, M. Fontaine, the most reasonable and intelligent of them all, declared that it was impossible. In fact, from the Place de la Bastille as far as and including the Place Louis XVI, the whole length of the boulevards was so full of building stone that three carriages could scarcely drive abreast, and even two often found it difficult. On the quays things were even worse. The Place des Victoires and the Place du Carrousel were both covered with vast mountains of stone, through which lanes had been opened just wide enough to maintain indispensable communications. I began by visiting all these places; then I drew up a list of open spaces, not on the public highway, where it was possible to set up building-yards and depots; and finally I issued instructions as to how this was to be carried out. All this was done under my personal supervision, in the course of which I several times visited every part of the town, which, as a result, was completely cleared up in the course of a few weeks.

As Prefect of Police, Pasquier was naturally aware of the growing discontent amongst the clergy as a result of the conflict between the Pope and the Emperor.

The dissatisfaction felt by the Chapter of Nôtre Dame with regard to the claims put forward by Cardinal Maury[15] began to manifest itself in a more noticeable manner during the course of November. I knew about it, but it was in no sense part of my duty to concern myself with it particularly. M. Portalis, now Comptroller of Printing and Publishing, with whom I was on friendly terms, came to see me, about the middle of December, and told me he was convinced that a pastoral letter from the

---

[15] Cardinal Maury, whose appointment had not been approved by the Pope, was at this time in open conflict with the Emperor, and claimed that the administration of the diocese had been relegated to him by the Chapter.

Pope had arrived in Paris forbidding the Chapter to hand over the administration to Cardinal Maury, and declaring that anything he might do as delegate from the Chapter was null and void. The government were fully aware of the letter having been sent to the Cardinal; but as no one could be more interested in keeping it secret than he, they could not suspect him of indiscretion in this respect. Thus, if this was the one that M. Portalis was referring to, it must have been sent to Paris under cover of someone else. In fact, in spite of the close watch that was kept upon the Pope at Savona, not only this pastoral letter, but another, and much more strongly worded one, had reached the hands of an ecclesiastic to whom His Holiness had sent it direct.

In giving me this information M. Portalis added that it was impossible for him to reveal how he had managed to get to hear of such an important matter, but that he could assure me that, unless steps were taken, the letter would be freely circulated in Paris before many days were out. He went on to say that he considered it to be very desirable that its publication should be prevented; and that if the Minister of Police were to send for certain ecclesiastics, whose names he gave me, and told them that he had been informed of the existence of the letter and that he had decided to hold them responsible if it became public, we could rest assured that they would find ways and means of preventing it from being divulged. Naturally enough M. Portalis authorised me to convey this information to the Minister of Police, and I at once informed him. He appeared to be well pleased, and said that he would act upon it; and indeed I believe that he followed the advice I had passed on to him, for, by the end of November, nothing had yet been heard of the letter.

However, the misunderstanding between the Cardinal and the members of his Chapter continued to increase. At the head of his opponents was the Abbé d'Astros, canon and vicar-general of the Cathedral, and closely related to M. Portalis. He had already drawn attention to himself by his resistance to the Chapter's intention of investing Cardinal Fesch with certain powers, and there had been some question at the time of banishing him. But the Cardinal, who did not want these powers and was only too happy to be spared the embarrassment of refusing them publicly, had succeeded in getting the order rescinded.

Faithful to the line of conduct I had laid down for myself, of never interfering in what was not within my province, and without seeking any opportunity for private conversation with the Emperor, once I had passed on the message I had received from M. Portalis to the Minister of Police I carefully avoided any word or deed which might have involved me more deeply in this affair.

On 1 January 1811, Cardinal Maury, having presented himself at the head of the Chapter to pay their usual duties to the head of State, Napoleon seized upon this opportunity of expressing his dissatisfaction, and addressing himself particularly to the vicars-general, he told them: 'Above all, gentlemen, you must be good Frenchmen, since that is the way to be good Christians as well. Let Bossuet's doctrine be your sole guide; with that, you may be sure of not going astray. What I am saying', he went on, pointing to the Abbé d'Astros, 'is chiefly addressed to you. I know that you are opposed to the measures prescribed by my policy, and that you are continually acting in an underhand way to prevent their execution. But I am aware of your plans, and I shall take steps to frustrate them.'

Everyone expected that, since he had made this speech before so many witnesses, it would be followed by severe measures. As soon as the audience was over, the Cardinal went up to M. d'Astros and asked him to accompany him to the Minister of Police who wished to have things out with him. Had he had the slightest tact, the least feeling for the proprieties, he would have realised how utterly shocking it was, how lacking in all delicacy, to suggest such an intervention between himself and his subordinate; the very most he should have done was to suggest a meeting with the Minister of Public Worship.

The Minister, assisted by M. Réal, first questioned the Abbé about the reasons for his opposition and the correspondence he presumably maintained with Savona. M. d'Astros, having answered all the questions that were put to him either negatively or evasively, the Minister finally asked him for his resignation, which he refused. In view of his refusal he was arrested, but before being committed to Vincennes he was taken home, so that he might be present while his papers were examined. Nothing escaped search; it was so thorough that they even examined his garments, and when they pulled out the lining of his hat they found the wretched pastoral letter that M. Portalis had told me about. I believe it was the one of which the first copy had been sent direct to Cardinal Maury; the second one was only discovered later. Asked about the use that he had made of this letter and about those to whom he had shown it, M. d'Astros was so inconceivably weak as to name three of them: M. de Lacalprade, a canon of the cathedral; the Abbé Guairard who worked under M. Portalis in the department responsible for the book trade; and M. Portalis himself. What could he hope to gain by this admission? Perhaps he wanted to give proof of his good faith, and to imply that, since he had confided in so few people, he had not acted from any evil intention.

I was still completely ignorant of this discovery and the admission made by M. d'Astros when, the following day, on my way to the Council of State, I happened to call at the Ministry of Police, and was most surprised to be told: 'If you meet M. Portalis going to the Council, whatever you do don't try to prevent him from doing so'. I asked the Minister what was the point of this recommendation, but he refused to give me any explanation. When I arrived at the Council M. Portalis was already there. Napoleon took the chair. Scarcely had he taken his seat than a scene began which, in view of the words the Duc de Rovigo had let slip, I could only suppose had been prepared in advance. Every effort was made, however, to make it appear simply as an outburst of anger that he could no longer contain.

Having enquired whether M. Portalis was present, the Emperor immediately went on to ask him, in the most offensive manner, 'How he dared to venture within the precincts of the palace when he was guilty of such treachery?' Then, after pointing out that his treachery consisted in his having known about and furthered a rebellious relationship with the Pope, the ruler of a foreign country, he declared that 'never had such shameless perfidy been seen, never in the course of his life had he known anything so repulsive, and this perfidy was the act of a man in whom he had placed special trust. He was at a loss for words to express his indignation'.

What I have here reduced to a few lines provided the material for a philippic lasting a quarter of an hour. The further he went the more terrifying became the tone of his voice, his gestures, his expression, and when he had finished everyone remained dumb with fear and bewilderment. M. Portalis, overwhelmed and almost prostrate, was scarcely able to stammer a word or two expressing his conviction that he had not failed in any of his duties by refusing to betray a relative and childhood friend whom he had, moreover, been at pains to hold back from the dangerous road on which he saw him embarking. Scarcely had he uttered these few words, than the Emperor started speaking again, with even greater vehemence, and managed to find still more savage terms in which to express his wrath. I felt that I was not justified in remaining silent and, seizing the first possible moment, I rose to my feet and said that it was my duty to come to the defence of M. Portalis and to supplement what his emotion had prevented him from saying. I then recounted what had passed between him and myself in the middle of the previous month, as well as the warning which, on his advice, I had given to the Minister of Police. I added that doubtless the Minister had made good use of it, since the Pope's letter had been kept completely secret, and would still be unknown had they not dared to act upon it. In conclusion, I expressed the view that the confidence with which M. Portalis had entrusted me ought to free him from any suspicion of treachery, and that it would perhaps be more justified to attribute to me, rather than to him, the appearance of culpability, seeing that I had not given as much weight to his warning as I might have done.

This short plea, which put the matter in a very different light and appeared to interest the Council greatly, produced an expression of angry impatience on the Emperor's face. After a moment's silence he began speaking again, apparently without paying the least attention to what I had said, and continued to abuse M. Portalis. I wanted to speak again, but was prevented from doing so by my neighbour, M. de la Valette, who begged me not to, and insisted that under the circumstances I should do more harm than good. And, indeed, what hope was there of arousing pity in a man of his kidney, when he had already gone so far? The scene concluded with these words: 'Get out, Sir, and never let me set eyes on you again!'

When M. Portalis had in fact left the room, the whole Council remained speechless for several minutes. Presently the silence was broken by Napoleon, who, in a much milder voice, expressed his deep grief at discovering what he still called an act of treachery in a body which he had hitherto always found loyal and devoted, on which, moreover, he had always bestowed the highest marks of his confidence, and to which he had been accustomed to reveal his innermost thoughts with complete freedom. It was a misfortune which all members of the Council would doubtless regret as much as he, and, in justice to them, he was convinced that they were deeply distressed by it. 'The Prefect of Police', he added, 'felt called upon however to defend M. Portalis. But he is a friend of his, and we must show indulgence towards the feeling that prompted him to do so.'

Thus he made no formal attempt to throw doubt on the facts that I had put forward, and it is clear that during the time he had remained silent he had been making up his mind what attitude it would best suit him to adopt towards me. The nuisance of having to find a new Prefect of Police if he dismissed me, and maybe the notion that it would be inexcusable to punish me for acting sincerely and conscientiously, doubtless determined the forbearance and the conciliatory tone of his last remarks to the Council. The blow had been struck, and everyone, Councillors of State, attorneys and auditors experienced a feeling of fear and sadness which it was beyond his power to dissipate. There is something profoundly disheartening in seeing an all-powerful being thus breaking and crushing his victim, without allowing him either time or means to defend himself. It offends those feelings most worthy of respect, and revolts even the most submissive consciences.

In vain Pasquier wrote to the Emperor in the hope of saving his friend.[16] *The only reply he received was instructions to inform Portalis that he had been banished to Aix-en-Provence. When he next met Napoleon, all the latter said to him was: 'I am afraid, Sir, that you do not fully understand the duties of a Councillor of State'; to which Pasquier replied: 'In this, as in all other matters, Sire, I believe that one is not likely to go far wrong so long as one obeys one's conscience.'*

'These were my literal words. He changed the subject without further comment, and from that time on he never said another word to me which had any bearing on this deplorable business . . . I had firmly fulfilled an obligation prescribed alike by my conscience and my personal feeling. As a result my position improved, not only in the Council, but among all those comprising the Government, and even those closest to the Emperor.'

[16] The original of this letter is preserved in the archives at Sassy. The final paragraph reads: 'Sire, he is a son, a husband and a father; he does not know where to go, what to do with himself, or where to hide himself. How many people will be made unhappy if Your Majesty does not deign to cast a pitiful eye on this wretched family!'

Leaving general politics aside for a moment, I should like here to give some details about the internal administration of the Prefecture of Police.

I had ascertained, amongst other confirmed abuses, what happened with regard to obscene books. Once they had been seized on a warrant from the Prefect, they never used to be destroyed, but were simply locked away in a room on the second floor of the Prefecture. The Inspector-General, M. Veyrat, and maybe others as well, had the key, and made no bones about giving these books to their friends as presents. It had been the same with M. Dubois. I was told that on several occasions, when his colleagues from the Ministry of the Interior dined with him, he had, as a gesture of politeness, presented each of them with a packet containing the most curious publications of this kind. But this was not the most serious aspect of the business, for a certain number of the works that were seized always found their way back into the hands of the booksellers and pedlars from whom they had been taken, and they were prepared to pay a very high price for them, either to M. Veyrat or his agents. This was an extremely lucrative business transaction. The only way to put an end to it was to destroy the books: I did not hesitate to give the necessary orders, and I insisted upon them being destroyed in my presence.

I decided that all the books that had been locked away should be burnt in the courtyard of the Prefecture. It was necessary to take some precautions to ensure that the burning of such a huge mass of paper did not set fire to the surrounding buildings. I remembered that there was a vast iron fireplace, that had been used for burning the *assignats* in the courtyard at the Treasury. I got them to lend it to me, and the whole operation was carried out without difficulty in a period of three hours.

It is worth noting that books that were seized on political grounds were always immediately sent to be pulped, only two or three copies being kept back to provide evidence where this was necessary, or to be used for purposes of comparison. It was in this way, for instance, that I came across the only two copies still in existence of the first work by M. de Bonald, *The Theory of Power*.[17] It was perhaps the most remarkable book he had

[17] *La Théorie du pouvoir politique et religieux dans la société civile, démontrée par le raisonnement et par l'histoire* was published at Constance in 1796. The Catholic and royalist opinions that were expressed in it led the Directory to seize the work

written, and as the author himself did not possess a single copy I gave one of them to him, while the other, I must confess, found its way into my library. This was a breach of trust for which I hardly reproach myself, however.

Amongst my staff, I made a discovery of a quite different kind, but even more distressing. One day, at the Council of State, M. Fiévée[18] told me that I had in my employment a very unfortunate man, whom he could confidently recommend to me, since he was a relation of his. M. Perlet, his brother-in-law, did in fact work in the secretariat of the Prefecture of Police. He had been deported at the time of the 18 Fructidor, together with MM. de Marbois, Pichegru and many other interesting victims, and the deportation had ruined him by destroying a paper which, at that time, he both owned and edited. On his return to France after the 18 Brumaire he had knocked at every door in the hope of restoring his fortunes, but without success; and he had been only too happy to find a refuge in the offices of the Prefecture. 'True,' added M. Fiévée, 'after his return to France his behaviour was not entirely beyond reproach, and I do not claim that he is blameless, but when a poor devil has been so roughly treated by life he deserves some indulgence.' I replied that I agreed with him in this respect, and that if I found an opportunity of being of service to his brother-in-law I should be delighted to do so.

The very next day I had M. Perlet sent to my office, told him of the promise I had made to M. Fiévée, and assured him that I intended to keep it. I was surprised by the eagerness with which he thanked me, and could not help noticing a certain exaggeration in the way he did so, as well as an air of humility that I found most displeasing, which almost made me regret the friendliness of my words. This disagreeable impression was confirmed by a letter that I received two days later. In it he told me that, taking advantage of certain connections that he had been able to establish, during his exile, with men devoted to the cause of the royal family, he had become a secret agent for the Imperial Government and, on the instructions of Desmarets and M. Dubois, maintained a correspondence with one of the best-known of the Pretender's agents in England: M. Fauche-

and have almost all the copies destroyed. The book, which had thus become extremely rare, was only reprinted in 1843, after the author's death.

[18] Joseph Fiévée had been the editor in chief of the *Journal de l'Empire*.

Borel.[19] The purpose of this correspondence was to discover the secrets of the royalist party, especially to get to know the men who were sometimes smuggled into France and thus to know precisely when to expect them. He had managed to convince them that a royalist committee existed in Paris, that he was its representative and always spoke on its behalf. In the end, he had been sent to England in order, as he said, 'to learn what were the hopes and the resources of the Bourbons and to discredit MM. de Puisaye and d'Antraigues in the eyes of the English government. The first was a man to be feared, since he was in a position to stir up dissension and to send agents to France'. And he added: 'I fully achieved the mission entrusted to me; you will find the proof of this in the original correspondence which is in the files of the Prefecture'.

Having thus been put on the scent by M. Perlet himself, it was easy for me to find out a good deal more than he had told me. I questioned the heads of the secretariat Division and of the first police Division, both completely honest men whom I had already recognised as being trustworthy. Both of them spoke of this wretch with horror, and informed me that he was born in Geneva, and as such was a compatriot of M. Veyrat, who had got him into the secret service and introduced him to M. Dubois. After Perlet got back from England, M. Fauche-Borel, in order to maintain the relations he had established with him in London, had sent him one of his nephews called Vitel, who had recently returned from India. The latter had no secrets from Perlet, his uncle's friend, and even confided in him that his instructions were concealed in his walking-stick. It was made of hazel wood, and was unlikely to attract attention. As soon as Perlet had got out of the young man everything he wanted to know, he had had him arrested by his friend Veyrat, who naturally discovered the documents concealed in his walking-stick; and the unfortunate Vitel, having been handed over to a military commission, was sentenced to death and shot on the parade ground at Grenelle.

From that time there had been some dissension between these two wretches, or at least so it appeared; though it did not require

[19] Louis Fauche-Borel, a professional conspirator, continued to plot on behalf of the Comte de Provence (Louis XVIII) throughout the period of the Directory, the Consulate and the Empire. He received but little reward however. Louis XVIII, on the advice of Blacas, refused to go on making use of him. For this interesting character see G. Lenotre: *L'Affaire Perlet*, Paris, 1930; J. Berteaux: *Secrets d'un siècle*, Paris, n.d.

much intelligence on my part to refuse to take this seriously. I
was informed by the head of the First Division that all minutes
of correspondence were in M. Veyrat's hands, and that he had
also been given a list of words, written on a large number of
cards, which served to disguise the names used in this correspondence. I sent for M. Veyrat, at a time when he would be
least expecting it, and ordered him to bring me immediately the
files containing the minutes and the cards. I flattered myself that
I was thus depriving him of the means of pursuing his odious
machinations without my knowledge; and in fact I heard nothing
more about the matter, until suddenly the Duc de Rovigo had
M. Perlet arrested, because he had kept back for several days two
letters that he had received from London without passing them
on to M. Desmarets. I was thus convinced that my precautions
had been of no avail, since, to all appearances, M. Desmarets
had a duplicate list of the agreed words. I was happy, therefore, to
be rid of this wretch.

Amongst the documents that M. Veyrat had to hand over to
me, I found two that deserve mention. The first was the minute
of a letter written by Perlet on 3 August 1806 to Fauche-Borel.
It was the joint work of M. Desmarets, Perlet and M. Dubois.
This item had its piquant side for me, because, having been
written at the time when I had just been appointed *maître des
requêtes*, M. Dubois thought he could take advantage of this
occasion to raise certain questions about me and to satisfy himself whether or not M. Molé and I were maintaining relations
with the Princes of the House of Bourbon; the passage referring
to us was all in M. Dubois' writing, and very adroitly written.

The second item[20] was a long note, written by M. Perlet but
revised by General Danican, an emigré living in London. It
contained some very interesting details about the kind of life
that all the French Princes living in England were leading, about
the men who were close to them, and also about the principal
people who were at that time in touch with the English government. The latter were, in general, very roughly treated in the
note, especially M. de Puisaye and M. d'Antraigues. Probably
the note had been prepared jointly by Danican and Perlet, and,
as part of his mission, he was to see that it was read by some
member of the English cabinet. When one finds M. Danican
plotting in this way with M. Perlet, and assisting him in his plans,

[20] The original of these two documents are preserved in the archives at Sassy.

it is difficult not to remember his appearance on 13 Vendémiaire as commander of the National Guard in Paris; and one
can scarcely help regarding the connection between the two
men as confirmation of the suspicions that his conduct at that
time aroused.[21]

In Perlet's report of his journey he reveals, in all its perfidy,
the part that he played with regard to Louis XVIII, who had
received him with the most touching kindness. I was to encounter this man once again: when he came out of prison in
1814 he had the impudence to present himself at the palace of
the Tuileries and demand an audience of the king. I was informed of this, and I considered it to be my duty to prevent His
Majesty from being so shamelessly deceived. He was shown the
door.

The rank-and-file at the Prefecture of Police had retained
some of the habits and customs dating from the Revolution. In
vain the Consulate and the Empire had replaced the Republic
and the Directory; in vain the Central Committee, consisting of
men from the lowest station of society, had given way to M.
Dubois, Prefect of Police, then to M. Dubois, Councillor of
State, and finally to Count Dubois, for in some of the offices
under his jurisdiction the public were still treated in very much
the same way as they had been in those charming days of
'equality'. By reducing everybody to the same level they
arrogated to themselves the right to treat everybody with the
same brutality. This kind of behaviour, however, had become
singularly anomalous in a country where dignities, titles and
decorations of every kind had eventually been restored to their
proper place in public esteem. No one knows how deeply the
people of Paris objected to this kind of behaviour, and how
grateful they were to me for putting an end to it.

Later, I had to take up the question of the very large number
of servants living in the capital, since it was desirable that, in
the interests of society as a whole but especially of their masters,
their behaviour could be easily supervised. Many thefts had been
committed in recent times; and it therefore seemed to me
necessary to introduce employment certificates for domestic
servants like those that are given to workmen, in which the

[21] Indeed General Danican, in command of the rebellious *sections* of Paris, had
led the attack against the Convention on the 13 Vendémiaire in a very feeble
manner.

name and status of their masters would be entered whenever they changed their employment. In this way they would no longer be able to conceal any misdemeanour, and anyone who engaged them would always be able to obtain such information about them as they considered necessary. In this way, also, the police would have, when they applied for their certificates, a means of checking whether they had previously committed some crime and whether they had been legally punished for it. They would also be in a position to warn such people as lawyers, cashiers and bankers; anyone, that is to say, who had special reasons for fearing domestic theft. However, the greatest difficulty in carrying out this measure came from the employers, despite the fact that it was so much in their interests. They were afraid that it might entitle the police to interfere in their business affairs; and, as a result, the regulations introduced by me were never fully applied, which explains why the use of these certificates was so easily given up.

In the administration of a great city nothing must be over-looked; and there is one aspect of it which, shameful as it is, nevertheless enables the authorities to render an important service. The existence of prostitutes is a necessary evil, inevitable perhaps as a means of preventing still greater licentiousness. But these unhappy creatures ought at least to be kept under supervision, and their health should be the object of special care since it exerts so strong an influence on that of young men.

The Paris police, in general so far-sighted before the Revolution, had in this respect nevertheless always displayed a negligence that it is difficult to explain. True, those prostitutes whom they knew to be sick were sent to hospital, but the police could only get to hear of their suffering from disease when it had already caused great damage and given rise to many complaints. My predecessor had had the happy idea of setting up a clinic, with the responsibility of visiting them, examining them in their homes, providing treatment for them and deciding when it was necessary for them to be taken to hospital. Unfortunately this idea had been rendered ineffective by the most revolting of abuses. Every prostitute had to pay a tax each month to meet the cost of the agents, doctors and remedies used by the clinics. The total sum came to about 30,000 francs, which was more than enough to provide everything necessary; but it was used for very different purposes. A surgeon, an old school friend of M.

Dubois, was put in charge of the establishment, and he alone was paid a salary of from 10–12,000 francs, though this did not prevent him from treating his position as a complete sinecure. Moreover, though I am almost ashamed to speak of it, M. Dubois' wife and mother-in-law were not above receiving from this fund 2,000 or 3,000 francs each, which they regarded as pin-money; while the remainder was shared by a few subordinate agents who, since there was no one to supervise them, either neglected their duties or treated them as an easy opportunity for blackmailing the poor girls into paying them to keep silent.

It took me some time to unearth these shameful facts. The surgeon, M. Dubois' friend, was then dismissed. I put a physician and a surgeon, both trustworthy men, in charge of the clinic, with authority to employ such assistants as they required, and I insisted that all the money provided by the tax, after paying the fixed salaries, should be spent on fees to those agents and surgeons who took the greatest care of the patients, paid the most visits and effected the most cures. I have never obtained more satisfactory results. Previously, one prostitute in eight had been sick: by the time I left the Prefecture, the number had been reduced to one in twenty-seven.

About the same time I had to carry out a reorganisation by which the city of Paris set great store. The fire brigade, so long famous for the excellent service it provided, had seriously degenerated during the last few years. When the ballroom at the Austrian ambassador's was burnt down, the Emperor had expressed great dissatisfaction with the way help had been organised. Thus one of the first recommendations that he made to me when I took over the Prefecture was that I should make a serious effort to establish the fire brigade on a better footing. There was, however, one great difficulty. While the services provided by this body came completely under my control, in so far as its finances, its organisation and the appointment of its officers were concerned, it was attached to the Prefecture of the Seine. The offices responsible for recruitment had admitted a considerable number of young men in well-protected positions, who had been prepared to pay highly for the privilege. Once their names were on the register, these young men, to save themselves the trouble and fatigue of performing their duties, had adopted the habit of paying elderly firemen to take their place on guard, and the latter were well satisfied with an arrangement which ensured them such a handsome wage. As a result, the new firemen never learnt their job, and, when a fire broke out, not only were they of very little help, but it also took a long time to find them. In addition to this the head of the fire brigade was a drunkard, and the majority of the officers under him should have been in the Invalides. Moreover, M. Frochot, the Prefect of the Seine, the most honest of men and in theory one of the most enlightened, was so easy-going and had such exaggerated confidence in all the people who had access to him, that the abuses were bound to increase under his administration. He must, however, have had an excellent disposition, for probably no one ever opposed him on really important matters more than I did, and yet, since he could not accuse me of any wish to harm him, we always lived on very good terms with one another.

Previously, the firemen had been selected from amongst the tradesmen, working on their own account when they were not on duty, not living in barracks and, in consequence, only obliged to take their turn on guard on the days assigned to them. In order to get a clear idea of the kind of reforms that were necessary, I had a great many meetings with competent men; especially a certain Morat, a man who had really founded the brigade before the Revolution. He was the only man who had made a success of it, and, as a result, had won a considerable reputation. He was very old, and he clung to the old methods and the free and semi-voluntary organisation that had served him so well; but times had changed.

I came to the conclusion that an essentially military organisation was much to be preferred. Such an organisation would involve the provision of quarters, and therefore considerable initial expense, but it would also have the advantage that it would provide the town with a crack body of men, which might even be made responsible for mounting guard at some of the principal establishments, thus relieving the ordinary garrison, which was already overburdened by the number of places for which it had to supply sentries. I had some difficulty in getting this idea accepted, but in the end I succeeded. The matter was discussed in the Council of State on a report by the Minister of the Interior, and eventually the Emperor endorsed a draft decree embodying my views. He would never agree, however, to any of his conscripts being used, either as the original basis of the brigade nor even as part of an annual draft, though the number of the latter would have been very small; his main concern was not to interfere in any way with the laws governing conscription. Notwithstanding these obstacles, I still managed to create a fine body of men.

After one unfortunate choice, the general in command suggested as the head of the new brigade an officer of the engineers, M. de Plazanet; he had served with great distinction, especially at the siege of Saragossa, where he had received wounds that made further active service impossible. It is to him that we owe the excellent organisation of the fire brigade, which is still under his command and against which no complaints has ever been raised.

I devoted the spring and summer of 1811 to visiting the various public establishments that required special attention. This tour of inspection had good results and enabled me to remedy a number of abuses. I discovered plenty of them. For instance, the marketing of wood, coal and meat had been handed over to monopolies, which were against the interests both of the consumer and the producer. I tried to reorganise the Poissy meat-exchange[22] on a less restrictive and more genuinely useful basis. Was this exchange really indispensable? For a long time I thought so, but today I am doubtful. There are plenty of such organisations, which, originally serving a useful purpose, continue to exist long after their usefulness has completely disappeared, and when only their drawbacks remain.

From a general point of view here is what may be said about the regulations that govern the supplying of the capital. Dating from before the Revolution, they were all done away with in 1789. In the early stages this inevitably led to considerable confusion; given time and political peace, this might perhaps have been overcome, but instead we almost immediately had the *assignats*, rioting, the Terror, then the 'Maximum'[23] and wide-

[22] La Caisse de Poissy, created in 1680, suppressed in 1715, re-established in 1743, again closed down by Turgot in 1776, and restored once more by Necker in 1779, disappeared during the Revolution. It was reconstituted in 1802, and effectively reorganised by Pasquier on 6 February 1811. Originally it was composed of officers selected from the cattle merchants, who received one sous in the pound on the value of the animals sold and who, in return, were under an obligation to make an advance to outside merchants on the price of all animals sold to the butchers of Paris. Under the Empire the Caisse was responsible for the sureties imposed on the butchers.

[23] In 1793, at the instigation of the Paris Commune, a decree was passed

spread destitution. Then came a period of extreme scarcity; everything was in short supply, even the prime necessitites of life. When order was restored after the 18 Brumaire, and everything had to be reorganised, it was simplest to revert to the mistaken methods in use before the Revolution.

The consequences of the complete freedom of trade which, in 1789, was granted to those responsible for supplying the capital with food, were mistakenly confused with those resulting from the terror, the 'Maximum' and the lack of capital caused by the abuse of paper money. Consequently, regulations that should have been regarded as temporary were adopted as definitive measures. I am convinced that eventually the defects of this system will be recognised, and that gradually it will come to be understood that it is necessary above all to rely upon competition. This is what the present government is already attempting, on a very broad scale, as regards the meat trade; and I believe it is on the right road.

I was at great pains to establish regular communication between myself and the forty-eight police superintendents. Meetings took place every week, at which I put questions about everything and got them to talk and even to discuss with me. In this way I was able to discover their capabilities, and to decide which of them were most deserving of my esteem and trust. I also learnt to understand a mass of detail which would otherwise have escaped me. I must be forgiven for continually reverting to the past like this, and I can only hope that it may have for the reader as much interest as it still does for me. It is twenty-two years ago that I began my career as a public servant, I have since held many positions and, under difficult conditions, I have perhaps rendered some real service to my country, but nowhere have I so fully experienced the satisfaction of doing good and preventing evil, within the limits of my strength, as during the time when I was Prefect of Police. It is not suprising therefore that my thoughts revert to that period with some measure of self-satisfaction.[24]

enforcing a uniform price, or *maximum* as it was called, for bread and other necessaries. As the decree was extended to include corn, it was regarded as insufferably 'extremist' by all owners of property, despite its value to the poorest classes in the city. Pasquier's hostility to it, as revealed in the following pages, throws an interesting light on his political views. (Trs.)

[24] In fact, if we are to judge by the opinion of specialists, Pasquier seems to have been a good Prefect of Police. Cf. Claveau: *De la Police de Paris et de ses abus*,

*In 1811 the appointment of his protector and friend, the Duc de
Bassano, to the Ministry of Foreign Affairs, gave Pasquier the opportunity to make contact with 'a quite new world'. 'There I used regularly
to meet the principal figures in the diplomatic world and came to understand much better than I had previously done the secrets of Imperial
policy; I began considering them with more perspicacity, and consequently with more fear and apprehension.'*

*To the uneasiness that the bad news from Spain and the increasing
conflict between the church and the Emperor had already aroused in
Pasquier's mind, economic difficulties were soon to be added.*

The outlook for the 1811 harvest had been extremely favourable,
and as late as June there were still high hopes of it. The way in
which the baking industry and the sale of bread were organised
in Paris depended upon prices being kept down, since bread
must always be available to those who were least well off. When
the price of corn went up the government had to come to the
help of the bakers, either by supplying them with flour at a price
related to that of bread, or by paying them a subsidy to cover the
difference. This was an immense burden for the government.
Unless it had stocks of flour in hand it was forced to buy dear
and sell cheap; and, as a result of this operation, it was bound to
contribute to the raising of prices, which nevertheless it had to
fight against.

In any case, the expense of subsidising the consumer on such a
scale was enormous, and, if it was not to get out of hand, it was
necessary for the government to guard against any kind of fraud,
especially on the part of the bakers. If they were supplied with
the flour that they required, they did their best to obtain more
than was actually necessary and then resold it at the current
price; if they were indemnified by money payments, this method
had the drawback of making them quite indifferent as to the price
they had to pay; and this often meant that, in agreement with the
shopkeepers, they forced the price up in order to make a higher
profit later on.

In addition to the fraud perpetrated by the bakers, there was
also that of the consumers, always hounded by the fear of going

Paris, 1831; Parent du Chatelet: *De la prostitution dans la ville de Paris*, 2 volumes,
Paris (1857). His natural prudence led him to concentrate his energies on purely
administrative questions, as may be seen in the hundred and eighty-two Ordinances
that bear his signature.

short and therefore demanding more than they needed, and sometimes even supplying those living outside Paris with the surplus they managed to acquire, and thus carrying on a very lucrative trade at the expense of the government. Furthermore, the administration had also to protect itself against all those people who daily flocked into the capital, and especially against those who came to bring other essential foodstuffs. As far as possible, and it was a very difficult business, it was necessary to stop them taking away in return not only the bread that they themselves required, but also enough to supply in part the villages and towns to which they were returning.

In many provinces, the good weather in June soon broke. Nevertheless, in the Departments nearest the capital, such as La Brie, La Beauce and almost the whole of Picardy, the harvest was still good, but it would have had to have been still better to make up for the failure in Normandy, in the provinces of the Nord and of the Midi, where conditions were extremely bad. Directly this situation became known, demand increased in the most favoured Departments, which happened to be precisely those from which the capital is usually supplied and, from August onwards, I was obliged to draw the attention of the Minister of the Interior, M. de Montalivet, to a situation which was deteriorating every day. At the beginning of September the Minister took the wise precaution of setting up a Food Committee to consider what measures could be taken. I was on this committee, together with M. Frochot, M. Réal and M. Maret, a Councillor of State.[25] The last of these had for a long time been in charge of catering for the army in the field, and some eighteen months previously the Emperor had also entrusted him with providing a reserve supply for Paris. What at that time was the extent of this reserve? An agreement had been concluded in 1807 with a company known as the 'Paulet Company'; the person chiefly concerned being, I believe, a certain Vanlenbergh, a highly experienced corn merchant. This company, which was obliged to maintain a permanent stock of 300,000 metric quintals of corn and 30,000 sacks of flour, had to compete with the trade in supplying Paris and, whenever required to do so by the Prefect, it had to send there and sell at the current price the amount of grain and flour that it was ordered to. When necessary, it had to immediately renew its stocks to the extent of what had been

[25] The brother of the Duc de Bassano.

sold, and it had to do this by means of purchases made outside a radius of thirty leagues from the capital or, if necessary, abroad.

The reserve that was organised in this way had a concession for supplying the hospitals, prisons and charitable institutions. This was a way of ensuring a steady turnover for its corn and flour, so long as they could be replaced; and it appears that during recent years the market had been very advantageous for the contractors. The Emperor always made the serious mistake of regarding high profits as a kind of theft against the State, and he was always trying to put a stop to it. This was what he now tried to do with the Paulet Company, and their trading rights were anulled by a decree published in 1810. The enterprise was replaced by a government body administered by M. Maret, but for this purpose he had to take over its warehouses, and he was naturally unwilling to do so until the quantity and quality of grain had been checked. This involved considerable difficulty and many disputes, and in the end it was not until November that M. Maret's management began.

During this six months' interval, the Company had continued to supply hospitals, prisons and charitable institutions, but there had been no replacements. By that time, prices were no longer favourable and M. Maret was in no hurry to order purchases to be made. Unlike the Paulet Company, he was not subject to inspection by the Prefect of Police; there was nothing to prevent him acting as he thought fit. By the time the difficulties began, all that remained in the reserve warehouses was 115,000 metric quintals of wheat instead of 300,000, and 11,000 sacks of flour instead of 30,000. With such small resources the reserve could only be operated on a very modest scale; M. Maret was unwilling to run any risks before he had increased his supplies; he therefore started buying, and, despite what was said to the contrary by his agents, his purchases were made in the region that normally supplied the capital.

By 15 September the bakers began to demand a new increase in the price of bread, but as the price of a 4-lb. loaf already stood at fourteen sous, no one was in a hurry to grant it. The Emperor was most reluctant to see this figure exceeded. The bakers were told that the high profits they had been making over a long period would enable them to put up with a temporary loss.

The result of this resistance to any increase in taxation was that, by the end of September, bread was becoming scarce, not only in the central markets, but also in the suburbs and the most populous districts. Anxiety increased and the price of bread inevitably had to go up. Towards the end of October the government decided to give the bakers a subsidy of five francs on every sack of flour that they bought. This measure proved ineffective however; bread became scarcer and scarcer, crowds besieged the bakers' shops, and by nine o'clock in the morning their shops were empty. The price of all foods that could take the place of bread increased at the same rate as flour; this was then selling at seventy-six francs a sack, which raised the price of bread to sixteen sous for a 4-lb. loaf.

By the beginning of November, in the hope of bringing down prices, a decision was taken to get the reserve to sell in the central market. By that time all that remained in its warehouses was 98,000 metric quintals of wheat and 24,000 sacks of flour. M. Maret had given orders for considerable purchases to be made at Hamburg and on the banks of the Rhine where the harvest had not been too bad; but the resources that these purchases represented were a long way off; transport was difficult to arrange and extremely slow, and the blockade of all ports, which was strictly maintained by the English, made it almost impossible to bring it by sea.

At this juncture we suffered considerably from the unintelligent way in which the administration then dealt with these problems. This was due to the hostile, or at least distrustful, attitude that the Emperor always adopted to those engaged in commerce. He had no confidence in them whatsoever, and was convinced that one was bound to be cheated by them; in consequence he insisted that all financial operations should be carried out through some agency responsible to his government. Thus, for his purchases at Hamburg, Lubeck, and later even at Danzig, M. Maret sent his own men with instructions to find, buy and despatch food. At first the loss of time was considerable; often the men he employed were not very skilful, and, moreover, however zealous they might be, they were no match for the lively intelligence of merchants whose connections were already established and who, in carrying out any business entrusted to them, always had the stimulus of profits. His mania for doing everything himself reached the point where, in order to ensure government transport from the Baltic to Paris, he ended up by having a string of auditors based at intervals along the roads and canals, who were entrusted with preventing any delays. Now there was certainly nothing for which their education had made them less suitable.

The general administration of supplies for the Empire changed hands with the creation of a Ministry of Trade; it was taken away from M. de Montalivet and handed over to M. de Sussy. We had no complaint to make about this change. M. de Sussy, who had for a long time been in charge of the customs, had a better understanding than M. Montalivet of the nature of the operations that had to be carried out. Moreover he had greater independence of mind and was better able to resist the Emperor's unsound ideas on this question.

On 1 February the price of flour on the open market was ninety-two francs a sack, and it was only possible to maintain supplies to the capital without raising the bread tax beyond the existing rate by making available from the reserve, at the price of seventy-nine to eighty francs a sack, as many as 1,300 sacks a day, which had to be bought wherever possible at the current price. It was then that Napoleon summoned the Food Committee to meet him, and from then onwards it met frequently under his chairmanship. Its discussions soon became important, because we had to oppose the Emperor's idea of imposing a general tax on the price of grain, in short a 'maximum'. Though he was aware that this measure would meet with some resistance, he was so accustomed to seeing everyone give way to his wishes that he was persuaded it would eventually be carried out, and that this would be the end of all our difficulties. Apart from M. Montalivet and M. Maret, who always displayed the greatest humility, all the other members of the Council boldly expressed their disagreement. M. Regnault in particular lost no opportunity of making clear the dangers we were bound to run into if we accepted this false solution, and I supported him as strongly as I could.

I did my best to show that there were only two ways of dealing with our difficulties: in the first place, to purchase as much wheat as possible abroad and, to this end, to accept the services of whoever was prepared to help; and secondly, to maintain and encourage its free movement inside the country, and especially to do everything possible to support the public markets so that no one was afraid to use them for the disposal of their produce. Although these views were not always in agreement with the Emperor's ideas, I must in justice admit that he never turned them down with the least display of ill-temper, and even appeared to be grateful to me for the firmness with which I expressed them. Since, fortunately for me, no serious disorders broke out during this period in the capital, and the police appeared to be both vigilant and effective, this was the time when I most incontestably enjoyed his esteem and when he appeared to set the greatest store by my services.

Before long the price of flour reached one hundred and eleven francs per sack; by 1 April it had gone up to one hundred and twenty-five francs; and by 15, to one hundred and fifty francs, with the price of wheat increasing proportionately. Anxiety began to give way to terror. Those who were buying outdid those who were selling, however exaggerated the latter's pretentions might be, and their wildness affected the price of everything sold in the market. Vegetables, even tailings, could scarcely be had for love or money, and the grocers' shops were besieged by crowds in search of rice and vermicelli. This excitement spread to all the neighbouring markets; at some of them the people even took to violence and shared out the corn amongst themselves. At the same time, such vast amounts of bread were taken from Paris for the armies in the field that if this had gone on we should soon have had to use government supplies to feed not only Paris but those living within a radius of ten leagues. At this juncture the Emperor considered it advisable to call an extraordinary meeting of the Food Committee, which, in addition to the usual members, was attended by M. le Comte Defermon, president of the Finance Division, M. Pelet, Councillor of State and M. Dubois, the former Prefect of Police.

When it became generally known that the Emperor was personally studying the seriousness of the situation and considering ways of alleviating it, public opinion was somewhat appeased. Immediately, the gates of Paris were closed to prevent the export of bread, and in order to temper the harshness of this measure a hundred sacks of flour were distributed to each of the neighbouring communes.

The scarcity grew worse; in some departments it was terrible. In Normandy, where bands of starving beggars roamed the countryside, there were dangerous signs of revolt amongst the people; in the neighbourhood of Caen there were risings and pillaging, and several mills were burnt down; in such circumstances the blind fury of the people starts destroying precisely what it is most important to preserve. This rising was only put down by the arrival of a regiment of the Imperial Guard, sent post-haste; the repression was very severe, and, in the executions that followed, even women were not spared. Such extreme ruthlessness was doubtless deplorable, but would anyone be bold enough to maintain that, in all the circumstances, it was not the only way to prevent worse disaster?

At the end of April one or two meetings of the Food Committee were held, at which the Emperor insisted more strongly than usual that vigorous steps must be taken to ensure the people's food supplies against the greed of those who were holding them up and monopolising them. The imposition of a tax was again proposed. And once again we did our best to show that it was both dangerous and useless. But our efforts were unavailing; on 12 May a decree, dated 8 May, was published in *Le Moniteur*, which had been drawn up without the participation, or I may say knowledge, of the Committee, explicitly imposing a tax on wheat in the six Departments which were the only ones then supplying the trade. These were the Seine, Seine-et-Oise, Seine-et-Marne, Aisne, Oise and Eure-et-Loir. By this decree the price of a hectolitre of wheat was fixed in these Departments at thirty-three francs. In the Departments which obtained their supplies outside this territory this price could be increased by adding the cost of transport, fixed by the Prefect on the instructions of the Minister of Trade and taking into account the distance as well as the legitimate commercial profit.

Napoleon was leaving to take command of his army, and he therefore saw this as a fitting kind of farewell to the most necessitous part of his subjects; in this way he hoped to ensure that they would remain contented during his absence.

This was only a minor consideration, however, compared with the drama that was being prepared.[26]

[26] Napoleon's preparations included even the printing of false roubles. Pasquier's agents having discovered a den of counterfeiters, 'the Duc de Rovigo came to see me in a state of utter consternation. The whole of this enterprise was carried on at the orders, and under the direction, of M. Desmarets, head of the Secret Police, by a printer called Fain, whose brother was one of the Emperor's private secretaries. It therefore had to be admitted that this had been thought out as a way of paying for the supplies that the French army would require in Russia.'

On the eve of his departure [9.5.1812], I had a short conversation with the Emperor which did little to dispel my anxiety. This took place after a morning audience; he kept me behind in his study, and, after one or two casual references to the work of my administration in general and to the special attention I should have to give to it during his absence, he came to the question of food supplies. In his usual way, treating the facts he wanted people to accept as being already established, he said to me: 'As to the famine, that's pretty well over. The harvest has begun, and in a fortnight's time you'll have nothing to worry about'. I replied that this was not how I saw it; that in the Paris region harvesting only began in the course of July, and often not before the end, and that therefore it would be nearer mid-August before bread could be on sale; that this would mean we still had three months to get through; and that these three months might well prove to be the most difficult of all, since supplies were continually declining. Nor should he forget, I added, that his absence was going to make the situation all the more dangerous, in that the actions of the government would necessarily lose some of their authority.

'For instance,' I said to him, 'when the revolt broke out near Caen, it was Your Majesty himself who gave the necessary orders for sending a regiment of the Guards there. These orders were carried out with a speed and energy that might well not be the case when the Emperor is four hundred leagues away from his capital. If by ill chance any serious insurrection were to occur, is there not reason to suppose that it might have disastrous consequences both at home and abroad? It is my duty not to conceal from Your Majesty the dangers that I foresee.'

Napoleon was struck by these brief reflections. When I had finished he remained silent, walking backwards and forwards between the window and fireplace with his hands clasped behind his back like a man lost in thought. I was following at his heels, when, turning abruptly towards me, he uttered the following words: 'Yes, undoubtedly, there is truth in what you say; it is just one more difficulty on top of all the others that I am bound to meet with in the greatest and most difficult enterprise I have ever attempted. But what has been begun must be carried through. Goodbye, my dear Prefect.'

Throughout the summer and autumn of 1812 disturbing news continued to arrive from Russia, despite the victory at the river Moskva and the capture of Moscow. 'It was inevitable that the anxiety felt in Paris by those most devoted to the Imperial Government should arouse in those who were hostile to it the hope of overthrowing it.[27] At the end of October we had proof of this . . . I refer to the Malet conspiracy.'

It is worth recalling the origin of this extraordinary episode. General Malet, 'an ardent patriot at the beginning of the Revolution', already compromised in earlier conspiracies and, to begin with, imprisoned at La Force, had later succeeded, thanks it would seem to Fouché, in getting transferred to a mental asylum in the Faubourg Saint-Antoine, under more or less nominal police supervision. There he struck up a friendship with a certain Abbé Lafon, who had been active in the Chouan rising and who had more recently been arrested for 'papist plotting'. It is not only birds of a feather that flock together: though Malet called himself a Republican and Lafon was a Royalist, they were united in their hatred of Napoleon.

Their plan was simple: to announce the death of the Emperor; then to present themselves at the entrance to two barracks and read out a fictitious proclamation and decree, setting up a Provisional Government and investing General Malet with full command of the armed forces; and finally to do everything in their power to win over the Paris garrison.

To begin with everything went splendidly. The details had been worked out by two confederates, a certain Boutreux, utterly devoted to Lafon, and a corporal Rateau, who, while visiting one of his relations in the asylum, had fallen under General Malet's influence.

Malet and Lafon left the asylum on 23 October at eight o'clock in the evening. The general donned his uniform, in the room of a Spanish priest who was one of their accomplices, and then—after losing valuable time in drawing up the proclamation and decree and having them copied—turned up at about half-past three in the morning at the Popincourt barracks, occupied by national guardsmen. The amazing thing is that the colonel and commander of these troops accepted the order to hand over without a word of argument. Malet now found himself with twelve hundred men at his disposal. Some of them were despatched to the Hôtel de Ville, while he himself led the others to the La Force prison, which he entered, without striking a blow, at half-past six, releasing two of his friends whose anti-Bonaparte feelings were known to him, Lahorie,

---

[27] Was this the reason why Pasquier 'advised' Chateaubriand to keep away from Paris on 4 September 1812?

former chief of staff to Moreau, and Guidal, recently involved in another plot. [28]

    Lahorie, supported by Guidal, had orders to arrest the Prefect of Police and the Prefect of the Seine, while Malet betook himself to military headquarters in the place Vendôme. [*The story is continued in the next chapter.*]

[28] Also freed at the same time, probably without his knowing why, was another very obscure prisoner, 'a certain Boccheiampe, a Corsican by birth, recently brought to Paris from Parma, where he had been imprisoned by the State for a number of years'.

V

The End of the Empire
1812–1814

THE MALET CONSPIRACY – BUSINESS STAGNA-
TION – CREATION OF PARIS GENDARMERIE –
GENERAL PESSIMISM AFTER LEIPZIG –
STRUGGLE BETWEEN THE EMPEROR AND THE
LEGISLATIVE ASSEMBLY – CONVERSATION
WITH NAPOLEON ON THE EVE OF THE FRENCH
CAMPAIGN – SETTING UP OF A NATIONAL
GUARD – PASQUIER'S SECRET SYMPATHY FOR
TALLEYRAND – CAPITULATION OF PARIS –
TALLEYRAND'S FALSE START – EMERGENCY
MEASURES FOR THE OCCUPATION OF THE
CAPITAL – DISCUSSIONS WITH THE TSAR –
ENTRY OF THE ALLIED SOVEREIGNS – DIS-
CUSSIONS AT THE HOTEL SAINT-FLORENTIN –
SHOCKING BEHAVIOUR OF CERTAIN ROYALISTS
– PASQUIER REMAINS IN OFFICE – INFORMS
NAPOLEON THAT HE IS JOINING HIS ENEMIES –
THE EMPEROR'S ABDICATION IN FAVOUR OF
THE KING OF ROME – FRUITLESS APPROACHES
BY THE MARSHALS TO ALEXANDER I –
NAPOLEON'S FALL ANNOUNCED IN THE
SENATE – FINAL ABDICATION

It had gone seven by the time Lahorie arrived at the Prefecture
of Police. I had just got out of bed when I heard a loud noise
coming from the room leading into my bedroom. My valet went
to find out what was the reason for it. Seeing a group of soldiers
he tried to stop them and defended the door of my room with
admirable devotion; but he was thrown aside with a bayonet
wound in his leg. As I was trying to reach the staircase leading
into the garden I was met by another body of soldiers, under the
command of an officer who made me return to my room, without

allowing his men to treat me with violence. I did not recognise this officer: he was wrapped in a cloak, while his most characteristic feature, his high forehead, was hidden by a large hat. It was General Lahorie. He informed me that the Emperor was dead, killed before the walls of Moscow, and showed me the faked decree though without allowing me to read it. He also told me that citizen Boutreux, who was with him, was going to take over my duties, and then he confined me to my room under the guard of a few fusiliers. He himself went off, leaving a picket at my house, which had previously been guarded only be a few disabled soldiers.

When he reached the Ministry of Police, there was a much more lively scene. The Duc de Rovigo, who was caught like me unawares, was in much greater danger. General Guidal, who nursed a particular hatred towards him, would willingly have seized the opportunity to get rid of him; he had found that some of the soldiers under his command were of the same disposition. General Malet had issued the most violent orders; what he expected of his lieutenants may be judged by what he himself did. He had been clever enough to select a body of men who had been torn away from their homes when they believed themselves to be too old to be called up, and who were therefore disposed to bear a grudge against the imperial government. They were commanded by officers almost all of whom were already worn out with age and exhaustion, and who were thus easily deceived. The soldiers that General Guidal commanded invaded the Minister's bedroom, and he was only saved by the firmness of General Lahorie. The profound resentment which he felt against the Duc de Rovigo yielded a little on this occasion to his natural generosity: he used the authority he had assumed to prevent any harm being done to him, but, as he declared later, the only way he could save his life was by taking him prisoner. 'There is nothing to worry about', he told Savary. 'You have fallen into good hands, and no one is going to kill you.'

The Duke was taken by General Guidal to La Force prison in a hackney carriage. Lahorie, as Minister of Police, signed the order for his detention; he assumed this office simply in order to save Rovigo's life, he said, and did not in any other way exercise its functions. But on this point he was not telling the truth, for immediately after installing himself at the Ministry, he sent for a tailor, from whom he ordered a Minister's uniform; then he got into his predecessor's carriage and had himself driven to the Hôtel de Ville, where he introduced himself as Minister of Police.

While all this was going on at the Ministry I remained in my bedroom. I completed my toilet, with my two fusiliers one on either side of me; then, wishing to know what was happening, I asked if I might speak to citizen Boutreux. He came, and was simple-minded enough to show me the decree and the proclamation. As soon as I saw them it was immediately clear to me that these documents were apocryphal, and had been fabricated by people who were quite ignorant of the customary forms. I contented myself with telling him that I was very surprised to hear of the Emperor's death, because only the previous day I had seen dispatches brought by the speediest courier, and that according to these he was quite well. When, a few minutes later, Mme Pasquier and my brother-in-law succeeded in joining me, I told them that everything that was happening was based on a gross imposture, which would soon be recognised as such.

I was debating the probable issue of this rash enterprise, when the second-lieutenant in charge of the picket came into the room; his name, as I later learned, was Lefévre. He was the bearer of an order from Lahorie, Minister of Police, and he informed me that he was going to take me to La Force. I therefore got into a hackney carriage with the second-lieutenant, which was at once surrounded by a dozen soldiers; half way there, noticing how small the escort was, it struck me that it might be possible to make the officer listen to reason. I took the line of assuring him that he was the victim of a clumsy imposture, and probably did not realise the consequences of taking part in such a criminal business, which might well cost him his life; I also insisted that the Emperor was not dead, and that the decree, in virtue of which he was acting, was a forgery. At first he was amazed; then, either thinking this was a trick on my part or else because he was afraid of the soldiers who were with us, he ordered the hackney driver to go quicker and the escort to mend their pace.

We arrived at La Force. My lieutenant hastened to hand me over to the porter, a very decent man called Lebeau, whose father, in the time of the Terror, had distinguished himself by the courageous services he had rendered to the unfortunate prisoners. It was to me that he owed his present place, and directly the gates were shut he put himself at my disposal. He informed me of what had happened at the prison that morning when Lahorie, Guidal and Boccheiampe had been set free. He also told me how the Duc de Rovigo had been brought to him, and that, as he was leaving, General Guidal had taken the precaution of handing over the outside guard duties to soldiers from the troops under his command. Finally, I learned that M. Desmarets, also conducted by an officer, had arrived shortly after the Minister and had also been committed to prison. After considering for some minutes what to do for the best and what steps should be taken first, I sent the porter's wife to find out whether another way out of the prison, which led into a different street than the main entrance, was also guarded by troops. I was waiting for her to get back, when who should come into the office but M. Saulnier, principal secretary to the Minister of Police, and the local adjutant, Laborde. They told me that everything was already over, that General Malet and Lahorie had been arrested, and that they had not lost a moment in coming to free me and the Duc de Rovigo.

We left together, the Duke and myself, in M. Saulnier's carriage which took us to the Minister's house. I had thus spent little more than a quarter of an hour in La Force, but though I had got no further than the office it had been an unpleasant experience, and I freely admit that I had been considerably upset by it. Here I should mention that on the way from the Prefecture to La Force I had not noticed any crowds or signs of unrest. The whole town appeared to be completely ignorant of what was going on. A few of the local inhabitants, who had recognised me in the hackney carriage, surrounded by my escort, had stopped, and appeared to be greatly surprised. The Minister of Police had noticed even less. The assertions contained in M. Lafon's account of the incident[1] are therefore completely untrue, for he speaks of the indignation that broke out against us as we were being taken away and of the threats to throw the Minister into the river. On our return we found a considerable number of people assembled on the Place de Grève, and there were many more on the Pont Neuf and on the quay opposite the Ministry of Police and the Prefecture. They already knew of General Malet's arrest, and were discussing the whole episode as an act of criminal folly.

This is what led to its collapse. On arriving at the Place

---

[1] *Histoire de la conjuration du général Malet*, Paris, 1814.

Vendôme, Malet repaired to the quarters of General Hulin,[2] the divisional commander. Leaving his escort at the door, he went up to the general's apartment accompanied by two or three officers and non-commissioned officers. He then informed the general of the Emperor's death; but noticing his expression of incredulity, he invited him to go into a neighbouring room in order to read the documents he had brought to show him. As soon as they entered the room, while General Hulin was glancing through the decree, Malet shot him in the head with a pistol, and he fell to the ground unconscious. This done, General Malet hastened to resume command of his troops, some of whom were attempting to force the door of the headquarters situated at the opposite end of the Place; but it had already been seen from there that something unusual was happening at General Hulin's apartment, and they were on their guard.

However, Malet managed to get as far as the office of General Doucet, the adjutant-general and chief of staff, who was already reading the decree, which had just been handed to him by the officer commanding the detachment that had arrived ahead of Malet, and realised that the document was a forgery. As he protested at this infamy, Malet was about to subject him to the same fate as General Hulin, when the adjutant Laborde, who was close behind him, seeing him reach for his pistol, hurled himself on him and stopped him, at the same time summoning to his help the soldiers on sentry duty outside. Those who belonged to Malet's troop no sooner realised what was happening than they hurriedly placed themselves under the orders of General Doucet and his adjutant Laborde, whom they were accustomed to obeying.

M. Saulnier, having heard of the Duc de Rovigo's abduction, betook himself to M. Réal's, who had already set off for the Archchancellor's, then to the Minister of War, and from there to the Military School, where he instructed General Deriot, commanding the Imperial Guard, to call out sufficient troops to restore order. Meanwhile M. Saulnier had himself driven to General Hulin's. He arrived there a few minutes after he had been shot by Malet, and found him in bed. The Minister of War,

---

[2] Hulin, who had taken part in the taking of the Bastille, was later in command of the Consular Guard and President of the Commission which condemned the Duc d'Enghien to death (1804). At this time he was commander of the Paris garrison.

having already been informed of Malet's arrest, had given the necessary orders for the troops who had been seduced from their duty to be taken back to Paris.

Thus, as far as General Malet was concerned, after only four or five hours of success everything was over. He had assumed that the orders he had sent out from general headquarters to all bodies of men throughout the division were bound to be implicitly obeyed, since they would have been transmitted through the ordinary channels. However much one may be impressed by the audacity of such a conception, it is impossible not to regard it as an act of madness. To succeed, it would have been necessary to have killed the Minister of War and his headquarters staff, and to have won over, disarmed or destroyed the general and the principal officers commanding those units of the Imperial Guard that the Emperor had not taken with him, and who were quartered in Paris and at Saint-Cloud. Now he must certainly have known that the Imperial Guard was not under the command of divisional headquarters. Its devotion to the Emperor, the Empress and the king of Rome was well-known; the greater part of it was quartered outside the town, at the Ecole Militaire at Courbevoie; its leaders would in consequence have been warned in time, and they had from four to five thousand men at their disposal.

On this occasion the adjutant, Laborde, behaved with the greatest energy. On leaving the Place Vendôme, where he had arrested General Malet, he hurried to the Ministry of Police and seized Lahorie, already established in the Minister's study, though beginning to feel anxious. He must have been beginning to wonder whether his credulity had not been abused by General Malet. Trusting in what the latter had told him, he had been to the Hôtel de Ville to find the government that was established by the decree, and had been utterly astonished to find no one there save the two companies of the 10th Regiment sent by Malet to occupy it. No one being able to give him the slightest information about the supposed Provisional Government, he had decided to return to the Ministry. Astounded by the tranquility that reigned throughout the town, where no one seemed to have heard of such a great event as the Emperor's death and the overthrow of his government, he was busy pondering upon these facts when Laborde appeared and took him prisoner. It was after this, and on orders from the Minister of War, that Laborde had gone to La Force, accompanied by M. Saulnier, to set us free.

On reaching the quay we encountered a column of grenadiers belonging to the Imperial Guard, which was drawn up in front of the Ministry awaiting orders. Its presence alone was sufficient guarantee that there would be no disturbance. It was therefore assumed that everything was finished, yet it was precisely then that I personally was in the greatest danger.

As my presence was required at the Prefecture of Police, I hurried off there as quickly as possible. I was imprudent enough to go on foot, without an escort. During my absence, the soldiers who had been left in charge of the building had gone to rejoin the company to which they belonged and had been replaced by a company from the battalion of the National Guard which had been sent there by Malet. It was commanded by Lieutenant Beaumont.

When I reached the entrance of the Prefecture, seeing the courtyard filled with soldiers, I sent for the officer in command and instructed him to take his men back to barracks. I assumed that the mere sight of me would be enough to convince him that everything had changed, but, as I should have realised, the military are not so readily prepared to accept orders from a civilian official. The change in the situation, abrupt enough in all conscience, was not accepted by the officer, and he, encouraged by a sergeant who appeared to be very excited, completely refused to obey my order, and shouted to his men to fall in. This was the signal for some disturbance, accompanied by shouts of 'Arrest him! Shoot him!' Fortunately I was still standing near the gate. I flung myself into the midst of a crowd of curious onlookers who had gathered there, and turned into the little rue de Jérusalem, intending to get back to the quay. The soldiers set off after me with fixed bayonets, and all I could do was to seek refuge in a shop at the end of the street. They wanted to smash down the door, but a number of policemen from the Prefecture who happened to be present persuaded them to be satisfied with guarding it, and not to resort to violence, which they convinced them was both useless and dangerous. So there I was, once more a prisoner, and there I remained for nearly an hour. An adjutant arrived, furnished with orders from the Minister of War instructing the company to return to barracks. But his authority was rejected, as mine had been, and he was arrested. All this hullabaloo only came to an end when it was reported that a strong squad of the Imperial Guard was on its way to the Prefecture of Police. Lieutenant Beaumont therefore decided to retreat with his company, and thus ended his resistance, though it was none the less to cost him his life.

Soulier, leader of the troops which, on General Malet's orders, had set out to occupy the Hôtel de Ville, did not get there until half-past seven. Halting his men in the square outside, he went upstairs to acquaint the Prefect with the orders he had received, but the latter was spending the night in his country house. Soulier was only able to speak to one of the clerks, who, knowing that the Prefect must already be on his way, sent a messenger to tell him to hurry up, informing him of the Emperor's death in a hurried pencil scrawl which merely said: *Fuit Imperator.* M. Frochot arrived on horseback at eight o'clock. The news had almost driven him out of his mind, and everything he was now told only increased his bewilderment; thus he learned that the Minister of Police had arrived, but without realising that this was Lahorie and that the Duc de Rovigo was in prison. Then he was informed that there was an order for the arrest of one of his clerks called Lapierre, whom he was very fond of. And, finally, a doctor attached to the Duc de Rovigo turned up to see him, sent by the Duchess, who was worried to death and wanted to know what had become of her husband. As M. Frochot attributed the Duchess's grief to the Emperor's death, he regarded it as confirmation of the fatal news.

In the orders transmitted to him by the commander of the rebel troops M. Frochot then read that the imperial government had been abolished and that a Provisional Government Commission had been set up, which was to function from the Hôtel de Ville; with an injunction that, in case of need, he was to appeal to the people by sounding the tocsin. All these revolutionary measures completely baffled him. 'Well,' he said to Soulier, 'what do you want? You'll have to have somewhere for the Commission, and somewhere else for military headquarters. There's enough room in the Great Hall for the Commission, but as for the staff, they will have to manage in the basement.' Then, leaving his office, he went to the Great Hall, called the porter, ordered him to bring a table and chairs, and, hurrying off to his private apartments, called for horses, determined to get to the Archchancellor's as speedily as possible. At that moment, the arrival of the adjutant Laborde was announced, with orders from the Minister of War to get rid of the rebel troops and replace them with others, and it was not long before M. Frochot learned from M. Saulnier how he had been misled. Thereupon he became as delighted as he had previously been dejected, and went off with Laborde to persuade the colonel to obey the new orders that had been issued, which the wretch was very tempted to reject. Eventually, however, not knowing which way to turn in the midst of so many extraordinary and contradictory events, he gave in, and led his men back to barracks. While all this was happening, the chairs and table that had been put in the Great Hall were removed; but not before these preparations had been noticed. M. Frochot, overjoyed at the unexpected way things had turned out, did not at all foresee all the difficulties and misfortunes that were to ensue from his credulity, pardonable as it may have been.

During the 24th, the two generals, the officers and non-commissioned officers who had most actively supported General Malet were arrested. General Guidal and Boccheiampe were caught in the house to which they had fled. Boutreux, who had had the effrontery to assume the duties of Prefect of Police, at first avoided all efforts to find him;[3] and the same with Lafon, who did not appear again until the Restoration. A Military Commission was appointed right at the start to try the accused.

Malet and his principal agents belonged to the revolutionary party, and it was here that investigations had to be carried out. However, the information contained in the documents taken from the conspirators was contradictory; thus the decree included as members of the Provisional Government men who were well-known for their royalist and counter-revolutionary views. Amongst them were M. Mathieu de Montmorency and M. Alexis de Noailles, side-by-side with the Abbé Sieyès. The decree went on to annul Napoleon's marriage to Marie-Louise, to declare the young Napoleon illegitimate, and to abolish conscription and some indirect taxes. The Papal States were to be restored to the Pope and a Congress was to be summoned to establish peace, which would be facilitated by France withdrawing within her ancient frontiers. The inalienability of land belonging to the nation was guaranteed, though this word 'inalienability' was open to very different interpretations.

[3] He was ultimately arrested and executed on 29 January 1813.

The order of the day signed by Malet was no less extraordinary: it handed over command of the troops to Generals Guidal, Desnoyers and Pailhardy, all three revolutionaries, while General Lecourbe,[4] a personal enemy of Napoleon's and an extreme Jacobin, was appointed commander of a central army which was to be quartered near Paris, and General Lahorie was to be its chief of staff. Promises of more pay and higher rank were made to officers and men who distinguished themselves by their zeal. Finally it was announced that those perverse and corrupt men who sought to use their influence to oppose the work of the Provisional Government were to be arrested without delay; orders were given that the troops who were to be used for this purpose should conduct themselves with order and moderation, but with all the energy demanded by a measure decided upon in the interests of public order. It is clear that the Abbé Lafon had had a lot to do with drafting the decree, while the order of the day was entirely the work of General Malet.

To begin with, there was some hesitation about carrying out investigations. The interrogation to which General Lahorie was subjected by M. Réal, before his appearance before the Military Commission, brought to light the craziness of General Malet's whole conception. The Duc de Rovigo insisted upon my being present, a duty I would willingly have been spared. M. Pelet was also summoned as well as M. Anglès, M. Saulnier and M. Desmarets. I therefore witnessed a scene which lasted for more than three hours. Until the final evidence was produced, Lahorie maintained that he had had no prior knowledge, and that the sight of a General presenting himself at the head of a considerable military force without any appearance of disorder had inspired confidence; that he had accepted the Emperor's death which, in itself, would not have been extraordinary; and declared that the revolution that was announced had not struck him as being improbable, since he had seen so many other changes of government, particularly that on 18 Brumaire. Wasn't it by decree that the First Consul had been made Emperor? Since the Senate had created the Imperial Government, didn't it have the power to abolish it? Awoken from sleep and taken completely una-

---

[4] General Lecourbe who, under Louis XVIII, was to become a Count and Inspector General of Infantry, was at this time living in disgrace at Ruffey, in the Jura mountains, because he had given evidence in support of General Moreau, who had been brought to trial in 1804 and banished for his republican views.

wares, he had been utterly fooled by a man who excercised un-disputed power, who could get the gates of the prison opened without any violence, and whom those who accompanied him were only too anxious to obey.

When he was shown the decree and asked how he could have been taken in by such a clumsy forgery and such incoherent proposals, he replied that he had scarcely glanced at it and, urged by Malet to put himself at the head of the men whose command had been entrusted to him, he had not had time to read it and had only heard what he was told. 'You are amazed', he added, 'that I could have accepted the genuineness of such a document. It would have been much more amazing if, after carefully examining it, I had been crazy enough to make use of it, to have accepted it as the basis for such a perilous undertaking. No one has ever accused me of lacking either judgement or in-telligence, and you must take me for the most stupid of men to assume that I would voluntarily have lent a hand to such a rashly conceived imposture. No, I was General Malet's first dupe, and now I am his most wretched victim.'

Asked about his behaviour towards the Minister of Police and myself, he let it be understood that, had he obeyed Malet's in-structions, we should have been killed; and it was mainly his desire to save our lives that had decided him to take charge of the troops sent to arrest us. Then, turning to me, he said: 'I hope you were not ill-treated?' He had already asked me the same question in the morning, when I had found him under arrest after returning to the Ministry with the Duc de Rovigo. Only as regards one fact did his defence strike me as being unworthy of the character he displayed. Against all the evidence, he persisted in maintaining that he had never intended to take over the duties of the Minister of Police. As proof of his good faith, and of the credulity which was the sole reason for his following Malet, he declared that it was his visit to the Hôtel de Ville that had begun to arouse his suspicions. The calmness of the people he had met on his way there, and the absence of all those whom he was ex-pecting to find assembled when he arrived, had seemed to him quite inexplicable. He had therefore returned to the Ministry not knowing what to make of what was happening; and, by the time that the adjutant Laborde arrived to arrest him, his mind was full of the gloomiest reflections.

All these assertions conveyed an impression of truth that it was impossible to disregard; but if Malet had thus succeeded in deceiving the man to whom he had entrusted the most confidential mission, what are we to think of the alleged secret correspondence referred to in the account published by M. Lafon? Are we really to believe that he had so many accomplices in the army and all the departments of state, and yet, with so many people at his disposal, that he had chosen as his principal agent a general who was in prison? As soon as he began to doubt the truth of the facts he had been told and the assurances he had been given he was bound to be assailed by fear and despair. Malet, for his part, insisted that he had had no accomplices, but had done everything on his own and had relied for the success of his undertaking on a general explosion of the feelings of hatred and indignation that must be widespread and could not fail to respond as soon as the signal was given. It would be difficult for me to convey all that I suffered during the course of the wretched Lahorie's cross-examination. There is nothing more painful than to watch a ruined man trying to defend himself without hope of success, for the sake of his conscience. When such a man has courage and nobility of mind, when the deed he is guilty of is of the sort that revolutions produce and that are justified by political conviction, the thought that the man standing before you, so full of life and strength and energy, is so near his end is heart-breaking!

The other members of the Commission, MM. Réal and Desmarets, doubtless accustomed to such sights, did not seem to share my painful emotions; indeed, M. Réal sometimes put his questions in a harsh and ironical manner that was most unseemly. Poor Lahorie could see the effect that this produced on the rest of us, and several times I caught his eye as he glanced in our direction as though thanking us for our understanding. In the end M. Pelet could stand it no longer and, getting up from his seat, he came over to where I was standing by the fireplace. 'I can see you feel as I do', he said. 'Réal distresses me. This has gone on long enough.' Then, turning to Réal, he said: 'That's enough for today. Believe me, it's time to adjourn. For the moment you will learn nothing further from this gentleman.' The cross-examination was concluded, and we were free to retire.

Malet, Lahorie, Guidal, Boccheiampe, as well as the ten officers and non-commissioned officers, were shot on 29 October. The Abbé Lafon remained in hiding until the Restoration. 'As to the Spanish priest, he was never found.'

It remained to be seen what impression these quite unexpected events would produce on Napoleon. The day after the conspirators had been executed, Pasquier sent the Emperor his report,[5] which one imagines must have required a good many drafts.[6] In it, he skated over the facts and concentrated on the consequences: 'What has happened is of little significance for the Emperor, but it is of the greatest importance for the King of Rome . . . What would have happened if the false report had turned out to be true?' And he therefore drew the conclusion that it was necessary, in the first place, 'to strengthen and consolidate all civil institutions', and secondly, 'to strengthen the Paris police with a force which would be like the horse and foot Guards in days gone by'; this would have the advantage of making it possible 'to keep an eye on the military'.

The Emperor heard of the conspiracy and its suppression at the same time. The dossier reached him at Viesma in the middle of a snowstorm. 'He gave vent to his feelings in an outburst of astonishment, humiliation and anger,' Ségur tells us. Pasquier received confirmation of this scene from Daru. The Emperor's wrath, however, did not fall upon the Prefect of Police. Pasquier maintains that, finding himself in Napoleon's presence the day after the latter's return to Paris (18 December), 'many people were expecting that I should have to put up with a very disagreeable scene. This expectation was belied . . . He accosted me in the most affable manner and, speaking in an undertone so that no one else could hear, he said: "Well, my dear Prefect, so you too have been having a pretty bad time of it. Life always has plenty of these in store." '

Was this consideration due to the intervention of Savary, who claims credit for it? Or was it not rather attributable to the growing esteem in which the Emperor held his Prefect of Police? 'Baron Pasquier is an intelligent man', he confided to Caulaincourt some days later. 'He has considerable talent and plenty of determination. I am trying him out at the Prefecture of Police, with a view to promoting him if he lives up to

[5] It is a curious fact that Pasquier does not mention this report in his *Mémoires*, and it was not until 1901 that it was ultimately published in the *Nouvelle Revue rétrospective*.

[6] Molé had already seen one of these by 24 October, but his comments on it do not square with the final text. Probably Pasquier was awaiting the Commission's report before deciding on his own position; on the other hand, it is possible that he drew up two reports, one relating the facts, the other expressing his views upon them.

my expectations[7] . . .' In any case, neither he nor the Duc de Rovigo were in any way disciplined. The Prefect of the Seine was made the scapegoat for this tragi-comedy, and as a result lost both his position and the title of Councillor of State.

'The most serious events distracted attention from General Malet's crazy undertaking . . .' Everyone knew that hostilities were about to break out again, but in what circumstances? 'Despite the very confident tone of the speeches made by the Emperor and his ministers at the opening of the session of the Legislative Assembly, public opinion was becoming more uneasy and more critical every day.' And all the more so as the economic crisis was growing worse.

Not a day went by but money became tighter,[8] and, as anxiety about the future led the wealthier families to restrict expenditure, this resulted in a considerable decrease in employment. This unfortunate state of affairs was still further accentuated by the fact that all the great dignitaries of the army, whose luxurious way of living usually supplemented that of the court during the winter, were now either kept in Germany or else busy restoring, as economically as possible, their households, which had been completely destroyed by the recent campaign. Now it was quite impossible for any of them to do this without suffering serious financial embarrassment.

On top of this, in order to support themselves during the recent famine, the workers had used up a large part of their savings. The account I have given, more particularly of the poverty that was beginning to manifest itself in the Saint-Antoine district, where the principal cabinet-makers' workshops were situated, led to orders being placed by the administrator of the Civil List for a large quantity of furniture. This was to be used for furnishing the Louvre and other palaces. After the Restoration, the stewards of the royal household were delighted when they found it in warehouses belonging to the crown. In the

[7] True, in one respect Napoleon had reservations. He went on: 'But I don't like his friendship with the Rémusats, who are wealthy intriguers about whom I have been greatly mistaken.' Napoleon's attitude to the latter had changed since the time of the Consulate, when Mme de Rémusat had been one of Josephine's ladies-in-waiting.

[8] The economic crisis of which there were already signs in 1810, had noticeably become much worse by 1812 and 1813, thanks to the progressive closing of the European market as a result of the defeats suffered by the French armies.

Saint-Marceau district, I was able to procure another form of relief. I knew that the Senate held considerable reserve funds in its treasury; I proposed that these should be used for carrying out the embankment and terracing which were necessary for the completion of the avenue that was to lead from the Luxembourg Gardens to the Observatory. This work gave employment to the poorest workers in the district, and it is to them that we owe the splendid avenue which exists today, and which is one of the most striking beauties of the magnificent palace of the Chamber of Peers.

Having taken the necessary measures to ensure employment, the Emperor was anxious to create a service which the Malet conspiracy had convinced him was indispensable. So long as the Paris administration did not have at its disposal, and under its immediate control, an armed force that could ensure respect, it could never be safe from insurrection. I had already, on more than one occasion, pointed out the usefulness of such an organisation, in a variety of circumstances, especially when large masses of people were assembled. If the police are to be used to maintain order, a degree of patience is necessary that can only come from habit, and soldiers on active service certainly do not possess this. They approach this delicate task in a rough and ready way which always has a bad effect, and can result in the most deplorable scenes. This was why, during public holidays, in the central markets, as well as when the theatres were emptying, there had more than once been deplorable accidents and scenes of violence which only brought authority into disrepute and made it unpopular.

The Emperor was struck by the truth of this, and in January he instructed his ministers to undertake the formation of a body especially concerned with the maintenance of order in Paris, which would be under the immediate control of the city administration. I prepared several memoranda on this subject, in which, having carefully studied all the organisational details of the old City Watch, I showed that we could not hope to do better than by taking this organisation as an example, and that above all it was essential that the new body should comprise both cavalry and infantry.

The Emperor accepted my view and had plans prepared for discussion by the Council of State. It was opposed by the army, who could not bear the idea of a military force being subjected to the sole command of a civilian administrator. It was on this head that Napoleon, defending the plan, uttered the words which justified my conduct in the Malet affair: 'When I got back to Paris', said he, 'I was not yet sure what to think of the behaviour of the Prefect of Police. But, after the fullest examination of the facts, I was forced to agree that one had no right to criticise in any way a magistrate so completely unarmed that, on his way home, he was very nearly murdered by soldiers who nevertheless belonged to a regiment known as the First Paris Regiment.'

It was as a result of this discussion that a decree was published on 10 April, establishing the Paris gendarmerie, which comprised, as I had proposed, both cavalry and infantry. It was made entirely dependent upon my administration, and I was given full responsibility for its overall command, though with the help of a colonel in immediate charge of the service.

In the course of my working life I have done few things that caused me so much trouble and unpleasantness as did this. Completely ignorant of the complicated rules of military administration and accountancy, I was obliged to study them. The Duc de Rovigo very generously helped me with advice; the most valuable service he did me being to supervise the choice of men who were to form the basis for this organisation. According to the terms of the decree this selection had to be made jointly with the Minister of War and the Minister of Police, and the men were to be drawn from all the armed forces of the Empire. This gave rise to the most lively resentment on the part of Marshal Moncey since, as Inspector-General, he was in command; and he behaved in the pettiest and touchiest manner imaginable. When I met him at the palace he came up to me, his eyes blazing with anger, and said: 'Well, Prefect, so you are going to take any of my men you care to pick on, and if I, a Marshal of France and Inspector-General, happen to come across one of these fellows in the streets wearing your uniform, I shan't even be able to ask the rascal what he means by having his hat on crooked!' To which I replied: 'My dear sir, you won't even do him the honour of looking at him. You'll take him for a civilian.'

Pasquier spent the greater part of the summer organising this gendarmerie. For a short period, hope was revived by the victories of Lutzen, Bautzen and Dresden, but it was almost extinguished by the catas-

trophe at Leipzig. By 9 November Napoleon was back at Saint-Cloud.

Scarcely had he arrived at Saint-Cloud when he summoned all his ministers, to consult them about the plans to be discussed next day at the Council of State.

I was present at this meeting, and the memory of it has remained deeply engraved on my memory. Before starting the Council we were received in audience; Napoleon's features displayed the most painful emotions. His first words were addressed to M. Jaubert, Governor of the Bank, whom he angrily admonished on account of some refusal or other by the Bank to furnish him with money or credit. M. Jaubert defended himself better and more courageously than one might have expected; the year previously he certainly would not have replied in this way. When the meeting began, we had to discuss a proposal that was adopted without difficulty and promulgated by decree the same day. It increased the tax on doors and windows, and on patents, by thirty centimes, and increased the price of salt by twenty centimes a kilogram.

A suggested decree was then read to us, putting at the government's disposal 300,000 conscripts a year from 1806 up to and including 1814. Faced with such a demand, what was there to be said except that, since 11 January of this year, 1,140,000 had already been conscripted? In order to dispose of all these considerations in advance, as soon as the proposal had been read, the Emperor took the trouble to give us an account of how matters stood, in which he insisted particularly upon the treachery he had been exposed to, and which ought to be avenged for the honour of the nation.

When he spoke about Bavaria, his imagination kindled and his eyes began to flash. 'Munich must be burnt to the ground, and it shall be!' he cried, in a voice that still echoes in my ears and which filled us with terror. What kind of future was he offering us? How could we help but fear all the reprisals that were threatening us?

We were worried about everything and could see nothing but misfortune which ever way we looked. We no longer had faith in anything; all our illusions were at an end. It was no use filling the columns of *Le Moniteur* with loyal addresses and expressions of devotion from every government body and every town; all this official language merely sounded stilted. It would have been far better if the government had maintained a dignified silence, the only appropriate response in such mournful circumstances.

'*In the two months preceding the Emperor's new and final departure for the army,*' wrote Victor, Duc de Broglie, '*official society, and even those who did not belong to it, was divided between two salons: that of M. de Bassano, who had been appointed Secretary of State after handing over Foreign Affairs to M. de Caulaincourt,*[9] *and M. de Talleyrand's, still in disgrace, but still very much alive as one of the great Dignitaries of the Empire. Both groups poked fun at one another and mutually denounced each other. The second demanded peace, at the top of its voice and at any price, the first still counted upon some miracle of imperial skill. In the second, they canvassed beneath their breath, and not without a certain satisfaction, the final collapse of the Empire; in the other, they passionately longed for its continuation.*'

Pasquier belonged unquestionably to the Talleyrand clan, though with all the prudence suggested by his nature and imposed upon him by his duties. Charles de Rémusat recounts that at about this time he heard the Prince of Benevento, in his mother's salon, arguing most eloquently that all was lost. '. . . *He had one object in mind, to convince M. Pasquier and prepare him for what might happen. The latter listened attentively and uneasily. His silence allowed it to be seen that he had certain reservations which he was afraid to express, and that M. de Talleyrand's confidences worried him more than they flattered him . . .*'

Behind the scenes, however, the Prefect of Police was doing all he could to persuade the Emperor to accept the allied proposals.[10] '*M de la Valette, who had considerable influence as Post Master General, as well as on account of the confidence he had always enjoyed, seized upon every opportunity of ensuring that the truth reached his master's ears; I too, did not spare myself in this respect, and I was able to do so by introducing into my daily bulletins circumstantial accounts of what was being said in the town.*' Clearly, Napoleon was under no illusions as to the seriousness

---

[9] On 20 November Napoleon had twice offered the post to Talleyrand, who, with his usual flair for disaster, had refused it.

[10] An Allied proclamation of 1 December spoke in general terms of the possibility of allowing France to keep her natural frontiers, i.e., the Rhine, the Alps and the Pyrenees. 'The Allied sovereigns guarantee the French Empire a larger extent of territory than France ever knew under her kings . . .'

of the problem. 'In this situation, [he] understood, perhaps for the first time, the possibility of a Bourbon restoration, and I am convinced that he had considered this idea as a necessary consequence of the existing state of affairs, long before it had been discussed in foreign cabinets. He referred to it at first in relation to his possible death.' "I assure you", he said one day to M. de la Valette, and he said the same thing to M. Molé, "that if I get killed, the succession will not devolve upon the King of Rome. As things stand now, only a Bourbon could succeed me".'[11]

The Legislative Body met on 19 December. The Emperor, 'delivered a very cleverly conceived speech, which made a great impression. Despite the firmness of purpose that still characterised it, if one compares it with earlier speeches, it may be regarded as the beginning of abdication. But, with Napoleon, the persistent desire for power proved to be stronger than any fugitive aspiration towards conciliation.

When, in the evening,[12] the Emperor was informed of these facts,[13] which he should have been able to foresee from the previous day's session, he could not contain his anger. He did not, however, know the exact words of the report, since the Commission had taken care not to give anyone a copy, and people only had vague and contradictory notions of what it contained. Impatient to be more exactly informed, and fully determined not to allow anything to be published that was too opposed to his own views, at ten o'clock that evening Napoleon instructed his Minister of Police to obtain a copy of the first proofs from the Legislative Body's printer and to forbid him to distribute anything until further orders. The Minister was to bring this proof the following morning to the first audience, and was told that he must be in a position to express an opinion upon it. There was, however, no question upon which the Duc de Rovigo was less capable of giving an opinion; he had the good sense to recognise this, and did not hesitate to call for help from the members of his Police Committee. We met at his house at about eleven o'clock; but we had to wait for the proof that we were to discuss until past midnight, and he then called upon me to read it aloud.

The language in which their wishes were expressed scarcely

[11] 'I am more or less convinced that it flattered his pride to think that he could only be replaced by this ancient dynasty', Pasquier comments further on.

[12] 30 December, 1813.

[13] The same day the Legislative Body had adopted by 223 votes to 31 a report in favour of restricting the Emperor's powers.

concealed the serious complaints they were making, for apparently they were demanding liberty, personal security, respect for property and the free exercise of political rights, simply because they had been unjustly deprived of them for so long. In addition, the circumstances under which these demands were put forward were such as to increase their gravity. In order to draw attention even to their most just demands, have not people always been obliged to seize upon those moments when their rulers are forced to turn to them for help?

I was of opinion that, however much it might displease him, the Emperor must resign himself to listening to these demands without too obviously betraying his annoyance. We needed to revive the spirit of the people, to call upon them for a mighty effort, and in these circumstances were we to break with the one body that might be regarded as having been popularly elected? If, by too great a display of susceptibility, we were to deprive ourselves of the assistance that this body could still render us, who should we be able to turn to in future? How could we hope to influence men's minds?

If, however, when the petition was presented to him, the Emperor were to receive it with apparent goodwill, a few words from him and a declaration that would only be binding upon him within reasonable limits, would probably be enough to give satisfaction to, even to arouse enthusiasm in, men who were today—it was no use pretending otherwise—sufficiently ill-disposed towards him. M. Pelet and M. Anglès agreed with me.

When it came to M. Réal's turn to speak, who up till then had remained very thoughtful, and the Duke said to him: 'Come now, M. Réal, you are a resourceful man, what line do you think we should take?', he replied: 'What line? Well, there always must be one that you can take, and it will have to be a tough one. But what are we to base it on? Where, today, are we going to find the men who are capable of carrying out a strong policy? During the last ten years haven't almost all the true patriots been dispersed, persecuted, annihilated—all those energetic men who rendered such great services at the most decisive periods of the Revolution? Does anyone believe that it is possible to find them now, to bring them back to life? And where are we to find their like? It took unique circumstances to produce such men, men with the sacred fire in their hearts; but no one realised what they were worth. And, now, here's the Emperor confronted by an Assembly that knows it has the whip hand, for it is easier to win three major battles than to stand up to an elected body that has public opinion on its side. To fight against it is beyond our present strength; to get rid of it is equally impossible. Therefore, whether we like it or not, we have to accept M. Pasquier's opinion, and we must have the courage to say so.'

This speech, so naïvely revolutionary yet so reasonable in its conclusions made a deep impression on the Duc de Rovigo. 'It's quite clear', said he, after one or two very embarrassed sentences, 'that there's nothing else to be done. But to give such advice is not going to be as easy as you appear to suppose, gentlemen.'

It seems that in the course of an after-dinner conversation with the Emperor he had already had occasion to realise that he was very little disposed to accept the point of view that had prevailed with us. However, after a moment's reflection, he resolved to try his luck; only he made M. Réal and me promise to be at Saint-Cloud early next morning. 'I shall get there', he told us, 'before the levee, and I shall put your arguments to him, which I personally accept. But if I find him too recalcitrant, I shall ask him to hear you.' We were there promptly on time, and he did, in fact, go in to see the Emperor before anyone else. But after a few minutes we saw him come out again, looking very upset. 'Come with me,' he said to me. I got into his carriage with him, and on the way he told me that he had left the Emperor irrevocably determined to dissolve the Legislative Body, in view of the fact that there was no possibility of obtaining any service from it that would offset the harm that would result from the publication of such a report.

It was therefore above all essential to prevent this publication, and I had to send someone immediately to seize the whole edition at the printer's, and to warn him that if a single copy was released he would be held responsible. 'Very well', I replied. 'But for that I must have an order signed and sealed. Remember what M. Réal said yesterday, about the danger of running foul of an elected body. I shall do nothing, therefore, that cannot be legally justified, and I intend to see that I am fully covered.'— 'Right,' he replied. 'Then you shall have the order in a quarter of an hour.' And indeed I did; and it was duly carried out.

On 31 December the Legislative Body was adjourned.

On 3 January, I remained behind after the levee, as I had to speak to the Emperor about an important matter concerning the town of Paris. 'Well Prefect,' he said, as we began our conversation, 'what are they saying in town? Do they know that the enemy armies have definitely crossed the Rhine?'—'Yes, sir, they heard it yesterday in the afternoon.'—'How strong do they suppose they are?'—'There's talk of 200,000 men.'—'Then they are a long way out. There are from 3–400,000, and they've crossed the river between Cologne and Basle at seven or eight different points. The Swiss have allowed them to violate their territory. What decision are they expecting me to take?'—'They are convinced that Your Majesty will be leaving at once, to put yourself at the head of your troops and lead them against the enemy.'—'My troops! My troops! Do they really imagine that I still have an army? Don't they realise that practically all the men I brought back from Germany have perished of that terrible disease which, on top of all my other disasters, proved to be the last straw?[14] An army indeed! I shall be lucky if, three weeks from now, I manage to get together 30,000 or 40,000 men.'

Then, after a protracted silence, he went on: 'Oh well! what is it you want?' I then pointed out to him that in his last decree on the National Guard[15] there was no reference to the town of Paris, and that I felt it was essential that some decision should be taken on the question. It seemed likely that Paris was going to find itself depleted of the small number of troops that normally served to garrison it, and that in circumstances which might well become critical I could not see how it would be possible to manage without a force capable of maintaining order at a time

[14] Napoleon was probably referring to the typhus epidemic which broke out at Mainz in the winter of 1813 and caused 'terrible ravages amongst the garrison and population'.

[15] Originally created in 1789 as a voluntary civil guard for Paris, under the command of Lafayette, within a few months the bourgeoisie all over France were organising themselves into National Guards. Soon afterwards membership for all men aged twenty to sixty became compulsory for 'active' citizens (i.e. those entitled to a vote). Under the Convention the force was democratised by admitting all citizens whether 'active' or 'passive', and it played a considerable part in establishing the Republic. Distrusted by Napoleon, it continued to exist on paper until reorganised in 1812 for home defence and maintenance of public security. In 1813, however, Napoleon destroyed the original civilian character of the National Guard by enrolling all its best men as regular troops for service in Germany. (Trs.)

when the populace might be exposed to great hardships, and would in consequence be difficult to control. If there was the slightest trouble in the capital while he was at grips with the enemy, might it not be the most severe embarrassment to him, and was it not necessary to take steps to guard against this eventuality? An immediate organisation of the National Guard, therefore, seemed to me essential.

'All right,' he said, 'but this National Guard of yours may well number from 20,000–40,000 men, and who can answer to me for their loyalty? If they became disaffected, would it not be a great mistake to have allowed such a force to be organised in my rear? Besides, how are they going to be armed? I shall need all my small arms for the conscripts that are being called up!' I replied that the careful choice of officers would avoid the danger he had referred to, and that I saw little to fear because, quite certainly, the main concern of the bourgeoisie would be to protect their property by maintaining order. As for rifles, it would be sufficient perhaps to provide enough to arm those who had to relieve the guard each day. I had dealt with these questions in a report, which I left with him and begged him to read.

My initiative had been planned in concert with the Ministers of Police and of the Interior, who supported my proposals so effectively that, by the 8th, a decree was published putting the National Guard in Paris on an active footing. The Emperor proclaimed that he would be its commander-in-chief, and reserved to himself the right to appoint all the officers on the recommendation of the Minister of the Interior. The decree also contained full details for its organisation. Marshal Moncey was appointed major-general and second in command. His principal lieutenants were General Hulin, Count Bertrand, Marshal of the royal household, Comte de Montesquiou, Grand Chamberlain, and Comte de Montmorency. The troop commanders were also men of substance respected in their own districts.

Thus was organised that National Guard which, three months later, was to render such great services, and which we were glad to be able to show foreigners as proof that we were still strong enough to command respect as a guarantee of the public order it was so important to maintain.

On 23 January, 1814 the Emperor took leave of the officers of the National Guard, and entrusted his son to their care. Pasquier was present on this occasion. 'I saw tears running down many faces. Everyone swore by acclamation to show themselves worthy of the trust imposed in them, and, at the same time, I am convinced that everyone did so with sincerity.'

'The next day Napoleon set out for Châlons-sur-Marne, where his headquarters were established, this in itself is enough to give some idea of how far the enemy had already advanced. . . . As soon as he left the capital there were signs of those dangers that had been foreseen in the more or less distant future, a catastrophe was regarded as inevitable, even by those most disposed to feel confident. But who could say what would be the consequences? What alliances could emerge from a coalition in which the interests were so different? Who would exert the dominant influences?'

One had to learn to keep silent. Bad news followed swiftly upon bad news. When Bourdeaux went over to the Duc d'Angoulême on 12 March it made a deep impression in Paris. 'When, according to custom, I presented myself at the Tuileries to pay my respects to the Empress, I remember, as I went in, finding M. Boulay de la Meurthe, surrounded by a group of Senators and Councillors of State, declaring that the rumour was quite unfounded. He called upon me to bear witness that the news was false. But I merely replied that I knew nothing about it. Few people were deceived by this reply, many shook me by the hand and said: "Look, it's all over now and we shall have to make the best of it. But what's going to be the upshot?" M. Molé, usually so confident, did not conceal his anxiety.'

Strange projects were being hatched in certain minds. If we are to believe Pasquier, Savary envisaged having a number of miniature infernal machines made, which, discreetly placed along the roads, would have settled the question of the Princes' return to France. . . . It was, in any case, an opportunity—the first, he insists—for the Prefect of Police to make himself agreeable to the opposite side. 'I was in touch with Mme de Vintimille, as she herself was with the Abbé de Montesquiou, who was authorised to act on behalf of Louis XVIII in France. . . . I begged her to let the Abbé de Montesquiou know how essential it was to warn the Princes, who might already have arrived in France, of the precautions they should take. The speed with which events moved soon made this advice pointless.'

About 25 March the rumour began to spread that the Emperor had to take up his position in the enemy's rear, leaving the road to Paris open.

Almost immediately it was learned that, after a moment of hesitation, the Allies had resolved to march on the capital. 'From then on one had to be sufficient unto oneself. Reduced to this bitter necessity, King Joseph, in his position as Lieutenant-General of the Realm, gave orders that all available front-line troops should leave the town, take up positions at Saint-Denis and Vincennes, and occupy the bridges at Charenton, Saint-Maur and Neuilly. The defence of the city's fortifications was entrusted to the men of the National Guard; twelve pickets, one from each Legion, were to be posted behind the walls.'

These dispositions having been taken, the question of whether the Empress should remain in the capital had to be decided; it was discussed on 28 March. The Duc de Rovigo asked me for my opinion, as he had been doing for some time past in all matters concerning the town of Paris. I had no hesitation in replying that the departure of the Empress would create a deplorable impression, that already it was no use counting on any great display of energy by the people of Paris, and that to take such a step would only destroy what little they had and still further alienate them, because, by depriving them of the only protection that could make them hope for some consideration on the enemy's part, it would leave them in no doubt as to how little anybody cared about their safety or the protection of their property. I added that, quite apart from the interests of the town, it must be realised that, if there was any question of opening negotiations at which the interests of the whole Empire were to be discussed, we should be in a better position to do so if we were speaking and acting in the name of the Empress, for whom it was impossible to suppose that the Allies, and especially the Emperor of Austria, did not still maintain great regard.

The Duc de Rovigo appeared to share my opinion; he took with him the note I had handed him and, before the Council began, he got several of those who were going to be present to read it. The discussion was a long one and those in favour of the Empress remaining were certainly in the majority. This view was supported particularly by the former appeal judge, the Duc de Massa, who was entitled to attend the Council as president of the Legislative Body, and who spoke with a warmth one would scarcely have expected from him. He even went so far as to make a very touching appeal to Marie-Louise, in which he spoke of her duties as a wife, a mother and an Empress; but the woman he was addressing was very little disposed to listen to him, and was impatient to get away. M. de Talleyrand avoided speaking, and only expressed his opinion by nodding his head, which might have meant anything, but chiefly seemed to mean that we must be prepared for all eventualities and should submit to the sad necessities of the situation.

When the Lieutenant-General, King Joseph, was quite satisfied as to what was going to be the outcome of the discussion, he cut it short by producing a letter from the Emperor which, primarily concerned for the freedom of his wife and son, urged that, at the slightest appearance of danger, they should be sent away from Paris to the Loire, where they were to be followed by the Ministers, who would establish a new seat of government there. The Archchancellor then announced that he had instructions of the same kind, and it appeared that the Empress had also received a letter to the same effect. All these had been written by the Emperor when he was falling back from Rheims upon Arcis. Thus the Empress's departure had already been agreed and settled. The decision was confirmed on the 27th. During the same evening, I met M. de Talleyrand at M. de Rémusat's; he and I were the only visitors and the conversation naturally turned to the Empress's approaching departure. I said what I thought about it, and that I was convinced it was bound to have disastrous consequences for the Emperor's cause. M. de Talleyrand already knew this to be my opinion. He was one of those who had read the note I had written to the Duc de Rovigo. He himself took the opposite point of view, and insisted that the only thing that now mattered to Napoleon was to prevent his wife and son falling into the hands of the enemy. I replied that everything depended on the importance one attached to the more or less prompt surrender of the capital and to the negotiations that this would give rise to. Our discussion was extremely lively.

Having been the first to leave, next morning I received an invitation from Mme de Rémusat to call upon her immediately. 'I was anxious', she said as soon as I arrived, 'that you should not be unaware of what M. de Talleyrand said yesterday directly you had left. These are his actual words: "I would never have believed that M. Pasquier was so hostile to the House of Bourbon; the advice he gave was quite against their interests". '—'Well,' I replied, 'tell him from me, cousin, that I am not an enemy of the Bourbons, far from it; that it would doubtless be just as easy for

me to go over to them as for him; that I am even one of the
people in all France who would most benefit by their return, for
a thousand reasons; but that at the same time I am a man of
honour, and whenever those who have the right to ask me for
advice do so, I shall give it to the best of my conscience.' Had I
been in need of any enlightenment as to M. de Talleyrand's intentions this would have sufficed. But I already knew where he
stood, and I only saw a little more clearly that the moment was
approaching when he would feel able to throw off the mask; and
that the fall of Paris was, without the slightest doubt, the
opportunity for which he was waiting.

*The Prince of Benevento did not have long to wait, 'The Allies were ad-
vancing with* 150,000 *men at least, we had only* 18,000 *with which to
oppose them, infantry of all arms,* 4,000 *of whom were conscripts and*
6,000 *men of the National Guard. To these may be added some* 5,000
*cavalry, but the nature of the battle made them almost entirely useless . . .
The action began on* 30 *March at six o'clock in the morning. I had gone to
bed very late the previous evening, and I was awoken with a start by the
noise of cannon, which was soon accompanied by rifle fire . . . My duties
did not allow me to leave the Prefecture of Police . . . this obligation was
infinitely distressing to me . . .*

*'The morning was spent admidst the din of artillery, with conflicting
news arriving at every moment. But I must say that within the town
everything remained surprisingly peaceful . . .' Towards midday King
Joseph decided to leave Paris and follow the Regency. 'He had no
hesitation in authorising Marshals Marmont and Mortier to capitulate
on behalf of the army in the capital, and ordered the appeal judge, M.
Molé, to inform the high dignitaries of state, all the ministers, all the
Councillors of State and all the chief functionaries, to leave immediately
for Blois. The Prefect of the Seine and the Prefect of Police failed to
receive this order. It had been agreed that they would stay behind to
maintain order, and to minimise as far as possible the catastrophe
threatening the town . . .'*

*However, 'the Marshals were not prepared to yield until the last pos-
sible moment. The action continued for several hours and was keenly
fought . . . after the capture of Montmartre [towards* 5 p.m.], *firing on
both sides completely stopped . . .'*

I learned of the departure of Lieutenant-General Joseph and the
Ministers from the Duc de Rovigo, who sent for me in great

haste around two o'clock. 'I am leaving with the other Ministers', he told me. 'You will remain behind, and it will therefore be up to you to do what you think best.' He then told me many things I did not yet know about, and said that the capitulation was already in train. But he had one service to ask of me, which he immediately explained by pointing to a large portfolio which he had just closed. 'You must keep this for me,' said he, 'it contains all that is most precious to me; all my correspondence with the Emperor since I've been with him is in it. Here are to be found the explanation and justification of my conduct on every issue.'

I pointed out that I was the last man he should entrust with such a responsibility, since, considering that I was to be left at the Prefecture of Police, I was bound to be kept under the closest surveillance. Possibly all my papers and those belonging to the Prefecture would be examined and seized; in short, I could not answer for anything. True, there was my private house, but, since it was empty, some enemy officer would surely be quartered there; it would be highly imprudent to attempt to hide anything in it. As it was of such importance to him, why didn't he take it with him, and what was there to prevent him putting the portfolio in his carriage? 'Who knows,' he replied, 'I may well be captured by the Cossacks before I get to Versailles and, whatever happens, this must not fall into the hands of the enemy. You take it, and if there is the least likelihood of your being picked up get rid of it by burning it. On this last point, you must give me your word of honour.'—'So be it, then,' I said. 'But it wouldn't surprise me if I had to burn it before tomorrow morning.' The portfolio was therefore taken to the Prefecture.

When I myself got back there I was so taken up with the innumerable jobs that normally fell to my charge that, fortunately for me, I was prevented from realising the full scope of the new task that had been imposed upon me, or from envisaging all the labour, worry and anxiety of every kind that I was to have to put up with during the next fortnight. Since it was above all necessary for me to keep myself up-to-date with what was happening between our troops and the enemy's, I sent some intelligent messengers to Marshal Marmont. I gave orders that they were to seek him out, even on the battlefield if necessary, and urge him to keep me informed of any agreement he succeeded in coming to; he would understand how important this was in the interests of the city of Paris, whose safety had been entrusted to me. At the same time I also sent to Marshal Moncey, in order to find out from him what was expected of the National Guard and what arrangements had been made in this respect. He was just leaving as my messenger arrived; and all he said was that I should come to an understanding with Major-General Allent, who was staying behind.

It was almost seven o'clock before I received a reply from Marshal Marmont; it had been extremely difficult to get near him. How great my anxiety was during this interval will be readily understood; I employed the time in taking every precaution that prudence enjoined, seeing the principal officers of of the Prefecture, especially those employed on outside duty, and begging them to show the greatest possible circumspection in everything they did or said. The officer who caused me the greatest uneasiness was Inspector-General Veyrat. I knew that he was hated by the people and was capable of every kind of treachery; I instructed him to await my orders, even on the smallest matters, and therefore not to leave the building.

While I was busy dealing with the most urgent measures that had to be taken, I received a very strange visit: M. de Talleyrand arrived about six o'clock in the evening, accompanied by, or rather brought by, Mme de Rémusat, for it was she who acted as spokesman. 'You know, cousin,' said she, 'that M. de Talleyrand has been ordered to leave and join the Empress. But don't you think that this would be the greatest mistake? It would mean that no one was left to treat with the Allies; no one, that is, whose name carries any weight. You, better than anyone, should appreciate the disadvantages of this, since it is you who have to bear the main responsibilty. As you will realise, this puts M. de Talleyrand in the most difficult position, for how can he refuse to obey? Yet at the same time it would be the greatest pity if he were really obliged to leave!' I replied that I understood all this perfectly well, but that I did not see what I could do. 'Nevertheless he has come to ask your advice.'

M. de Talleyrand then stammered a few involved sentences that simply repeated what Mme de Rémusat had just said. Whereupon she interrupted him and, after considerable circumlocution, eventually came to the point: they proposed that I should send some men, whom I could completely rely upon, to the city gate which he would be leaving, and that when he arrived they should appeal to the mob, telling them not to allow the town to be abandoned like this by those who had most to lose, and who therefore ought to have the greatest interest in defending it. In this way he would be forced to turn back. I replied that, in a situation where my first duty was to keep the people quiet, I was certainly not going to risk taking a step which might well arouse them. 'But,' I added, 'there is a much simpler way of achieving your purpose, and one without risk. M. de Rémusat is an officer in the National Guard, and is almost certainly responsible for guarding one of the gates. Let M. de Talleyrand choose to leave by that one, and let M. de Rémusat and his National Guardsmen do what you are asking me to get the mob to do.'

This was a perfectly simple idea, and I believe they must already have thought of it; but it would have suited them better had I taken the full responsibility for their scheme on my shoulders. Seeing that there was no chance of persuading me, they decided to accept my advice and the matter was arranged as I had suggested.

An hour later, M. de Talleyrand presented himself at the Champs-Élysées gate, where M. de Rémusat and his company were on guard, and was very politely invited to return home, an invitation which scarcely had to be repeated.[16] It is difficult to understand how so subtle a mind could have believed that he could avoid the slightest danger by means of such a crude trick, or how he could have supposed that the Emperor, if he succeeded in returning to power, would have been duped by such an excuse from a man against whom he already had so many grievances. M. de Talleyrand must have been under some illusion in this respect; and this at least goes to show that he was not yet irrevocably committed, that he was not yet quite sure what attitude would be adopted by the Allies. Maybe he was afraid lest the Emperor Alexander, once he was master of Paris, might yield to the Austrian influence and insist upon treating with his conquered enemy. In that case, the old diplomat would probably have been called upon to conduct the negotiations; his remaining in the capital would then have enabled him to make

[16] Things did not turn out exactly as described by Pasquier. Talleyrand went, not to the Champs Élysées, but to the Passy, gate, where, having been warned in advance, M. de Rémusat politely requested him to return home. On the other hand, 'the commander of the Guard, who had not been let into the secret, offered him an escort to take him to Versailles.' Talleyrand refused and returned to the rue Saint-Florentin by way of the Faubourg Saint-Honoré.

himself very useful and so to restore himself to Napoleon's good graces, and, once again, play a leading part in affairs.

It was seven in the evening before I received information from Marshal Marmont that the capitulation had been almost agreed, and was invited to go to his house in the Poissonière district. There I found the Marshal with a Russian officer, an Austrian officer and a Prussian officer, who were acting on behalf of the Allies. They were busy putting into writing what had been agreed verbally at La Villette between the two Marshals and the leading Allied generals. The articles the Marshal allowed me to see only concerned the army. It was to evacuate the town on 31 March, that is to say, next day, at seven o'clock in the morning. Hostilities could only be resumed two hours later. Then came the usual agreements about arsenals, military workshops and warehouses, hospitals and wounded; as far as civilians were concerned, that is to say the inhabitants of Paris, they were scarcely mentioned. The town was recommended to the generosity of the Allied powers; it was only stipulated that the guard, whether national or municipal, was to be completely suppressed, except for troops of the line, and it would be disarmed or disbanded according to the decisions of the powers.

I requested, and with great difficulty managed to get it agreed, that the municipal gendarmerie should be allowed to share the fate of the National Guard. For the rest, the Marshal told me that, according to the rules of war, it was essential that the municipal force should be despatched to Bondy during the night, in order to surrender to the Emperor Alexander; that I should lead this deputation, and in this way should be able to discuss with him everything affecting the interests of the town of Paris; and that he had no doubt that the Emperor would listen to me sympathetically. He went on to say that I should inform the Prefect of the Seine of the necessity of this step, and that we and the municipal police must both hold ourselves in readiness; he supposed that we might be able to set out about eleven o'clock that evening. The reason for this delay was that we had to wait for the capitulation to be ratified, and that in order to perform this ceremony he had to go to Bondy, which was the headquarters of the coalition.

After leaving Marshal Marmont, I went to see the Prefect of the Seine at the Hôtel de Ville, in order to acquaint him with what I had heard. There everything was in a state of great confusion. M. de Chabrol, a very honest man and a good administrator, was not well suited to deal with such a difficult and dangerous state of affairs; not that he lacked courage, he would have met his death honourably, but that he was very easily upset. Some of the members of the Municipal Council had spontaneously rallied to him. I urged him to summon the others immediately, and to warn General Allent that he would have to accompany us to Bondy. I drew his attention to the fact that, next day, we should be expected to provide all kinds of supplies; and, on my advice, he summoned the heads of his departments who were in touch with the storekeepers at the hospitals, prisons and other services, so that they might be in a position to supply the bread, meat, wine and brandy that would be requisitioned.

When I got home I had similar problems to attend to. I sent orders to the bakers to bake more bread, and warned the customs officials that more wine would probably have to be provided from the depots that they were in charge of. Many country-folk had already arrived in the town, fleeing from the enemy with all their personal effects, horses and cattle. I instructed the Police Commissioners to make arrangements with the Mayors about finding accommodation for them. Finally, before returning to the Prefecture of the Seine, I remembered the portfolio that the Duc de Rovigo had entrusted to me, and which I could scarcely leave in my apartment, for who could say whether, when I returned from Bondy, I should still be Prefect of Police; and the first thought of whoever was sent to take my place would certainly be to seize all my papers. I therefore sent for a divisional inspector in whom I had great confidence, and asked him to keep the portfolio, of which I had the key, until my return. As it was necessary that he should appreciate its importance, however, I made no attempt to conceal from him what it contained, and urged him to put it in as safe a place as possible. He was most unwilling to accept the responsibility, and insisted that he should be relieved of it the following morning.

Before handing the portfolio over to him, however, I thought I ought to open it, in order to judge for myself whether the Duc de Rovigo had told me the truth about its contents, and to make sure that it contained nothing else except the correspondence he had mentioned. While carrying out this check, which convinced me of his honesty, my eyes naturally fell on the documents at the top of the pile, which were Napoleon's most recent letters, those he had written as he was leaving Rheims. What was my astonishment to discover that these were largely concerned with the suspicion he felt about the Empress Marie-Louise, or rather, about his brother Joseph, whom he accused of having made the most odious approaches to her! The Duc de Rovigo was hauled over the coals for having failed to give any warning in this respect, and he was urged to keep the closest possible watch in future on what was going on in the palace. For a long time I believed that this accusation of Napoleon's against his brother arose from the abberration of a mind that was temporarily disposed by innumerable difficulties to indulge every kind of suspicion. Later, however, I was to discover from M. de Saint-Aignan who, considering his very close relations with the Duchesse de Montebello, must have been very well informed on this matter, that the suspicion was only too well founded, and that the Empress at this time had been considerably pestered by her brother-in-law and had every reason to complain of his importunity.

At eleven o'clock that evening I was at the Hôtel de Ville; there had still been no news from Marshal Marmont. The city Council was assembled in the great hall; and it is worth noting that in this crisis not a single voice was raised against the man who had been the cause of it. From this Council, which would soon have to take the most important decisions, there was not one complaint. We had to wait a long time for the order to leave. It was learned later that this delay was due to the fact that the Allied officer who was bringing the ratification of the capitulation from Bondy had been killed on the outskirts of Paris because he failed to reply quickly enough to the sentry's challenge. As he did not return they decided to send a second, who arrived safe and sound. But, in the meantime, many hours had elapsed, and it was past one o'clock in the morning before we left the Hôtel de Ville.

As I wanted to have a travelling companion to whom I could speak freely, I took M. de Lamoignon with me in my carriage, a man with a sense of humour, a very well informed member of the Municipal Council and one of my oldest acquaintances. We had a long retinue, and in consequence proceeded very slowly. When we reached the Pantin gate the head of our column was stopped by the sentry on guard, who refused to let us leave. As the delay was prolonged, I decided to get out and go and see what I could do about it. The guardroom was still occupied by grenadiers of the Imperial Guard. The officer in command told me that the most rigorous orders had been given to let no one leave the town. I pointed out to him that this could not apply to the municipal authorities, who were attempting to carry out the very onerous duty imposed upon them. 'Sir,' he replied, 'I know you are the Prefect of Police, because I have seen you more than once when I was on guard at the palace. So there can no longer be any possible doubt that Paris has been handed over to the enemy! We have lost the capital of our country and that's the only result of twenty years of fighting, of all the battles and victories I have played a part in; for I have been in the army since the year '92.' As he finished speaking, he raised his hands to hide the tears that were running down his face, but he could not conceal them. The patriotic grief of this old warrior—his moustache was turning grey—impressed me more deeply than I can say. I shook him by the hand, feeling as deeply moved as he was. 'There's nothing left but to surrender', said he. 'Come on then, you had better go.' And he gave orders for the gates to be opened. I never saw this brave fellow again; I have often regretted that I did not ask for his name. When we returned next morning he had been relieved, and had rejoined the army which was evacuating Paris.

We had difficulty in making our way along the road to Bondy, and we were astonished and shaken by the sights that met our eyes. What a brutal contrast with everything that had been dazzling our imagination for the last fifteen years: victories, glory, power, all that was over! Innumerable camp fires crowned the heights of Montmartre, of Belleville, of Chaumont, of Romainville, and the plain of Saint-Denis was covered with them; while in the direction of the road leading to the Étoile gate one could see, as far as the horizon, the lines of these fires, which surrounded the capital and penetrated deep into the outlying districts, attesting the presence of the redoubtable army that was to enter the city next day. Every few moments we met cavalry pickets on their rounds, and we made our way between groups of soldiers stretched out asleep beside their piled arms. As we approached Pantin, the spectacle became monstrous. It was here that the bloodiest fighting had taken place, and here was to be seen, displayed in all its horror, the aftermath of battle, for it was here that the Russians, blasted by the French artillery, had lost three or four thousand men. Not a corpse had yet been removed. Men and horses sprawled on top of one another. Never before had I beheld such heaps of dead. My companion, M. de Lamoignon, who had escaped from the slaughter at Quiberon, though not without receiving a terrible wound, might have been expected to be less astonished, yet he, too, was deeply moved.

Beyond Pantin we were able to proceed a little faster; between Pantin and Paris we had been continually held up. Here we had to show our pass to a patrol of Cossacks. A Russian orderly was carrying it, and he rode ahead of us, our only protection. We had no escort, for we had been obliged to leave the gendarmes who had accompanied us till then at the gate. Everywhere the road was choked with smashed carts and gun-carriages that we either had to go round or move out of our way. As a result it took us nearly four hours to cover a distance of less than three leagues. During these four hours, M. de Lamoignon and I had plenty of time to exchange ideas. He was one of those who were pledged to the former dynasty, and naturally felt on friendly terms with anyone who was prepared to work for them. What were his chances? Everything depended on the course that the Allied sovereigns would take. Apart from them, what could one hope to do for the Princes of the House of Bourbon, in a country that scarcely knew them any more and where it was greatly to be feared that the army would remain hostile to them? And yet we both felt that their return would be the most desirable outcome; since politically they could not afford to offend any party or harm any interest, nothing was so likely to lead to that general pacification, the need for which was so widely felt. The example of what had just happened at Bordeaux was most encouraging.[17]

By the time we got to Bondy, day was beginning to break. As we entered the château where the Emperor Alexander was quartered, I was struck by a number of quite personal impressions in addition to those that had been worrying me since we left Paris. During my earliest childhood my maternal grandfather had lived in this château; since then I had only visited it occasionally, but the memories it had left in my mind were all

---

[17] This refers to the fact that, as long ago as 12 March, Bordeaux had enthusiastically welcomed the Duc d'Angoulême, the son of the Comte d'Artois and husband of Louis XVI's only daughter, who played an active part in the Restoration. See below.

closely bound up with the kind of incidents that affect us so deeply at the start of life; and now here I was, brought back there by one of the greatest events that had occurred since the beginning of the monarchy. I was taking the surrender of the city of Paris to a sovereign whose country, only a century ago, was almost unknown to our forefathers, and who now, sweeping down from the confines of Asia and gathering up the whole of Germany in his train, had come to impose his rule upon the France of Clovis, of Charlemagne, of Henri IV, Louis XIV and Napoleon! And it was we who had gone to seek him out in those frozen wastes, we who, by the light of his burning capital and gutted towns, had drawn him and his Tartars in our wake! Could Peter the Great have dreamt of such a thing in the days when, journeying through the civilised countries of the world to study their institutions, art and customs, he had visited the palace of the Tuileries and, with every mark of respect, taken in his arms the child king who was his host?

We were taken into the salon on the ground floor, occupied by some officers of the guard. They told us that the Emperor was asleep, but that he would certainly be getting up soon, probably even at once when he heard of our arrival. Half an hour later, an officer of the General Staff came into the room and introduced himself in the most courteous manner, speaking good French, through with an Italian accent. It was General de Pozzo di Borgo. He did his best to engage us in conversation, but in spite of his extreme civility no one was in the humour to indulge in idle chat.

A quarter of an hour later another dignitary arrived; M. de Nesselrode. Though he did not actually bear the title of Minister, he was nevertheless a member of the Russian cabinet, responsible for foreign affairs, and one of his master's closest confidants. As he had been First Secretary at the Russian Embassy in Paris, we had often met at M. de Bassano's and our social relations had always been most friendly. Our meeting again was, to both of us, a source of genuine satisfaction, since we both felt delighted to have someone to whom we could talk freely. He immediately drew me aside, and his first words were to ask me whether I knew about the proclamation that the Prince of Schwarzenberg had made. I replied that I knew the sense of it, but had not read the text. He at once gave it to me.

The purpose of this important document, which had been published everywhere, was, as I have already said, to draw a distinction between Napoleon's cause and that of the capital of France. It contained the following characteristic words: 'The Allied sovereigns seek in good faith to discover *a salutary authority in France*, which can consolidate agreement between all nations and all governments and herself. In the existing circumstances, it is upon the town of Paris that the opportunity to hasten the peace of the world devolves. Her wishes are awaited with all the interest that such an event must inspire. Let her but say the word and, from that moment, the army that lies before her gates will become the mainstay of her decisions. Parisians, you know your country's position, what happened at Bordeaux, the friendly occupation of Lyons, the evils that have fallen upon France and the true feelings of your fellow-citizens . . .' Then came an assurance that the people of Paris would be treated with every consideration and respect; the whole document ending with the following words: 'It is with these feelings that Europe, in arms before your walls, addresses you. Hasten to respond to the confidence she feels in your love for your country and in your wisdom.'

It could not have been put more clearly: 'Overthrow Napoleon, and whoever you put in his place we will accept.' But how could so formal a declaration have been written by the Austrian commander-in-chief when, so very recently, the head of the government, the most intimate confidant of the Emperor Francis, had written to the Duc de Vicence:[18] 'You ought to be acquainted with our wishes, our principles and our outlook . . . these are in favour of a dynasty that is so closely related to our own.'

The fact of the matter is, the proclamation was not the work of the Prince of Schwarzenberg; it had been more or less sprung upon him by General de Pozzo di Borgo, who had first thought of it at a little village where the headquarters of the Allied sovereigns had halted on the way to Coulommiers; that evening he had got his Emperor to take over the drafting of it, and next

[18] Armand de Caulaincourt (1772–1827), created Duc de Vicence in 1808, distinguished himself both as soldier and diplomatist. Returning from a mission to St Petersburg in 1801, he became aide-de-camp to the First Consul. As ambassador to Russia in 1807 he succeeded in obtaining peace for some years; but when, against his advice, Napoleon decided on the invasion of Russia, Caulaincourt accompanied him on the campaign. In 1813 he replaced Maret, Duc de Bassano, as the Emperor's closest advisor on foreign affairs, and during the Hundred Days acted as Foreign Minister. (Trs.)

morning the latter had put it to the King of Prussia, who had given his assent, and to the Prince of Schwarzenberg, who had not dared to refuse his. His hand strengthened by this approval, all General de Pozzo had to do on reaching Coulommiers was to find a printer; there he hurriedly had the document set up, and ordered a large number of copies to be printed. But the Prince of Schwarzenberg had already forestalled him with the Emperor of Russia, and when it came to printing his signature alongside the others, the printer insisted that an Austrian officer had instructed him not to do so until further orders. Pozzo was not to be put off by this, and hurrying off at a gallop he caught up with his Emperor on the main road, as they were leaving for Meaux. The Generalissimo was riding beside him; Alexander immediately grasped the seriousness of the hitch that had just been explained to him, and, in order to get over it, had no hesitation about coaxing the Prince of Schwarzenberg into withdrawing his objections. Once again he gave his consent, and this was immediately reported to Coulommiers. Thus the proclamation was eventually able to appear and to be distributed bearing his indispensable signature.

The Prince of Schwarzenberg was a brave man and very good-natured, but he had a mediocre mind and his military gifts were even more second-rate. He had been appointed generalissimo of the Allied armies out of consideration for Austria, and in order to bind her as closely as possible to the common cause. The burden was such a heavy one that there was little fear of his exercising his command in too exacting a manner; what *was* to be feared was his indolence. He was always under the immediate control of his master and M. de Metternich. On this occasion, he found himself for the first time left to his own resources, and it was not difficult for a mind as subtle as General de Pozzo's and a prince as captivating as Alexander to monopolise his attention at least for a few hours. The success achieved through M. de Pozzo's skilful handling of the matter must be reckoned one of the greatest services rendered to the House of Bourbon, if not, indeed, the most decisive. While I was carefully reading the document that M. de Nesselrode had just handed to me, he was trying to judge from my expression what impression it was making upon me, and, as soon as I had finished, he lost no time in asking me what I thought of it. 'I am very pleased', I replied, 'with the concern it shows for Paris. It is most essential, in fact, if we are to avoid accidents that would only sadden the Emperor Alexander's generous spirit, that Paris should be treated with consideration.' 'On that score,' said he, 'you may rest easy, for it will depend entirely on the Parisians themselves whether or not his benevolence towards them increases and proves to be their most valuable safeguard. In any case, the Emperor himself will soon be giving you every assurance you could wish for. As soon as he gets up he will instruct me to introduce the deputation; I shall tell him that you are in charge; and he will certainly be only too pleased to discuss matters with someone so completely to be trusted. Whether you are answering his questions or asking him for anything, don't feel the least constraint. Tell him whatever you feel will be useful. But I warn you, he is rather deaf in one ear and you must speak up if you want him to hear you.'

He then asked me to introduce the Prefect of the Seine and the leading members of the deputation to him. After he had left us, we had to wait for a considerable time, while the salon gradually filled up with all the leading members of the Emperor's staff and the principal generals of the Allied army. They tried to converse with us in the most friendly manner, expressing high praise and even admiration for the fine resistance put up by the French troops, especially during the final struggle which took place at La Fère-Champenoise.

It was about six o'clock when we were taken to the apartment on the first floor occupied by the Emperor Alexander. After an introduction, in which M. de Nesselrode, with the help of information given him by me, presented all the members of our deputation to the Emperor by name and rank, His Majesty began to speak, paraphrasing the Generalissimo's proclamation. He was no more precise than the latter in indicating what was to take the place of the government they wished to see overthrown, but he was infinitely clearer and more positive when he came to express his implacable hatred of Napoleon. 'I have only one enemy in France,' said he, 'and that is the man who has deceived me in the most unworthy manner, abused my confidence, betrayed every oath he made me, and involved my country in the most iniquitous and hateful war. Any reconciliation between him and myself is henceforward impossible; but, I repeat, he is the only enemy I have in France. Apart from him, I am well disposed towards all Frenchmen. I feel the highest esteem for

France, and for the French people, and I only hope that they will give me the opportunity of being of help to them. I honour the courage and glory of all those brave men against whom I have been fighting for the last two years, and whom I have learnt to respect in every situation they have found themselves in. I shall always be ready to render them the justice and honour that are due to them. Therefore, gentlemen, tell the people of Paris that I am not entering their city as an enemy, and that it is up to them whether I shall be their friend. But do not forget to tell them also that in France I have one enemy with whom I will never be reconciled.'

This he expressed in a dozen different ways, but always with the greatest vehemence, walking from one end of the room to the other. We all remained completely silent. When he was satisfied that we had fully understood him, he addressed himself directly to me and asked me whether I had any demands to make in the interests of the town and the maintenance of order. I pointed out to him that under the terms of the capitulation the National Guard had been exempted from the stipulations agreed upon for the army, but that no decision had been taken as to whether they were to remain unarmed and whether they were to continue to act on his behalf, which I regarded as essential. 'All right,' he replied 'if you consider it to be necessary, I agree. It is a mark of the confidence that I feel in the people of Paris, and I hope they will prove themselves worthy of it.' Then, re-membering that the major-general of the National Guard, M. Allent, had been presented to him, he went over to him and said: 'Are you prepared to answer for the National Guard, sir?' —To which M. Allent replied in a resentful tone of voice: 'Yes, provided they are not asked to do anything detrimental to their honour and the oath they have taken.' He had been deeply hurt by the Emperor's declamation against Napoleon, but fortunately he did not speak loudly, so that, thanks to his deafness, all the Emperor heard was 'Yes.'

I then ventured to make the same demand on behalf of the gendarmerie of Paris as for the National Guard, and I did my best to stress its usefulness; but as it was a paid body, fully militarised, this was a more delicate question. Alexander decided to defer his decision, though meanwhile allowing the police force to be used provisionally. Having agreed this point, I drew attention to the fact that the Generalissimo's proclamation promised that the capital should not be burdened by any billeting of troops, and I took the liberty of stressing how important it was that this undertaking should be strictly observed, as far as the rank and file were concerned. Indeed, how was I to accept responsibility for what might happen, with a population of more than 700,000 people, unless we were to be spared the daily brawls that were bound to break out between the common people and the soldiers if the latter were billeted on them? The Emperor at once repeated his promise, in the clearest possible terms.

He then asked how many barracks there were in the town and suburbs. He was surprised that there were so many, when the Prefect of the Seine and myself enumerated them. We observed that, in addition, there were others quite near, and that the barracks of Saint-Denis and Courbevoie could be regarded as belonging to the town. When we had explained this, the Emperor very graciously added his personal promise that public property would be respected, and that anything in the nature of looting would be prevented. He then dismissed us, adding that orders were about to be given for moving the troops, which, under the terms of the capitulation, were to enter the town at seven in the morning. I therefore suggested to him that, assuming they would occupy some of the city gates at that hour, it was greatly to be desired that they should not advance further into the town before ten or eleven o'clock. Those of us who were here were the only public officials who could give the necessary orders to prepare for their reception. We had been obliged to be absent from our posts nearly all night; it would be eight or nine o'clock before we could get back, and we should need time to take certain necessary precautions; at the very least, to publish a proclamation and to inform the National Guard that it was not to be disbanded and would be responsible for maintaining order. On our way downstairs, M. de Nesselrode informed me that one of the Emperor's aides-de-camp would be returning to Paris with me in my carriage, in order to make arrangements for His Majesty's quarters. I therefore had to ask M. de Lamoignon to find a place in someone else's carriage, while M. de Wolkonski got into mine, which went ahead and was immediately surrounded by an escort of Cossack guardsmen. We had scarcely gone two hundred yards from the village of Bondy, when I caught sight of the Duc de Vicence walking along the road. As soon as he recognised me, he rushed to the door of the carriage, doubtless hoping to find out what had been happening and especially what had been said, for at that moment the slightest word spoken by Alexander carried tremendous weight. Soon afterwards I learnt that he had already been there for some time, but had been unable to get into the village despite all his efforts to have the Emperor informed of his arrival. I should have been only too glad to exchange a few words with him, but the Cossack escort, probably at a sign from M. de Wolkonski, would not allow my coachman to stop, and forced him to drive faster.[19] Thus the return journey was made more rapidly. As may be imagined, the conversation between my companion and myself was not very animated, though it was extremely civil and well-mannered.

The road had been cleared of many of the obstacles which had held us up on our previous journey. This had been necessary in order to allow free passage to the numerous columns of troops, which were already being drawn up to the sound of military music, and in the midst of which we drove from Pantin as far as Paris. All the men of these advancing troops wore green sprigs in their caps, and white scarves on their arms. When I drew attention to this, my companion explained to me that the green sprig had been adopted in compliance with a custom of the Austrian soldiers, who always wore them when they took the field. As to the white scarf, the decision to wear this had been taken before the battle of La Rothière, so that the troops of so many different nations might recognise one another when there was any hand-to-hand fighting. It was almost eight o'clock by the time we passed through the city gate, which was already occupied by foreign troops, though they had not advanced any further. A little further on I found the detachment of gendarmes, whom we had left on our way out. They formed up on one side of my carriage and the Cossacks took the other, and in this manner I traversed the greater part of the town on the way to the Prefecture of Police.

[19] Caulaincourt's version, in his Memoirs, is rather different. 'About a league from Bondy I met some carriages which were taking the Paris municipal authorities home . . . The Prefects, surprised to see me and embarrassed at the thought of talking to me in front of the foreign officers who were watching them, behaved in a most chilly manner . . . They told me that the imminent arrival of foreign troops in Paris made it essential for them to get back at once, and scarcely gave me time to say that I would see them at M. Pasquier's when I got back.'

This first appearance of foreign soldiers inside the capital made a deep impression, and I could see in the eyes of almost all those who watched us go by a look of mournful dismay. Many thought that I had been made prisoner, and took this to be a most baleful omen. Before leaving Bondy, I had agreed with M. Allent that as soon as we got back he would give the National Guard orders to remain on duty, and to split up into numerous patrols to prevent any disturbance of the peace. I summoned the commander and principal officers of the gendarmerie, and informed them that the corps was to carry on until further orders; and that I hoped before long to obtain a definite decision. They were, on the whole, well disposed towards me and very keen to make themselves useful; but, at the same time, as one-time soldiers (they had all served in the army, and served well), they felt considerable dissatisfaction at being obliged to remain separate from the army; several of them were deeply devoted to Napoleon. I talked to them as best I could, and tried to make them understand that, in the circumstances in which we found ourselves, there were few greater services they could render their country, or for that matter the Emperor himself, than to see to the preservation of the capital and protect it from the calamities that might threaten it. In the end they all promised to do so, though some of them with a pretty bad grace.

I was busy drafting a proclamation to the people of Paris,[20] when the Duc de Vicence was announced. He had come in search of the information that he had been unable to obtain when we met on the way from Bondy, and I gave it to him as frankly as possible. Before doing so, however, I asked his permission to finish what I was writing, explaining to him how important I considered it to be. When I had finished he expressed a desire to see my draft; I willingly agreed, and even showed that I accepted some of his comments by changing one or two words.[21] He then told me that the previous evening Napoleon had reached a

[20] In it, Pasquier described the capitulation as 'most honourable', and added that there was no other solution. 'The National Guard', he told the Parisians, 'will stay behind for the purpose of protecting both you and your property. On this grave occasion remain calm, and display the admirable spirit for which you are already well-known.' Referring to these events, Mme de Chastenay comments: 'People found a certain coldness in the style of M. Pasquier's proclamations.'

[21] According to Caulaincourt: 'M. Pasquier received me in a somewhat chilly manner, but by the detailed account he gave me he proved that his foresight and loyalty had been greater than those of the authorities.'

position three leagues from the capital, between Cour-de-France and Villejuif. There he had encountered the head of a column of cavalry commanded by General Belliard, who had informed him of the capitulation. His first reaction had been to continue on his way and enter Paris; but what could he have done there? To keep troops in Paris who had already capitulated and undertaken to leave, would have been to violate all the rules of war.

On the other hand, the army which was following up behind him could not have reached the capital before 2 April. He was therefore obliged to retrace his steps, and he had decided to return to Fontainebleau. He had then sent the Duc de Vicence to the Emperor Alexander, with instructions to negotiate at all costs if there was still time. This was how it came about that we had met on the outskirts of Bondy; he admitted that he had had no better luck after I had gone than before, and had found it just as impossible to reach the Russian Emperor. He flattered himself, however, that he would be granted an audience immediately after Alexander's entry into Paris. When I stressed the very categorical way in which he had expressed his hostility towards Napoleon, he replied: 'I think I know him pretty well. Certainly he has been hurt, deeply hurt, but he is capable of generosity and moderation. This last great success he has just achieved will perhaps enable me to make him understand better and more easily that he would be unwise to expose the undeniable fame he has today acquired to the hazards of events. He has before him a great example, his rival's; I shall draw his attention to it, and I shall be very much surprised if I fail to make an impression on him.' To which I replied: 'I am afraid that you may be flattering yourself. But it needs confidence to act and to succeed, so I will not attempt to shake yours.'

The departmental chief to whom I had entrusted the Duc de Rovigo's portfolio lost no time in returning it to me as soon as I got back from Bondy. When he saw the Cossacks arrive at the Prefecture with me, and remain downstairs in the courtyard, he had firmly made up his mind that he was not going to be left with it on his hands. But what was to be done with it? It was difficult to foretell what might happen during the next forty-eight hours. The little I had seen of the correspondence contained in the portfolio had considerably increased what I already regarded as the serious consequences that might result from its disclosure, in view of the large number of people and interests that must inevitably be compromised by it. After a few moments hesitation, I decided to throw the whole lot in the fire; five minutes later it was completely destroyed.

When, three weeks later, the Duc de Rovigo asked me to return what he had entrusted to my discretion he could not help realising that I had acted prudently,[22] though he added that its loss was an irreparable misfortune for him since it contained the justification of his whole political career. Doubtless I had destroyed documents of the greatest historical value; but when I think of the use to which they might have been put, and realise the part they might so easily have played in paying off old scores, I tell myself that, although this had not been precisely my intention, nevertheless I had done a number of my contemporaries a very good turn. Had I been influenced by personal considerations, I should have argued that, in the event of any decision being taken that might lead to a breach with Napoleon and would, if he remained victorious, have exposed me to his harshest vengeance, it would be prudent to keep in my own hands a pledge, for the restitution of which the guarantee of my own peace of mind would not have been too high a price to pay. Such a breach of confidence shocked my sense of honour, and I remained true to the promise I had made to the Duke.

The Allied sovereigns entered Paris on 31 March. At the end of the day the Tsar, the King of Prussia, the Prince of Schwarzenberg, the Prince of Lichtenstein, M. de Nesselrode and General Pozzo di Borgo met at Talleyrand's house in the rue Saint-Florentin. French interests were represented by the Prince of Benevento, the Duc de Dalberg, the Abbé de Pradt, the Archbishop of Malines, and Baron Louis.[23]

Talleyrand, who was incontestably the master mind, argued that the restoration of the 'legitimate king' was the only possible solution.

M. de Nesselrode had written me a note which I received before

[22] Indeed, in this respect Savary's *Mémoires* in no way reproach Pasquier. 'I handed over to him', says he, 'a portfolio containing all the letters that the Emperor had done me the honour of writing to me during my term of office; he undertook to look after it for me on condition that he should be allowed to burn it if he himself was in any danger. In fact this proved to be the case, and the valuable documents I had entrusted to him were destroyed.'

[23] For Dalberg and Pradt see below, footnotes 26 and 36. Baron Louis, the indispensable Minister of Finance in both Restorations, adhered to the small group of Constitutional Royalists known as the *Doctrinaires*, to which Pasquier, de Broglie, Guizot and Royer-Collard also belonged. (Trs.)

five o'clock, urging me to come as quickly as possible to M. de Talleyrand's house, where the Emperor Alexander was due to arrive, as it would be necessary for them to come to an understanding with me. The large number of orders that I had to issue had not allowed me to leave immediately, and by the time I arrived the meeting was just breaking up.

I went up to the first floor, which M. de Talleyrand had reserved for himself. M. Louis came down and told me what had just been agreed, asked me whether I was willing to have a hand in it, or whether I should refuse to pledge myself, as he had just done, to a cause whose success could alone ensure the salvation of France and restore peace and happiness to her. No one's authority was less likely to influence me than M. Louis's; while admitting his intelligence and gallantry I had very little opinion of his judgement. Before I could make up my mind I needed to hear other opinions as well as his, and my answer was therefore evasive. 'I understand', he replied, 'that the decision is a hazardous one, and one would need to reflect carefully before taking it. But here comes M. de Nesselrode. I will leave you with him as his words will doubtless carry greater weight with you than mine.'

In fact, I spent nearly an hour with him. He went into the greatest detail about what had been said and done at the Council, mainly insisting on the unshakeable decision never to treat with Napoleon or with his family that had been taken by the Tsar and his allies. This decision, unless it resulted in immediately separating Napoleon from France, or rather of inducing France to abandon his cause, would lead to a continuation of wars and disasters, the end of which not be foreseen. Was not this, then, the moment to make an effort to avoid so great a disaster? Did not true patriotism demand that, at the risk of whatever personal danger, one should support the only policy that was capable of ensuring the safety of the country?

I had already given much consideration to the grave situation I should have to face, and I had not concealed from myself either the dangers or the sadness inherent in an irrevocable decision. From that moment, I resolved to use all the means in my power to facilitate the Restoration, and to ensure victory for the cause of the Bourbons. I did not conceal from M. de Nesselrode the difficulties of the undertaking nor the necessity of doing everything possible to persuade the people that nothing was being imposed upon them, but that they should act freely, obeying their own feelings and disregarding all foreign pressure. The feeling of national pride would have to be very carefully handled, especially as regards everything that might affect the army. In Paris there were swarms of disabled soldiers who must be reassured. I knew that many of them wanted to be moved outside the town. 'I can assure you in advance', M. de Nesselrode told me without hesitation, 'that the Emperor will accept whatever you suggest with regard to these soldiers. You may rest assured, moreover, that directly your intentions are clearly known to him you will enjoy his fullest confidence; and, what is more, he himself will give you this assurance, for you have to see him during the evening.'

I expressed a desire to read the text of the declaration that had been endorsed by the Council, since I was in a position to know whether its effect on the people of Paris would be good or bad. A proof reached me an hour later at the Prefecture of Police, and I changed a few words. This declaration had certainly been prepared beforehand by M. de Talleyrand or M. de Pozzo, for it would have been impossible at such a short meeting of the Council to produce a written draft in which all the essential points were so clearly touched upon with such admirable restraint.[24] Thus, the wishes of the French people being assured, they had not been afraid of suggesting that, while the conditions of peace must stipulate the strongest guarantees when it was a question of curbing Bonaparte's ambition, they could be much milder if France herself were to give unmistakeable proof that she desired the peace that the whole world was longing for.

The Allied sovereigns proclaimed that they would no longer treat with Napoleon, nor with any member of his family; that they would respect the integrity of the former France, as it had existed under its legitimate kings. They might even have gone further, for they had always professed the principle that it was necessary for the well-being of Europe that France should remain great and strong. The greatest criticism that anyone could have made of M. de Talleyrand was for failing to make more of this important concession. Finally, the sovereigns pledged themselves to recognise and guarantee the Constitution chosen

[24] Pasquier's supposition was in fact correct. The Tsar's declaration in the name of the Allied powers was adopted by the Council in the late afternoon of the 31st, but it had been drawn up in the morning by Talleyrand and his advisors.

by the French nation. They invited the Senate to designate a Provisional Government, which would be in a position to provide the necessary administration and to prepare the Constitution which would be best adapted to the wishes of the French people.

M. de Nesselrode wanted to keep me with him, and assured me that the Emperor, who had gone to his study to give certain orders, would receive me in less than half an hour. But I pointed out to him that my presence was too necessary at my own office for me to remain absent for so long, particularly at that time of day. It was agreed that I would return in the evening, M. de Talleyrand having told me that he would invite a small number of people with whom he wanted to discuss matters to meet at his house at nine o'clock.

On getting back to the Prefecture, I was informed in detail about everything that had happened in the town since the entry of the Allies. Except for that part of the town lying between the Boulevard des Italiens, the Place Louis XV and the rue de Richelieu as far as the Palais-Royal, where the first royalist acclamations had been heard, everywhere else there had been great consternation. At several points, notably in the Hôtel de Ville district and towards the Faubourg Saint-Antoine, a pretty lively opposition had broken out on a number of occasions. Fortunately it had been kept under control by the numerous patrols of the National Guard, which that day had begun the active and intelligent service which it was to maintain with such admirable perseverance throughout the duration of the crisis. It was apparent that the slightest incident might lead to an explosion, not so much against the Allied troops, whose strength was too imposing for anyone to dare to brave them, but against those who came out in favour of the Bourbons, whose rowdy merriment and friendliness towards the foreigners were regarded by a very large number of citizens as an insult to the people's grief and a betrayal of the national cause. Now, in the existing state of affairs nothing would have been more fatal than a movement of this kind. The administration therefore took every possible care to avoid this danger, and I can vouch for it that, with so many different and equally passionate feelings, the task was no easy one. I must say in fairness to all those who were there under my orders, that I found them to be as willing as they were zealous. I was fortunate enough to have inspired considerable confidence in them during the three years that I had been in charge of them;

and on this occasion I reaped the benefits of it. Thus, when I called together the police superintendents and officers of the peace to give them my instructions, they all assured me that they had decided to obey me blindly, since they were convinced that I should give them the best possible leadership according to what circumstances demanded for the greatest good of the town. When studying the reports that were submitted to me about the events of the day in the various districts, there was one which I could not help feeling might have had serious consequences. It had started in the Place Vendôme, about five o'clock in the evening. A number of royalists, who had gathered at the foot of the column surmounted by Napoleon's statue, had conceived the notion that pulling it down would create a decisive effect; they therefore began proclaiming their intention at the top of their voices. One or two of them had even climbed to the top of the column and started ineffectually attacking the statue. Darkness had put an end to their attempt, but it was to be feared that further similar ones might be made. The supporters of Napoleon were bound to resent this insult to him; besides, the spirit of the nation and army were sure to be deeply disgusted by this attack upon a monument which was so magnificent a tribute to the glory of French arms.

The greatest problem that day was distributing food to the very considerable number of troops that had entered the town. Delays occurred that might well have had very serious results, had it not been for the strict orders issued by the Allied sovereigns for the maintenance of discipline. Thus it was not until seven in the evening that the Russian troops received their first supplies of bread. I wrote to the Prefect of the Seine, since this was a matter that concerned his administration, and sent for all the leading officials charged with this special responsibility, doing what I could to stimulate their zeal. Our greatest difficulty was supplying so many cavalry, for there were very few fodder merchants in Paris; yet we were assured that it would be easier to get the Cossacks to go without food for themselves for a couple of days than to persuade them to put up with a delay of three hours in the distribution of rations for their horses. We decided to make an appeal to the principal contractors in Paris, and they were asked to meet me next day.

Between nine and ten o'clock, I returned to M. de Talleyrand's house and was at once taken to the Emperor Alexander's apartment. He could not have welcomed me in a more friendly manner, and he repeated in great detail everything that his ministers had told me in the morning. He assured me of his confidence in me, and said he had instructed the general whom he had selected for the command of Paris to make all the necessary arrangements with me and that I should find him a brave and reliable man. And, indeed, General de Sacken fully deserved this recommendation. The Emperor concluded with these words: 'For the rest, if anything upsets you, or if you feel there are certain measures that could usefully be taken, come direct to me; or if you yourself cannot come, send me a letter by an orderly and I will see that you have a reply within half an hour.' I availed myself of this invitation more than once, and always successfully.

On leaving this audience I went down to M. de Talleyrand's apartment. The antechambers and his outer study were already filled with crowds of people, most of them doubtless brought there by the purest motives, but amongst whom it was easy to pick out a number of men in a great hurry to get on. I noticed M. Laborie[25] talking to M. de Bourrienne and looking very pleased with himself; before long he was to find himself appointed to the secretariat of the Provisional Government. From that moment I was convinced that it would be a poor lookout for anyone who trusted him. When I reached the study, I found that the Duc de Dalberg,[26] M. Louis and M. de Jaucourt were already there with M. de Talleyrand. They were discussing the best way of getting the Senate to take action. It was agreed that as many Senators as possible should be informed, and that a meeting should be called at the Luxembourg for next day at three o'clock. I knew that, during the afternoon, M. de Caulaincourt had obtained from the Emperor Alexander the audience he had been counting on, although, in the event, its

[25] Roux de Laborie had a genius for intrigue. Beugnot says about him: 'After the 9 Thermidor he managed to get himself employed by the Committee of Public Safety, and from that time until the Ministry of the Prince de Polignac (who formed a reactionary government in 1829 under Charles X) inclusive, he never ceased to be the most active, the most subtle and the most tireless agent on behalf of all the governments that succeeded one another.'

[26] The Duc de Dalberg (1773–1833) who, according to Queen Hortense, was 'devoid of principles on any subject whatsoever, liberal, high-minded and cunning at the same time, profoundly demoralised by boredom and society', was, with Baron Louis, one of the men who did most to keep alive Talleyrand's hatred of Napoleon. A Minister of State in 1815, in the following year he went to Turin as ambassador.

results had disappointed his hopes. It had been made abundantly clear to him that any negotiations which sought to preserve the crown for his master were henceforward useless, and even out of the question.

The 1 April was going to prove whether the Senate would fulfil our hopes of it. If it were to disappoint us, the position would be critical, for we should find ourselves isolated, without any legal support in the country. There can be no doubt that never in his whole career did M. de Talleyrand manoeuvre more successfully than he did on this occasion, for, as everyone knows, everything he wanted, everything he felt to be necessary, was promptly agreed to and carried out. That evening, as I was about to go home, we learned that a deputation had just asked to be received by the Tsar; it had been sent by a group of royalists who had been meeting at M. de Mortefontaine's. The nucleus of it consisted of the young men who, during the morning, had sported the white cockade: M. de Sémallé had managed to get himself accepted as the Comte d'Artois' representative; M. de Chateaubriand and M. Ferrand had been present at the meeting; and they were all three members of the deputation. They brought with them an address, in which Napoleon was treated as a monster, no longer acceptable to the country, begging the Allied sovereigns to restore France's exiled king. The Emperor instructed M. de Nesselrode to inform them that neither he nor his Allies would ever treat with Napoleon, and that a solemn declaration to this effect was about to be published. By a curious coincidence, the man in whose house this first public meeting of the royalists was held had married a daughter of the regicide, Lepeletier de Saint-Fargeau.[27]

Returning home late that night, after all I had seen and heard I had plenty to occupy my mind; but fortunately, at times like this, men are sustained by the sheer speed of events, as well as by their sense of duty and the responsibilities they have undertaken. Confronted by a host of problems that had to be dealt with, and involved issuing orders, I had no time to brood upon things; I was lucky if I managed to snatch an hour or two's rest.

Next day I found myself even more preoccupied; food supplies were already beginning to cause serious anxiety. For the past three days nothing had reached the market; it had been generally assumed, outside the town, that the gates would be

[27] See above, Chapter II, footnote 9.

closed. The countryfolk were thus afraid to come near; while those who were prepared to run the risk did so only to seek refuge from the violence of the foreign soldiers who, quartered in the villages, and therefore out of sight of their officers, had already been committing excesses. On the other hand, there were plenty of people inside the town who, taking advantage of a period of calm that perhaps might not last, decided to find safety for themselves and their most precious possessions. The military were in a delicate position, for a large number of sick and wounded officers of all ranks had been obliged to leave the army and set up home in the capital. Having been unable to avail themselves of the short time that the terms of capitulation allowed the army for evacuating the town, they were afraid of being taken prisoner by the foreign troops; and since the Minister of War had left with all the other ministers, taking with him the leading officials in his administration, I was the only person left to whom they could turn in order to find out whether they were to hide themselves or whether they were to be moved out of the town in safety.

Nothing had as yet been decided; I did not know what authority would be given me to ensure free movement. I went to M. de Talleyrand's to discuss the matter with M. de Nesselrode; at my suggestion it was agreed that I should grant whatever passports I considered to be necessary, but to make certain that these would be respected by the various foreign military authorities, it was decided that they should be countersigned by the officer commanding the city, General de Sacken, and that one of his staff officers should be seconded to the Prefecture to issue the visas on his behalf. It was further decided that I should be authorised to announce in the name of the Prince of Schwarzenberg, by means of a printed notice to be as widely distributed as possible, that all the gates of the town would be open as usual. Thanks to these measures, which were made public with the greatest possible speed, couriers and public conveyances would be able to leave that evening: this was of great importance, in order to reassure the country as to what was happening in the capital.

There remained the question of the sick and wounded soldiers. I pointed out to M. de Nesselrode that nothing would be so likely to win people's confidence in the Tsar, which he was so anxious to have, as an act of generosity that would completely reassure them. He went upstairs to ascertain his sovereign's views, and when he came down again asked me to draw up the declaration I wanted myself, and the Emperor would then immediately sign it. It was the one that appeared in *Le Moniteur* on 2 April, in which Alexander declared in the name of himself and his Allies that: 'Soldiers of all ranks who are at present in Paris, either as a result of recent events or because they are suffering from exhaustion or honourable wounds that require treatment, have no need to hide, they are as free, as completely free, as all other French citizens. They are called upon to accept those measures which will decide the great question now under consideration, upon which the happiness of France and of the entire world depends.' This declaration produced an excellent effect; it restored tranquillity to men's minds. For my part, the satisfaction it brought me amidst all my worries was extremely gratifying.

On 1 April, the Senate, under the chairmanship of Talleyrand, appointed a Provisional Government, in which he reserved the place of President for himself. In addition to him, it included Comte de Beurnonville, Comte de Jaucourt, the Duc de Dalberg, and the Abbé de Montesquiou. Except for the last, all these men had filled important posts in the Imperial administration.[28]

On the same day, the Paris Municipal Council adopted a violent proclamation, in which its members 'abjured all obedience to the usurper in order to return to our legitimate ruler'. The Prefect of the Seine, after reflecting upon the matter for twenty-four hours, added his signature. Should Pasquier do the same? Pressure was brought to bear upon him, but he evaded the issue. 'I had to avoid upsetting many people whom I was working to bring over'; moreover, 'I found the insulting tone of the proclamation utterly repugnant . . . The hot-headed royalists who used to meet at M. de Mortefontaine's did not fail to notice the absence of my name at the foot of a document with which they were overjoyed; this was the origin of their distrust of me . . .'

For the moment, however, no one contemplated replacing Pasquier, who had made himself indispensable by the confidence he had inspired in the occupying powers. Indeed Talleyrand even offered him the Ministry of

---

[28] According to Beugnot: 'The émigrés, and in general the royalist party, were annoyed that the honour of welcoming the return of the House of Bourbon should have fallen to men who, with one exception, had grown old in the service of the Revolution or of the Emperor'.

Police. '*I refused it for two reasons: firstly, because I did not want to continue my career in the police any longer, and was, in fact, anxious to give it up; secondly, because at the moment the Prefecture of Police was of greater importance and I felt it would not be right to combine the office with that of the Ministry. I therefore, preferred to get M. Anglès appointed, as I knew him to be a good-natured man and most un-assuming. From the point of view of my personal interest it was a mistake, a great mistake. I remained in a secondary position, which allowed such enemies as I might have to attack me and prejudice my position.*'

'*I made up my mind to inform the public officially of the line that I intended to pursue, and of the decisions I had taken. I was most anxious that there should be nothing offensive in what I had to say, and I took the greatest pains to ensure this . . .*' This declaration of intent took the form of a circular to the employees at the Prefecture of Police, which was published in Le Moniteur of 4 April. It ended with these words, very characteristic of the times: '*Honoured by the confidence of the Paris authorities, who have kept me in office, I owe it to myself, I owe it to you, to acquaint you with my feelings and to indicate the nature of your obligations. Happy that the evils afflicting our country are at an end, I have accepted this new opportunity to serve her, my devotion to her is complete, and I look to my fellow-workers to share that devotion, to do their utmost to carry out whatever orders may be given them without the slightest hesitation . . .*

'*. . . Following my example, the Prefect of the Seine also issued a circular. Whereupon people flocked to join us.*'

But Napoleon was still at Fontainebleau, and the question of his abdication had still not been decided. Many people believed that hostilities would be renewed.

Happening to be at M. de Talleyrand's one day, discussing with the Duc de Dalberg the possibility that the war might continue and that battle might be joined maybe within the next four days, I could not help mentioning what I had heard about the fears and anxieties that the Allied high command still entertained with regard to the Emperor: 'If the generals, in the position they are in and with such a superiority of strength, are so obviously afraid of the man they have to fight, how can one expect them not to suffer a serious defeat?'—'You are right', replied the Duke. 'That's why other safety measures have to be taken.'—'And where do you hope to find them?'—'Steps have already been taken; we shall forestall the danger that is rightly to be feared.' He then went on to explain that a number of determined individuals, led by 'an energetic b . . . . . '—to use his own word—were to put on the uniforms of the *chasseurs de la garde* taken from the warehouses of the École Militaire, and then, either before or during the battle, thanks to this disguise, they would surround Napoleon and rid the country of him once and for all. The indignation I felt on hearing this odious proposal was so obvious from my expression that I sought in vain to obtain any further information. Only when I asked him where they had managed to find men capable of striking such a blow, he answered, 'Oh, that wasn't difficult. There are plenty of them about—Chouans, Jacobins, and so on.'

After this conversation I returned home, my mind full of the most sombre thoughts and deploring the associates one is committed to during great political crises and in times of revolution! Scarcely had I sat down, than I received a note from M. de la Valette, obviously written in great haste. 'I know', he said, 'that you are utterly incapable of being mixed up in the infamous plot against the Emperor's life that is now being considered. Maybe you are unaware of it. I therefore ought to warn you about it, convinced that you will do everything in your power to foil it.' How had he found out about it? That I never discovered, but his note proved that, as the preparations had leaked out, they must already be well advanced. Almost at the same time I received similar information from an inspector of police, Foudras, in whom I had the greatest confidence. Like M. de la Valette, he, too, had been warned. I have rarely been in such a difficult position. To be in possession of a secret, but having a very imperfect knowledge of the details and without knowing the name of any of those concerned, what could I do to avert an act which filled me with horror? Whichever way you looked at it, there were snares; the most determined loyalty might well be taken for treachery.

At the end of the day, still in a state of great anxiety, a note was brought to me at midnight, which had been left in my antechamber by some fellow from the country. He had promised to return the following day, before noon, to get my reply. I recognised the writing as the Duc de Bassano's. On behalf of the Emperor, he asked for detailed information of what was going on in Paris, adding that what they had heard appeared most improbable. I at once decided to take advantage of this opportunity to utter two warnings: in the first place, that the Emperor ought to take the greatest possible care for his personal safety; and, secondly, that he could no longer look to me to perform any service for him.[29] I decided to show M. de Bassano's note, on the following morning, to M. de Talleyrand, and to let the latter know that I intended to answer. To my great surprise, the Duc de Dalberg happened to be there; he approved of the advice that I was proposing to give, and assured me that it would help.

I then scribbled a draft of the answer I proposed to send; it was the Duc de Dalberg who thought I should mention that there were Jacobins amongst those who intended to insinuate themselves into Napoleon's presence. I kept a copy of my note, and here it is: 'These are the facts: the Senate, with eighty-two members present, has set up a Provisional Government; it has also announced your downfall. The government has issued an appeal to the French army. Several generals have already declared their adherence; amongst them, Generals Nansouty, Montelegier, Dangranville, Montbrun. Marshal Victor is taking steps to effect a reconciliation. General Dessolle is at the head of the National Guard. General Dupont is Minister of War. I understand that there are several plots on foot to get near the Emperor, and that amongst those who are committed to this idea are a number of Jacobins. The bankers are offering twelve million francs. The Legislative Body is meeting this morning. It will be even more committed than the Senate. The National Guard, under its new chief, is displaying a remarkably good spirit. No further approaches should be made to me on any account; the position I have adopted must be understood.'

The man who had called the previous day came back as agreed and took this note, which was written and folded so as to take up the least possible room. I heard that it had been handed to M. de Bassano in Napoleon's presence, and that he, recognising my writing, had hastened to read it. For a while he remained plunged in a brown study, then he said: 'This fellow's in a great hurry. Anyone would think he'd put on his hunting gear in order to go faster.'[29] During the night of the 3–4, the Duc de Vicence had

[29] From what Caulaincourt says, however, it appears that Napoleon spoke in the most generous terms of the stand taken by the Prefect of Police. 'Pasquier,' he is quoted as saying, 'is the only one to have behaved properly. A man who makes up his mind before an issue has been finally decided is acting courageously: he is taking a chance and, if it turns out not to be justified, he deserves to be

arrived and, on a number of questions, had given him much more detailed information than mine, though he was not yet aware that Napoleon had been deposed.

The account I have just given of what M. de Dalberg had confided to me, and his approval of the warning I had sent to the Emperor, was later to provide the key to an incident that gave rise to the most distressing rumours, and that many people have not yet been able to make up their minds about. I mean the expedition that took place under M. de Maubreuil's leadership.[30]

Marshal Marmont's defection was known in Paris during the morning of 4 April. 'The news was a great relief to us . . . I know what has been said, and what one is fully justified in thinking, about Marshal Marmont's conduct . . . nevertheless he rendered a great service. I feel bound to confirm this because so many people have expressed doubt on the question: what he did, he did without any attempt to impose conditions, without demanding the least personal advantage; whatever his private thoughts may have been, he neither asked nor stipulated anything for himself . . .'

On the same day, Napoleon, under pressure from his marshals, abdicated, on condition that a regency should be appointed in the name of his son.

The members of the Provisional Government, as they were in the habit of doing, met at M. de Talleyrand's between eight and nine o'clock in the evening [4. 4 . 14]. They were solely concerned with an event that was expected to occur during the night, and which they hoped to have news of the following morning when the Marshal's troops reached Versailles. Being completely absorbed by this one matter to the exclusion of all others, it was a short meeting; and between ten and eleven o'clock many of those present had retired. I decided to do the same, and I had just reached the bottom of the stairs when who should I see but M. de Saint-Simon, hurriedly dismounting from his horse. He asked me where he could find M. de Talleyrand, as he had news of the greatest importance for him; and asked me to accompany him.

Hurrying into the study, he announced the impending arrival

forgiven. To warn someone is not the same as to betray them. I used to think well of him, and I am delighted that his conduct has justified my opinion.'

[30] For the 'Maubreuil affair', see chapter VI, p. 194 ff.

of the Marshals[31] and the Duc de Vicence, who must already have reached Villejuif and would be here in less than three-quarters of an hour. Though he had overtaken them at Essonnes and ridden at full speed, he was sure that they could not be far behind. He told us about the mission they were charged with; they were bringing the Tsar Napoleon's abdication, on the one condition that a regency be appointed in the name of his son. Had it not been for M. de Saint-Simon, both the Government and the Emperor Alexander would have been taken completely unawares, and in that case there is no knowing what might have happened. It is possible that Alexander might have been induced to give some unconsidered pledge.

Having informed M. de Nesselrode of what we had just heard, M. de Talleyrand asked him to pass the information on to his master, and to enquire whether he wished to receive the Marshals as soon as they arrived, or whether he felt that it might be preferable to put off any meeting until the morrow. M. de Nesselrode returned a few minutes later to say that his master was determined to receive the deputation at once, but that as soon as he had heard what they had to say he would be very pleased to discuss any proposals they might make with the Provisional Government. Those who had already left were therefore sent for, and all of them, apart from the Abbé de Montesquiou,[32] returned. As M. Dessolle was there, M. de Talleyrand invited him, as well as myself, to remain. Thus we were about to take part in a great discussion. We settled down to wait in the Emperor's outer drawing-room, where we found M. de Nesselrode, M. de Pozzo and one or two Russian officers belonging to Alexander's suite.

It was around midnight before Napoleon's plenipotentiaries were introduced, and they appeared extremely surprised to see us there. Both sides greeted one another civilly, and after a few words of general conversation everyone began chatting to his neighbour, M. de Talleyrand to the Duc de Vicence. Happening to find myself next to Marshal Macdonald, I exchanged a few words with him. He said we ought to be well pleased with the proposals they were bringing, which they had only managed to obtain with

[31] Ney and Macdonald who, on their way through Essonnes, had called upon Marmont to accompany them.

[32] The Abbé de Montesquiou-Fezensac had accompanied Louis XVIII during his exile and, as one of his closest advisors, was a member of the Provisional Government in 1814 and subsequently Minister of the Interior. (Trs.)

considerable difficulty. I replied that, in my view, a regency offered none of the conditions for future security that were to be desired, though this did not prevent me from recognising the great service they had done by persuading Napoleon to take this first step. I added that he should not count on us to support the proposals they had been instructed to put forward.[33] Shortly afterwards, the door of Alexander's study opened, and they were invited in. The meeting started with a suggestion that they should negotiate directly with the Provisional Government, but this they declined. Indeed, neither they nor the Government was prepared to accept this method of proceeding. Half an hour later they came out and it was our turn to be received.

The Emperor Alexander remained standing, while we formed a semi circle facing him. In the clearest possible terms, he gave us an admirable account of all the arguments that had been used to induce him to accept Napoleon's offer. Carefully, even warmly, he stressed all its advantages: 'It would settle everything; it would ensure that France had a government that would respect recent developments and new interests; it would remain in the hands of men who, for many years past, had occupied leading positions, it was bound to have the necessary ability. Inside the country, everything would be perfectly safe. Abroad, once the man who had inspired such universal distrust had been removed, there would no longer be cause for anxiety. Satisfactory relations with the whole world would be established without difficulty. On top of this, the very lively interest that Austria was bound to take in the imperial dynasty would provide a sure guarantee that no other power would attempt to take advantage of France's rather weak political position as a result of her being in a minority; finally, and this appeared to be the decisive reason in his eyes, by accepting this proposal we should be sure of the army's approval, and in this way dispose of the one real difficulty in the situation. No more fighting, no further possibility of opposition; peace would be genuinely established, at once and everywhere.'

Our answers to this could be neither so concise nor so clearly argued, for the simple reason that we had far more to say. M. de Talleyrand, to whom it fell to speak first, dealt with the principal points; then the Duc de Dalberg and M. Dessolle[34] said a few

[33] Macdonald does not mention this conversation in his *Mémoires*.

[34] Who had been appointed commander of the National Guard by the Pro-

words. They had no difficulty in demonstrating that any such attempt to arrive at a rapid conclusion by accepting a regency was a mistake, since it offered no security; that with a man like Napoleon, with all the resources of his enterprising genius, there would be no way of preventing him, in a year's time, perhaps sooner, from once more seizing the reins of power. No one, presumably, suggested keeping him in prison. Such a step would be incompatible with the direct negotiations with him that had been accepted; it we were to resort to it, it would arouse support for him on all sides.

What was to be done with his family? What part were they to play? Many of them were ambitious, unruly men. The greatest difficulty would arise from the Bourbon's revived claim for the restoration of their rights. After being forgotten for several years, recent events had given them a new vitality, a new strength, which could not be denied. Though the name Bourbon had so far not been mentioned in any official proclamation, everybody was nevertheless aware of what had been done to prepare for their return. The entire Senate had rallied to the idea; at the earliest opportunity, maybe within forty-eight hours, it was bound to pronounce in their favour.

Could we pretend that these obvious and important facts were to be regarded as non-existent? One of the largest towns in France, Bordeaux, had come out in favour of the ancient dynasty. A similar outlook obtained in several towns in the Midi; in the capital a large number of people had loudly voiced their opinion without any hostile reaction from the mass of the population. If we lost this opportunity of restoring the House of Bourbon, while at the same time insisting upon conditions that would benefit everyone, no one could answer for what the Bourbons might do later on if their cause were to triumph. For how many years had we seen their supporters carrying on their agitation inside France, often enough with a considerable chance of success? At that time, however, they had had to struggle against the Republican spirit produced by the Revolution, which had had time to develop and was then at its strongest. This spirit had since been stifled by the ascendancy of a man of genius, who had succeeded in reviving the feeling for the monarchy in

visional Government. 'His acceptance produced a very considerable effect', Pasquier added. 'He was the first officer of general's rank who had shown himself not to be afraid of accepting the new regime . . . '

his own interests, and who, in order to found his Empire, had done his utmost to destroy and uproot all the customs and ideas opposed to this form of government. Was there, in the whole of history, a single example of the founder of a sovereign dynasty who had succeeded in bequeathing to his descendants what he had failed to keep for himself?

During this first discussion, no one attempted to remind Alexander of the solemn engagement he had entered into *never to treat with Napoleon or any other member of his family*. It was, I think, a tactful omission, and one for which he was grateful to us.

Having heard us out with the greatest patience, the Emperor dismissed us, telling us to wait in the other room. He then re-called the members of the deputation. From what I heard later, he repeated to them everything we had said with the same care and precision that he had repeated their views to us. They had not expected this conflict of opinion. They pressed home the argument which always had the greatest effect on Alexander: if their proposals were accepted they were assured of the army's universal support; if they were rejected, the army would be justly indignant that so little consideration had been accorded to the great sacrifice made by the man who was still the object of their devotion. Their loyalty to him would take on renewed strength; we should have to be prepared for a most determined struggle. It would be a mistake to assume that the army had been as badly shaken as had been generally supposed; in a few days, the world would be amazed to discover how many men had rallied to Napoleon and gathered beneath his flag.

These gentlemen were once more dismissed; we took their place; and matters proceeded as before. The Emperor repeated the Marshals' latest argument, appearing to be considerably im-pressed by the force of their reasoning. It was necessary to op-pose them again. The abdication was bound to upset even those who were most passionately devoted to him, it could not fail to cool their ardour. The rank and file of the French army had too much common sense not to realise that the cause of a man re-duced to such an extremity was irrevocably lost. In the end they would realise that they were not fighting for Napoleon but for his son, for the interests of a child, and this was hardly likely to stir their imagination. The absolute devotion attributed to the army had been exaggerated; in reality, their devotion was to

their country rather than to Napoleon; once the distinction between these two causes became clear to them, with very few
exceptions they would rally to the country's flag. The proof of
this was to be seen in the ease with which the negotiations with
Marshal Marmont and his army corps had been concluded. It
was important to wait and see what effect the agreement would
have; the Marshals knew nothing about it, as was clear from
their continuing intimacy with Marshal Marmont.

Finally, we had to use the argument hitherto held in reserve:
the Emperor must remember that the members of the Provisional
Government, and all those who had been drawn to follow their
example and their advice, had only made up their minds on the
basis of the promise he himself had made on behalf of himself
and his allies: not to treat either with Napoleon, *or with any
member of his family.* All those who had trusted in his word were
exposed to certain danger; sooner or later they would be the
victims of an implacable vengeance; the wisest, the most
fortunate, would be those who decided to become expatriates,
and who obtained permission from him to follow him and find
asylum in Russia.

General Dessolle grew very heated on this question; though
he spoke very well, in the course of his improvised speech he
allowed one or two phrases of rather too soldierly an eloquence
to escape him. At the time, it was felt that this freedom of language, far from producing any ill effects, had exerted a powerful
influence on Alexander's mind, and had struck him as being
evidence of the general's forceful convictions. This has been
asserted, and, indeed, printed; but it was a mistake, as was later
to be proved to me beyond doubt.[35]

By the time we withdrew the Emperor was considerably
shaken. During his preceding discussion with the Marshals, he

[35] 'In 1818, after the conclusion of business at the Congress of Aix-la-Chapelle,
the Emperor Alexander took it into his head to pay a short visit to the King of
France in Paris . . . The ministers who remained in Paris—the Duc de Richelieu
was still at Aix-la-Chapelle—thought it would be a good idea for General Dessolle
to welcome the Tsar at the frontier. Great was our amazement when we heard
from the Duc de Richelieu that, far from being pleased by this choice, the
Emperor had been genuinely upset by it and had formally complained that it
seemed strange that anyone should have thought of sending him a man who had
behaved with such grossness on the occasion when the question of the regency
had been discussed in his study. I think he felt that it would have been more
proper for one of the Princes of the blood to have come to meet him, and that
his annoyance on finding that no one had thought of this had increased the ill
humour that he evinced towards General Dessolle.' (Note by Pasquier.)

had also received a note that was passed to him by M. de Pozzo, which contained certain warnings and arguments against the regency. Thus from all appearances his mind, if not completely made up, was at least very nearly so when he finally dismissed us, saying that he needed to reflect upon everything he had just heard; that it was, moreover, necessary for him to discuss the matter with the King of Prussia; and that we should be informed of the decision he had reached at nine o'clock next morning. He had doubtless made a similar appointment with Napoleon's emissaries.

It was by then two o'clock in the morning, and we had been present at one of the most extraordinary scenes known to history. A monarch, arriving from the confines of Asia, had insisted upon coolly discussing the existence of a dynasty founded by the greatest man of modern times, and the restoration of the oldest ruling dynasty in Europe, which had been driven from its throne twenty-two years previously by the most terrible of revolutions. And he had put an end to the discussion by saying: 'I will let you know my decision at nine o'clock tomorrow'. One can only assume that, despite the tranquil air he affected, the Tsar himself must have felt the gravity of the decision he was about to take.

It has been said, and it is by no means impossible, that the Duc de Vicence had managed to arrange a further meeting with him, at which he made a considerable impression upon him by his lively description of all the difficulties and dangers that were bound to ensue from the restoration of the Bourbons, which others had represented to him as such a simple and easy matter. What must particularly have preoccupied him, was the necessity of making up his mind in the absence of the most powerful of his Allies, who was so directly involved in the matter. As long as it had only been a question of taking steps to overthrow Napoleon, Alexander had been able to go ahead without hesitation; but, after the abdication, it would be a matter of preserving the crown for his son, for the grandson of the Emperor of Austria, his beloved daughter's child. Obviously, this was bound to be an embarrassing position for the man whose advice would settle the question. There was only one way to get out of it, which was to insist that the abdication would simply be an illusion, that the regency would be tantamount to a continuation of Napoleon's government until such time as he himself boldly resumed control of it. This was the thesis that the Emperor Alexander maintained with his allies. He had no difficulty in convincing the King of Prussia, whom he called upon at six o'clock next morning and who agreed that abdication on condition that a regency should be appointed should be utterly rejected.

It remained to convey this refusal to the interested parties. The Duc de Vicence and the Marshals, with the exception of the Duc de Raguse, had, in their impatience, arrived at the Tsar's quarters well in advance of the appointed time. He received them without delay; the position had changed to their disadvantage. It was difficult for them to insist any more upon the feelings and views of the army, for the movement of men that had been agreed between Marshal Marmont and the Prince of Schwarzenberg had been carried out during the night, despite the Marshal's absence and without awaiting his orders. General Souham, in agreement with General Bourdesouile, had taken this decisive initiative on learning, according to them, of the steps taken by General Lucotte to warn the Emperor Napoleon of the danger that threatened him as a result of the defection of his advance guard.

Be that as it may, General Souham arrived at Versailles at the head of his troops, and news of this had reached the Emperor Alexander by daybreak. I have it from M. de Pozzo that, having spent the night in one of the salons leading to the Emperor's study, and having gone to the window to watch the sunrise, his attention was attracted by someone laying a hand on his shoulder. It was the Emperor himself. He had just received the news, and wanted to share his satisfaction with somebody. He therefore passed it on to M. de Pozzo, adding, with that mystical insistence that was already becoming habitual with him: 'You see, the will of Providence has now manifested itself; no more doubts, no more hesitation.'

The plenipotentiaries soon realised that they had nothing more to hope for, and announced their intention of returning to Napoleon to inform him of the failure of their negotiations and to discover his latest views. The Emperor had formally intimated to them that a straightforward abdication, on the part of Napoleon's whole family as well as himself, was the sole condition for the cessation of hostilities, which would otherwise be renewed with the greatest energy, taking full advantage of the abandonment of his forward positions, until recently occupied by the army corps that had just deserted his cause.

As may be seen, the situation had changed very rapidly.

On 6 April, Napoleon signed an act of unconditional abdication. Without awaiting his final decision, the members of the Provisional Government had been busily engaged during the last few days in drawing up a new constitution. Talleyrand entrusted Lebrun with the responsibility for drafting it.

This choice of Lebrun as the drafter was generally well received. In addition to his talent as a writer, he had a longstanding reputation for his ability in all matters concerned with government and administration; he had been a member of the Constituent Assembly and, ever since the *Conseil des Anciens*, had continued to occupy important posts in all succeeding governments. He appeared to accept the commission with the utmost willingness. On the evening of 3 April we all met at M. de Talleyrand's to hear his proposals, the abdication having been proclaimed in the morning.

The gathering consisted of from twenty to twenty-five people; all the members of the Provisional Government, plus General Dessolle, M. Louis, the Abbé de Pradt[36] and myself; from the Senate, as far as I am able to recall, there were M. de Marbois, M. Lanjuinais, M. Abrial, M. de Pastoret, M. de Fontanes, M. Fabre, M. Cornet, M. Emmery, M. de Malleville, M. Lambrecht, M. Vimar, and one or two others whose names escape me; and finally, representing the Allies, MM. de Pozzo, de Nesselrode and, I think, M. de Hardenberg. When everyone was seated, sitting in any kind of order in a very small room on the first floor, M. de Talleyrand, having installed M. Lebrun on his right hand, opened the proceedings with his customary eloquence. He informed us that the Duc de Plaisance had been good enough to undertake some preparatory work, which coming from a man so enlightened and so profoundly versed as he in these

---

[36] The Abbé de Pradt had been successively appointed Almoner to the Emperor, Baron, Bishop of Poitiers, Archbishop of Malines and ambassador at Warsaw. But in this last post he upset the Emperor, who, on his way back to France in December 1812, had, in the presence of Caulaincourt, had a similar kind of scene with him to the one that Talleyrand had been subjected to on 28 January 1809. In 1814 the Abbé de Pradt, convinced that his moment of revenge had come, played an active part in setting up the Provisional Government.

difficult matters, might well shorten our labours and greatly assist our deliberations.

We were all listening with the greatest attention, convinced, indeed, that we were about to hear the most carefully considered proposals. There was complete silence. M. Lebrun, having with some difficulty taken from his pocket a splendid volume bound in red morocco, then said in that gruff, mocking tone of voice that he invariably employed: 'As you will see, gentlemen, the job has not given me much trouble; I discovered it had been already done. It did not require much reflection on my part to convince me that, however, hard I worked at it, I could do no better, probably not as well. Believe me, you can take my word for it, it's never too late to return to something that is unmistakably good.'

Whereupon, he laid his handsome volume on the table, which proved to be simply the Constitution of 1791. We all looked at one aother, dumb with astonishment; the most embarrassed, the most discomfited of all being M. de Talleyrand. He did his best to utter a few phrases which, without being too unfriendly to M. Lebrun, nevertheless made it clear how badly let down he felt; and then, while doing justice to the merits of certain parts of the 1791 Constitution, he went on to point out, without much difficulty, that it could not possibly be adopted to the present situation; and seizing upon the point which he felt sure would be most readily agreed, he said: 'For example, in this Constitution there is only one legislative body and one chamber; we have to have two. We already have a Senate, which we cannot do without. This in itself is bound to produce considerable difficulty as regards their respective powers. What we have to decide upon is some kind of declaration of principles, the establishment of some solid basis with which all dispositions of detail can later be co-ordinated.'

Everybody applauded the way in which he had brought the discussion back to the real issue. MM. de Marbois, Lanjuinais, Emmery, de Pastoret, Lambrecht and the Abbé de Montesquiou took part in the discussion. I recall that when they were insisting upon the importance of the Senate, and the need to make it as prominent as possible, a word or two was said on the subject of the endowments it possessed, the Senatorships with which many of the Senators had been invested, and the need to consolidate these. This was the prelude to that unfortunate provision, shortly

afterwards inserted in the draft Constitution, which did the
Senate so much harm and eventually robbed it of all significance.

On this subject, I ventured to say that no one had mentioned
the sole condition which would ensure the Senate an existence
proportionate to the part we wanted it to play; that as soon as
one had two chambers confronting one another, it was, in my
opinion, only the hereditary principle that would enable the
Senate to offset the influence that the elected Chamber exercised
over the country as its immediate representative. My observations
were taken up very warmly by M. Emmery, who appeared to be
far from satisfied with the importance that was attached to
financial interests. As we were leaving, he said to me: 'I am afraid
these folk haven't enough commonsense to realise that the hereditary principle would assure them of much greater benefits than
these Senatorships they set such store by preserving.'

Very skilfully, M. de Talleyrand allowed it to appear that he
regarded the restoration of the House of Bourbon as so inevitable that he only referred to it at the end, when he took the
quite natural opportunity of praising the man who was to
become King. 'You must remember, gentlemen,' said he, 'that
the task you are about to embark upon will be judged by a man
of very superior intelligence. The Prince who will have to accept
the constitution and give life to it, upon whose collaboration it
will depend, is in a better position to criticise it than anyone else.
His natural abilities are reinforced by the experience he has inevitably acquired during his long stay in England with regard
to these important matters, with which, as you know, he has
always been deeply concerned. You will probably not have
forgotten that he expressed his opinions and principles as long
ago as the Assembly of Notables.[37] He is thus in a better position
than any of us, perhaps, to discuss article by article what should
be included in a wisely moderate Constitution; make no mistake,
we shall be dealing with a tough customer, and we should get
short shrift if we were to offer such a Prince a feebly conceived
Constitution which failed to satisfy either his strong reasoning
powers or his high intelligence. And this means, therefore, that
what we produce must be good; and, above all, we must not

[37] The part played by the Comte de Provence, as Louis XVIII then was, at
the Assembly of Notables in 1789, had consisted mainly in assisting the obstructive
tactics employed by the privileged classes, especially by the clergy, towards the
projects of reform that were laid before them.

allow ourselves to get bogged down in detail.' No one could have shown greater skill in bringing out those aspects of the future King of France's character that could be most usefully popularised. This first meeting enabled M. de Talleyrand to give the Constitution the appearance of an achievement resulting from long deliberation between men whose names commanded great authority with the public.

In fact, by next day, 4 April, the Constitution had been drafted; it was submitted on the 5th to a commission of the Senate, approved by the Upper Chamber on the 6th, and by the Legislative Body on the 7th. The new Constitution had to be submitted to the approval of the French people; as everyone knows, its character was profoundly changed by the Charter.

VI

The First Restoration
1814–1815

THE COMTE D'ARTOIS RETURNS TO PARIS –
THE ULTRAS' CHARGES AGAINST PASQUIER
– THE MAUBREUIL AFFAIR – LOUIS XVIII
ENTERS PARIS – BLACAS' INFLUENCE – PASQUIER
APPOINTED DIRECTOR GENERAL OF ROADS
AND BRIDGES – EVACUATION OF THE CAPITAL
BY THE ALLIES – SUBMISSION OF THE CHARTER
TO THE LEGISLATIVE ASSEMBLY – TRAVELS IN
THE PROVINCES – DISCONTENT OF AN IMPOR-
TANT PART OF PUBLIC OPINION – CONVERSA-
TION WITH TALLEYRAND BEFORE HIS
DEPARTURE FOR THE CONGRESS OF VIENNA –
NAPOLEON LANDS AT THE GULF OF SAINT
JUAN – THE ROYALISTS IN CONFUSION – PLANS
FOR RESISTANCE – CONVERSATIONS WITH
VITROLLES AND THE ABBÉ DE MONTESQUIOU –
DEPARTURE OF THE KING AND THE EMPEROR'S
ARRIVAL

For a long time Monsieur, the Comte d'Artois,[1] had been
staying so near Paris that they must have intended him to
enter the capital as soon as there could be no objection to his
presence there. Above all it was essential that the Prince's

---

[1] The youngest brother of Louis XVI, who therefore, since Louis XVIII had
no children, succeeded to the throne on the latter's death in 1824. Having fled
abroad in 1789, he had lived mainly in England, continually conspiring against
the Revolution and the Empire; and after the Restoration he continued, as leader
of the *Ultras*, the party of extreme reaction, to plot against his brother, who said
of him: 'He conspired against Louis XVI, he conspired against me, he will end
by conspiring against himself.' On his accession to the throne in 1824 he refused
any compromise with the liberal opposition and imposed the government of the
Prince de Polignac, the incarnation of clericalism and reaction, on the country.
His virtual suspension of the Constitution and attempt to rule by ordinance were
the immediate causes of the 1830 Revolution which overthrew him. (Trs.)

appearance should not be the pretext for any outburst of opposition. The collapse of the imperial regime had been proclaimed,
and the restoration of the Bourbons decreed, by the Constitutional Act; Napoleon's abdication could be regarded as certain,
only awaiting the return of his plenipotentiaries and the ensuing
negotiations with them. It was felt that the time had come to
take the initiative; the Comte d'Artois was invited to leave his
quarters at Nancy and to make his way towards the capital. M.
de Vitrolles, who had remained in Paris attached to Allied
headquarters, was sent by M. de Talleyrand and the Duc de
Dalberg to give him all necessary information.

The king was kept in England by an attack of gout, which
prevented him from fixing the date of his departure. It was
essential to put an end, as quickly as possible, to a precarious
situation which was not without danger. Thus we were about
to take part in an historical event as strange as it was unforeseen.
After twenty-two years in exile, during which he had been
almost completely forgotten, after so many events and battles
in which he had not been involved, the people were about to see
once again that member of the royal family who had been the
first to flee abroad, and who had therefore been the object of
special dislike. He was about to appear as the angel of peace, as
the once certain pledge of all the happiness that people were
longing for. In this capital, where the blood of his brother the
King, of his sister and of his sister-in-law, the Queen, had been
shed upon the scaffold, where three weeks previously not one
person in a thousand had even been aware of his existence, his
return was going to be regarded as a blessing and he himself to
be acclaimed on every side. The National Guard, in which, as
late as 31 March, not a single company could have been found
to which it would not have been dangerous to suggest changing
the colour of their cockades, which had agreed to his return
only four days previously, and then with the greatest hesitation,
were about to rally to him, carrying their new colours as
ardently and enthusiastically as if they had never entertained any
other feeling.

On 11 [April], it was learnt during the morning that
Monsieur had arrived within three leagues of Paris. All those
who had been attached to him in the past, all those who had
been in touch with him either in the old days or recently,
hastened thither to pay homage to him. The little village of

Livry where he spent the 11th, was overrun that evening by a huge concourse of people, amongst whom were a number of National Guardsmen, very naturally drawn thither by zeal and curiosity. Monsieur readily received them and was most gracious; everyone was delighted with him. They came back wearing, in addition to their white cockades, white ribbons that had been distributed by Mme de Damas and Mme de Chastellux, who were entertaining Monsieur for the night.

Leaving Livry early on the 12th, Monsieur found detachments from every legion of the National Guard awaiting him at Bondy, and they accompanied him as far as the Pantin gate. He was on horseback, wearing the uniform of the National Guard, and he reached the gate shortly before three o'clock, where the Provisional Government, the Municipal Council and a considerable number of general officers led by the Marshals had been waiting since midnight to receive him. Speeches were made by M. de Talleyrand on behalf of the Provisional Government, and by M. de Chabrol for the Municipal Council. His replies were in excellent taste, though they are not to be judged entirely by what was printed next day in *Le Moniteur*. The printed versions, as one would expect, had been touched up by M. Beugnot,[2] and it is to him that we owe the admirable phrase: 'At last I am back in France, where nothing has changed, except that there is one Frenchman the more.' There is no doubt that this was due to the author I cite; he had agreed upon it with me.

M. de Talleyrand's speech, no more than five or six lines, was remarkable because it gave the impression of being simply a short, spontaneous outburst of affection.[3] M. de Chabrol went further, and most appropriately brought France into the picture. His speech, too, was a great success; everyone recognised in it the skilful and elegant hand of his father-in-law, M. Lebrun.

The ceremonial entry was greeted by splendid weather, and

[2] The Comte de Beugnot, having given proof of his considerable capacity as an administrator in Germany in 1810, remained nevertheless a consistent supporter of constitutional monarchy. After the Restoration he was a member of the Provisional Government and was one of those responsible for drafting the Charter. For Pasquier's opinion of him, see below, p. 209. (Trs.)

[3] How spontaneous may be judged from the text of his speech: 'Your Highness, the happiness we feel on this day of regeneration is beyond all expression. Accept, sir, with that celestial goodness of heart that distinguishes your august family, the homage of our religious feeling and respectful devotion.'

was a magnificent spectacle.[4] The procession proceeded through the suburb and street of Saint-Denis as far as Nôtre-Dame, where the Prince attended a service of thanksgiving and listened to the *Te Deum*. He drove through an immense crowd, who acclaimed him enthusiastically. The Allies had had the tact to confine all troops to barracks for the occasion. Thus only the National Guard was to be seen, carrying out all guard duties and lining the route. In this way the ceremony was entirely French, and all distressing thoughts were as far as possible laid aside. The streets through which the procession passed on its way from the city gates to Nôtre-Dame, and from Nôtre-Dame to the Tuileries, were those that might be regarded as belonging more particularly to the merchants and middle-class, and in consequence to the National Guard. The windows were filled with their wives, sisters and daughters, delighted to see the part their husbands, brothers and fathers were taking on this great occasion. Everywhere there were signs of sincere joy. One might say that it was to the National Guard that the honour and glory of this brilliant occasion were due. On every side one heard shouts of: 'Long Live the House of Bourbon! Long Live the King! Long Live Monsieur!' In many places the walls were hung with tapestry, as they used to be in the old days on Corpus Christi; white flags fluttered from every window, and people threw bunches of flowers in the path of the procession. The joy that was expressed had all the marks of being genuine and spontaneous.

In the account I have just given, I do not think I have in any way exaggerated.[5] No one was in a better position than I to see what was going on. I was taking part in the procession and was very close to the Princes, so that I was able to see a great deal with my own eyes, and the reports that I received at the end of the day convinced me that, even where I could not see for

[4] Pasquier's instructions to the police on this occasion began: 'Wishing to do everything in our power to maintain the most perfect order during this great and memorable ceremony, and at the same time to ensure to all citizens of every class the opportunity of expressing their joy, and of approaching as near as possible the august Prince whose return puts an end to the evils that have weighed on them for so long and guarantees peace and happiness for them and their children ...'

[5] Pasquier's evidence agrees with that of Beugnot. The latter, however, noted the presence in the procession 'of Russian, Prussian, Austrian, Spanish and Portuguese officers, at the head of whom the Prince appeared like an angel of peace in the midst of the great European family'.

myself, it had been the same: not a hostile voice was to be heard. The common people were less enthusiastic than the bourgeoisie, but even amongst those who could be said to have been half-hearted there was not the slightest expression of dissatisfaction.

'From that day forward, it is true to say that the political scene completely changed; the reign of the Provisional Government was at an end . . .'

On the 14, the Senate conferred upon the Comte d'Artois the title of Lieutenant-General of the Realm, 'but the King's obligation to accept the Constitutional Charter as the primary condition for his assuming power was scrupulously adhered to'. Monsieur gave his assurance that Louis XVIII would not seek to evade this duty; though at the same time he surrounded his pledge with certain reservations. Then he set up a provisional Council of State which included, in addition to the members of the Provisional Government, Marshal Moncey, Marshal Oudinot and General Dessolle. Vitrolles was appointed secretary, as a reward for the services he had rendered to the cause of the Bourbons since the beginning of the year.

It was not long before differences of opinion began to appear. 'It was scarcely to be hoped that good relations could for long obtain between men of such different outlook and origin, and whose interests were so contradictory. On the one hand were officials, who for the past fifteen years had given proof of their undeniable ability; and, on the other, men embittered by misfortune and exile and all the suffering they had endured for a cause which had at last triumphed, who were impatiently awaiting the reward for their loyalty and were very little disposed to give much consideration to those who had served under the preceding regimes, which they had always detested and fought against. As far as I was concerned, I soon became aware of the veiled hostility that surrounded us, and of the efforts that were being made to instil into the Prince's mind the most unjust prejudices against us.

'Later on, I discovered that Monsieur had been inspired with such prejudice against me that, on the day after his return to the Tuileries, he had said to M. Beugnot: "Look, M. Beugnot, I shan't be able to sleep in peace as long as M. Pasquier remains in charge of the police." '[6]

The curious Maubreuil[7] *affair was, moreover, about to bring the Prefect*

---

[6] Beugnot does not mention this remark in his *Mémoires.*

[7] On this question see Maurice Garçon: *La tumultuese existence de Maubreuil,* Paris, 1954. The author draws largely upon Pasquier's account, which he considers to be in the main correct.

of Police a good deal more into the limelight than he probably cared to be.

One has to bear in mind the measures taken by the Provisional Government (which I was at pains to enumerate above), to ensure that the monies, taken on orders from Napoleon or the regency during the last days of March, were repaid to the Treasury or into various State accounts.[8] Commissioners had been despatched all over the place to enforce these decrees, and M. Dudon had been especially charged by M. Louis with the recovery of the diamonds and the civil list appropriation which had followed Marie-Louise to Blois under the care of M. de la Bouillerie, the treasurer of the civil list.[9] M. Dudon had had no difficulty in arranging for the return both of the government funds and of M. de la Bouillerie, who was only too pleased to restore them. But, on reaching the gates of Paris, the convoy fell in with a troop of soldiers, led, if I am not mistaken, by a certain Lagrange, who had been instructed to seize the money. As to who had instructed him, I have no idea. Instead of being deposited at the Treasury, the cases were to be taken straight to the Tuileries. This incident had led to a very lively dispute between M. Louis and Monsieur's advisors, who wanted to establish a private hoard with the eight to ten million francs that had been returned. They based their claim on the fact that these monies had accrued from the civil list. In M. Louis' opinion, it did not much matter where they came from, the essential thing being to maintain the public services; and he argued, not unreasonably, that in the penurious state of the Treasury this assistance was indispensable.

During this dispute, I remember, the cases were left in the courtyard of the Tuileries, without being emptied, and guarded by a detachment of National Guardsmen and gendarmes to whom M. Louis had appealed for help. The Commissioners, despatched by the Minister of Finance, were not, therefore, as we have just seen, the only agents actively engaged in looking

[8] A decree of the Provisional Government on 9 April called upon anyone possessing bonds taken from Paris before the capitulation, or otherwise withdrawn from the public treasury, to declare them immediately with a view to refunding them.

[9] Napoleon approved of La Bouillerie's ingenuity and zeal. He used to say of him that he was 'a sack that never gets a hole in it'.

for and recovering these monies: in this respect, the royalists were also displaying considerable zeal. One of them, M. de Maubreuil,[10] had particularly distinguished himself by his energy. He had, in the person of M. Laborie, a special protector; and M. Laborie, as assistant secretary of the Provisional Government, had since the start been in a position to introduce to M. de Talleyrand's ante-rooms a swarm of people anxious to offer their services, for whose ability, enthusiasm and sound opinions he was prepared to vouch. Unless they had actually seen them, nobody would believe what a crowd of people used to be packed into so small a space, nor what an incredible mixture it comprised; men from every rank of society, of every shade of opinion, of every conceivable temperament were to be found there. This spectacle was all the more extraordinary because, on the floor above, the Tsar was installed with his principal officials, and the courtyard and staircases of the building were filled with his guards.

No doubt M. de Maubreuil, under the wing of his protector, M. Laborie, had on a number of occasions been one of this crowd, and had been introduced to M. de Talleyrand and to some of the members of the Provisional Government. And doubtless he had been received with the polite and meaningless words that are freely used on such occasions with all comers. But he was not content to be fobbed off like this; he was determined to strike a blow, and this is the plan he conceived.

According to this Lagrange, the man who had so conveniently intervened in the recovery of the civil list funds, Maubreuil claimed that two of the cases containing valuables, possibly some of the crown jewels, were still missing, because they had been sent to Napoleon; and he offered to go in search of them wherever they might be. It appears that at first he tried to obtain authorisation for carrying out this search from M. de Sémallé,[11] but when the latter turned him down he applied to the Minister

[10] Maubreuil, who had previously taken part in the Chouan insurrection against the Republic, later became an equerry to King Jerome, then speculated in army supplies and, on the fall of Napoleon, attracted attention to himself by his excessive devotion to the royalist cause; he was one of the crackpots who had attempted to overthrow the Vendôme column. He was said to have been so lacking in good taste that he used to ride about with his Legion of Honour Cross tied to his horse's tail.

[11] M. de Sémallé was a supporter of the Comte D'Artois. He had reached Paris ahead of the Prince, with full authority as his personal representative.

of War, General Dupont, from whom he obtained on the 16th
an order to the military authorities, and to any French troops
he happened to meet on the way, to render him every assistance.
What induced M. Dupont to take this initiative? Why, without
being authorised by any of his colleagues, did he give this order
for a matter so far removed from his competence? He appears
to have retained no precise recollection of what occurred
between M. de Maubreuil and himself; he even thinks that this
order may have been extorted from him on the pretext of
trying to find certain valuable objects that had been stolen from
the army depot, that is to say, the plates from which Cassini's
military maps were printed.

However that may be, M. de Maubreuil had to have a passport; it should be noted that he did not dare to come to the
Prefecture of Police for it, since he was too well-known there.
He therefore applied to the Ministry of Police. After some
difficulty, M. Anglès decided to grant him one after seeing the
order from the Minister of War; and he added a similar order,
addressed to the civil authorities. Provided with such good
credentials, he had no difficulty in obtaining from M. de
Bourienne a permit enabling him to travel post wherever he
wished.[12] Even more surprising, he managed to get an order
made out by General de Sacken and the chief of staff of the
Allied forces, which placed any foreign troops he might
encounter at his disposal, in the same way as General Dupont
had done with regard to the French forces. Armed with all these
documents, he set out on the 18th with a certain Dasies, whom
he had taken into partnership, and with whom he appears to
have been associated since the attempt to pull down Napoleon's
statue in the Place Vendôme.

On this same day, the 18th, the Queen of Westphalia, the
Princess of Würtemberg,[13] set out to return to Germany, taking
the Nemours route. M. de Maubreuil had served as equerry in
her husband's household in Westphalia; the relations he had

[12] Bourrienne (1769–1834), a diplomatist who had accompanied Bonaparte to
Egypt as private secretary and was with him at the time of the 18th Brumaire.
He subsequently acted as French envoy to the free city of Hamburg, but was
recalled in disgrace in 1813. In 1814 he supported Louis XVIII and was appointed
Postmaster General in the Provisional Government. (Trs.)

[13] Catherine of Würtemberg was the second wife of Napoleon's youngest
brother Jerome, who was made King of Westphalia in 1807. In 1814 she was
crowned Queen in her own right. (Trs.)

maintained with his entourage made it easy for him to ascertain the time of her departure and the route that she was taking; he felt convinced that she would be taking with her the jewels, diamonds and other valuables that belonged to her. Everyone knows how, having requisitioned a squadron of cavalry and mameluks at Montereau, he lay in wait for her near the village of Fossard, forced her to get out of her carriage and go into a barn, and finally refused to let her continue her journey until she handed over the eleven cases containing her jewels, her diamonds and 84,000 gold francs. He also demanded the keys of all her trunks, which she was obliged to give up, except for one that had been kept by her husband. The excuse he gave for this attack on the Queen was that he had been ordered to seize her baggage as she was suspected of having appropriated some diamonds belonging to the crown.

All this took place on the 21st. On the night of the 23rd–24th, at one o'clock in the morning, having got back to Paris after making a number of detours (very exactly described in the extract, published in 1827, from the depositions taken at Douai in May 1818 by the attorney-general to the crown of that city), the audacious Maubreuil had had no hesitation in turning up at M. de Vitrolles' apartment in the Tuileries.[14] He had with him four sacks of gold, according to him, and these, together with the remains of a case that had been smashed on the way, comprised the balance of what he had taken from the Queen of Westphalia; the other cases had been brought to M. de Vitrolles by M. de Vanteaux earlier in the day. All these things had only been restored, or rather deposited, because of a rumour that the Allied sovereigns, and especially Alexander, were extremely angry at hearing of such hateful violence, such a preposterous insult, against a princess of the royal blood who had so recently been crowned. As she was travelling on a passport made out in the name of all the sovereigns, her arrest, and the theft of which she had been a victim, constituted the most impertinent violation of every right. The ministers of the foreign powers had therefore been instructed by their masters to demand, with the greatest insistence, the immediate restitu-

[14] The Baron de Vitrolles was employed by the Comte d'Artois as a secret agent throughout the emigration. After the Restoration he continued to intrigue on behalf of the *Ultras* against Louis XVIII who, in 1818, dismissed him from the Privy Council for his part in a royalist-military conspiracy. (Trs.)

tion of everything that had been stolen from her, as well as the punishment of those responsible.

When the provisional secretariat of State, which had been installed in the Pavillon de Marsan, saw this case arrive, and later the sacks containing the money, they therefore considered themselves to be extremely fortunate. They fondly imagined that this was the end of the matter. But both M. de Vitrolles himself and his clerks had made the incredible mistake of accepting everything without checking it, without insisting upon the cases being opened and without examining a single sack. They had been satisfied with the declaration that the keys had not been handed over with the cases. Next day, when they sent for the locksmith who had made the chests to open them (a man called Biennais, well-known for this kind of work), they were found to be almost completely empty, while the sacks contained nothing but silver coins worth twenty sous, instead of twenty-franc gold pieces. They were profoundly disappointed. It could be foreseen that M. de Maubreuil would claim that he had handed over everything exactly as it was when he had taken it, and that he would thus divert the charge from himself to those with whom he had deposited the goods. No one knew what to do.

This state of uncertainty persisted throughout the day of the 24th. Meanwhile, M. de Maubreuil was strolling about Paris, apparently utterly unconcerned. Infuriated by this insufferable impertinence, the Allied powers lodged a complaint and eventually it was decided to arrest him. He and his associate, Dasies, were therefore summoned to the Tuileries, on the evening of the 25th, to give some explanation. M. Anglès was there with a Police superintendent, who interrogated both of them, then drew up a report and sealed both the cases and sacks of money.

This done, M. de Maubreuil and M. Dasies were brought to the Prefecture of Police; it must have been midnight, for I was already in bed. M. Anglès had me woken up, and informed me that these two gentlemen were my prisoners. He added that I had been asked to pursue the matter as energetically as possible, and to recover what had been stolen. Up till then I had had nothing to do with the handling of this affair, but I was aware of its seriousness, since the ministers of the Allied sovereigns had already called for my intervention several times. It was

possible that the tactless royalists in Monsieur's entourage might
be compromised. It was scarcely believable that such an audacious
plot should have been attempted without considerable encouragement, without some assurance of the most powerful support.
I therefore felt it was necessary to get to the bottom of the
matter as soon as possible, this being the only way to prevent
the most tiresome suspicions. To achieve this, nothing was
neglected; houses were searched and people were interrogated.

The first thing to be discovered was a diamond, which was
found in one of the apartments occupied by Maubreuil; he had
two or three in Paris, this one was in the rue Neuve-du-Luxem-
bourg. The diamond, which was found on the bed, was obviously
one of those belonging to the Queen, which proved that they
must have been handled here. I had dispatched some very
intelligent agents to make enquiries along the whole route
taken by the thieves, and I was expecting their report to throw
some light on the matter; but to do the job well took time, and
their return was delayed. This delay aroused the impatience of
the Allied sovereigns, and gave rise to new and more pressing
demands from them. They could not be convinced that we were
not showing consideration towards the guilty, were not
attempting to save them. Scarcely a day went by but some
Officer was sent by the Emperor Alexander to ask me what was
happening.

Finally things reached the point where M. Talleyrand, unable
to evade their tiresome importunity any longer, authorised me,
in order to bring things to a head, to offer M. de Maubreuil, if
he was prepared to return everything, a sum of money, as well
as a promise that his future safety would be guaranteed. I therefore had him brought to my study: this was the first time he
had appeared before me; he had often been interrogated, but
by police agents highly skilled in this kind of investigation.
Throughout our conversation he remained unshakeable, always
maintaining his complete innocence; he insisted that the only
motive for everything he had done was his desire to render an
important service to his country without any thought of personal
interest.

However, the agents I had sent to cover the route he had
taken, had acquitted themselves with great skill and very
successfully. They eventually returned with the most circumstantial details of everything that had happened at Fossard, and

later on. Retracing his footsteps, they had eventually discovered that Maubreuil had abandoned the direct road to Paris on his way back, and, on reaching Croix-de-Bernis, had taken the one to Versailles. Once they had established this fact, they had had little difficulty in discovering which of the inns in that town he and his accomplice had stayed at, and they had managed to find out everything that had passed between these two wretches. Having taken a room at the back of the building, they had sent for a locksmith who, on their orders, had opened with a skeleton key the one case for which they had none. This was the one that contained the most valuable objects. The same man had been sent for three or four hours later to lock it up again. All this was established by formal affidavits, obtained in the course of interrogation. There was no longer the slightest doubt as to where the cases had been opened or who had been responsible. I was therefore in a position to provide the government with precise and conclusive information.

The first thing to do was to question Maubreuil again. He was not in the least disconcerted, and persisted in denying everything. It was now that he produced for the first time a completely unexpected line of defence: 'He fully realised that they wanted to get rid of him, that they had made up their minds to sacrifice him for failing to justify the horrible trust they had imposed in him. The truth was that he had left Paris having been commissioned to assassinate the Emperor Napoleon, and it was M. de Talleyrand who had given him his instructions; that despite his horror of the mission he had been charged with, he had undertaken it for fear it might be entrusted to someone else. He had so arranged matters as to evade the criminal intentions of those who had employed him, and had flattered himself that, by obtaining all these valuables for them and so satisfying their greed, he would manage to avoid their displeasure. He had had everything taken to M. de Vitrolles', because he knew that nowhere else would such a gift be so welcome; and, indeed, it appeared that they had made no bones about making use of it.'

It was useless pointing out to him the obvious falsity of this account, that it was contradicted by incontestable evidence; nor was it any use telling him that, even supposing one were to accept the first part of his story, this would not dispose of the facts established at Versailles, which proved conclusively that the chests had been emptied by him at an inn in the town; nothing would persuade him to abandon his new line of defence. I reported the position to the government. They now had to decide what they were going to do about him; and it was an extremely embarrassing problem. At first sight, the most natural thing was to bring him to trial, but remember the position they were in; just imagine the effect it would have had if allegations like those being put forward by Maubreuil were made public; and, above all, consider what an impression they might have made on the army, particularly on the rank and file! In matters of this kind, even the biggest lies always achieve some measure of credence.

It was therefore decided to do nothing rash, but to keep the accused in prison and look to time and the march of events for help and counsel. Even the Allied sovereigns had to assent to this approach, for they, too, were compromised. Maubreuil did not hesitate to assert that the mission he had undertaken had been entrusted to him in the common interest and with the agreement of all the interested parties, in the forefront of whom he put Monsieur, the Emperor Alexander and the King of Prussia. In proof of this, he referred to the orders he had been furnished with by General de Sacken and the Prussian general, both of whom had authorised him to call upon the Allied troops for help at any time. Such a mark of confidence was, in fact, extraordinary, especially when bestowed upon such a man; to explain it, it was difficult not to believe that some very considerable service had been expected of him. Thus it may be seen with what diabolical cunning this wretch had succeeded in protecting himself by managing to compromise those in the highest positions. The whole responsibility was attributable to the first order, which had been given him by General Dupont. His passports, his permission to use post horses, and the two other orders had all ensued from this, if not inevitably, at least very understandably; this could not but appear all the more serious in view of the fact that General Dupont was suspected of nursing a burning desire for vengeance against Napoleon.[15]

[15] Dupont de l'Etang (1765–1840), after fighting brilliantly in the revolutionary and imperial campaigns, was created count by Napoleon after the occupation of Madrid, but shortly afterwards was defeated and capitulated at Baylen, for which he was deprived of his rank and title and imprisoned from 1812–14. He therefore supported the Restoration and was appointed Minister of War in the Provisional Government. (Trs.)

Was this strange affair in any way connected with the plot which the Duc de Dalberg had told me about in confidence? It sometimes happens that the most glaring lies are based upon some point that offers an appearance of truth. When he told me about the plan for getting rid of Napoleon, M. de Dalberg had said that the conspirators were to wear the uniforms of the *chasseurs de la garde*. M. de Maubreuil had also mentioned, both in his depositions and interrogations, that the same disguise had been suggested to him. As soon as I got to know about this particular detail, I felt certain that the leader of the expedition that the Duc de Dalberg had spoken to me about, had at last been found.[16] True, that plan had been abandoned, when the danger that had led to its inception had disappeared owing to Marmont's disaffection. What all this seemed to point to was that Maubreuil had, as he insisted, been approached: but that, as regards the sordid deed that he boasted of not wanting to commit, though it had been agreed upon to employ him for it, this had been at a much earlier date than his expedition against the Queen of Westphalia. Since that time, no one had dreamt of reviving the loathsome plot, which had been abandoned, if, indeed, it had ever been seriously considered. Maubreuil flung himself into the enterprise, convinced that the confidential knowledge he possessed would force the government to treat him with the greatest leniency. The fact that the moment chosen by him to carry out this attempt happened to coincide with Napoleon's departure, was a stroke of luck for him: it provided him with a basis for the story he had invented. Thus an abandoned plot had been the real cause underlying Maubreuil's audacious attempt. The repercussions of this adventure were to persist for a long time. Even as I write this, after a lapse of thirteen years, it has just served as a pretext for a calumny against M. de Talleyrand, that has struck a most painful blow at him in his old age by suggesting that he may have been privy to a plot to assassinate the Emperor Napoleon.

I have recounted everything to do with this affair that came to my knowledge with complete honesty, and there is not the slightest foundation for this odious accusation.[17] In the whirl-

---

[16] *See above*, p. 175.

[17] In his *Mémoires* Talleyrand dismisses this accusation as being 'even more absurd, if that is possible, than infamous.' Maubreuil was released, then arrested again, and finally condemned in his absence to five years imprisonment in 1818.

pool of events in which M. de Talleyrand was then involved, he may well have met Maubreuil, without attaching the least importance to it. It is extremely likely that the latter was introduced to him, like so many others, by M. Laborie, and they may have exchanged a few friendly words, but they certainly did not have a long conversation as claimed by Maubreuil. The Prince was far too experienced, far too astute, to discuss serious matters with someone he did not know; a few vague and utterly commonplace phrases were all he would have addressed to him.

The Comte d'Artois retained his position as Lieutenant-General for seventeeen days: 'Napoleon's departure led to a palpable improvement in the conduct of affairs; but though the dangers decreased, pretensions and passions that had hitherto been held in check now began to assert themselves with greater assurance; from then on our most serious difficulties arose from the unreasonable demands of the royalists. The ineptitude of their speeches, their stupidly expressed scorn, their denigration of everything that had happened, the high and mighty airs affected by a considerable body of people suddenly reappearing on a stage from which they had so long been absent, were bound to sow the seeds of uneasiness and discontent amongst the public.'

Pasquier, from what he says, was continually drawing Monsieur's attention to the concern he felt in this situation. 'The violence of the royalist party provokes similar violence in the party of the revolution.' But no one listened to him. ' . . . There was a tendency to distrust anything that appeared to be established.' Shortly before Louis XVIII returned, however, the Abbé de Montesquiou gave him an assurance that he was to remain in office. 'He insisted that I should agree to remain in charge of the police for a year or two and said that, to get me to make up my mind, they would make whatever arrangements I asked for.'

The king, who 'was in no hurry',[18] *entered Paris on 3 May.*

Carefully prepared, the king's entry was admirable; every day saw fresh displays of magnificence; what perhaps had nowhere

In 1827 he made himself even more notorious by striking Talleyrand in public, for which, after a rowdy trial, he was condemned to two more years in prison. 'He hit me with his fist, Sire,' Talleyrand told Charles X when asked what had happened.

[18] After wandering about Europe for nearly twenty years, Louis, like so many other political refugees, had settled in England in 1807, at Gosfield in Essex, moving two years later to Hartwell in Buckinghamshire, where he remained until the Restoration, at which time he was prostrated by an attack of gout. (Trs.)

been encountered to such a degree previously, was the spontaneous enthusiasm of vast numbers of people. The weather was superb, as it had been on 12 April; the same itinerary, the same decoration of houses and windows, the same transports of joy, above all on the part of the bourgeoisie. Henri IV's statue had been set up once more on the bastion of the Pont Neuf as though by magic, and the king's carriage stopped so that he could read this simple and elegant inscription on its base:

Ludovico Reduce Henricus Redivivus.[19]

So great was the crowd at this spot, that it was only with the greatest difficulty that the road was kept open for the procession to pass. All the way, stands had been put up wherever there was an open space, and these were crowded with spectators. In the first open carriage sat the old king, his handsome features, so typical of his ancient race, still wearing a kindly expression, despite misfortunes and infirmities; and beside him was the Duchesse d'Angoulême, the daughter of Louis XVI and Marie-Antoinette, who had been imprisoned in the Temple, and whose melancholy expression recalled so many unhappy memories. Facing them was the Prince de Condé, father of the Duc d'Enghien and the last survivor of his family, while on either side of the carriage rode Monsieur and the Duc de Berry. Even today I still find the memory of that day profoundly moving. I recalled those sad times when I used to look up at the high walls of the Temple with a heavy heart; I recalled the Place de la Révolution, the death of the King and of my father, and so many occasions when the stoutest hearts were overwhelmed with despair! Who, in those days, would have thought that this family, scattered by the storm, would return in triumph, acclaimed by the people of Paris?

All foreign troops had been carefully confined to barracks. The French soldiers behaved to perfection, seeing the King and the Princes surrounded by their most distinguished leaders, the men for whom they had long felt the highest respect. Marshal Berthier rode in front of the King's carriage, with a group of generals. The other Marshals accompanied Monsieur and the Duc de Berry. It would have been almost impossible for the troops not to have shared in the enthusiasm of the crowd.

---

[19] Beugnot claims to have been the author of this inscription, and reproaches Lally-Tollendal for trying to make Louis XVIII believe that he too had thought of it.

The Imperial Guard, who occupied the leading position in the escort, appeared to be deeply conscious of this honour. Seeing them go by, in many places there were cries of '*Long live the Guard!*' and this, mixed with shouts of '*Long live the King! Long live the House of Bourbon!*', produced an admirable effect. Had one of the Princes gone to them next day and told them in the King's name: 'Comrades, you have become the Royal Bodyguard, the King and his family put themselves in your hands and seek no other guarantee of their safety but your courage and loyalty', all these old warriors would have been irrevocably won over.

Having left Saint-Ouen at ten o'clock in the morning, the King did not reach the Tuileries until six in the evening; an immense crowd packed the Carrousel, and all the courtyards and gardens. Several times during the course of the evening His Majesty was obliged to show himself on the balcony, with the Duchesse d'Angoulême at his side. The day ended with a display of fireworks and the illumination of the city.

I was delighted that there were no accidents for me to report in my evening bulletin, a rare enough state of affairs on such a day. Unhappily the following day turned out to be less lucky. The Russian, Austrian and Prussian troops were drawn up from early morning on the right bank of the Seine, from the Arsenal as far as the Louvre. At three o'clock the King took up his position at the window of the Pavillon de Flore. Beside him stood the Emperors of Russia and Austria, the King of Prussia, the Duchesse d'Angoulême, Monsieur and the Duc de Berry.[20] The march-past began immediately and finished at six o'clock. It was under the command of the Grand Duke Constantine. This military pageant was certainly very splendid, but all the way along the route it led to a lively agitation, mainly caused by a custom that I have already referred to. The Austrians, whenever they go into battle, all wear a sprig of green in their helmets; both the Russians and the Prussians had adopted this custom; and there was a general feeling that they were wearing this decoration as an emblem of victory. Grumbling broke out on all sides, amongst the National Guard as well as the people.

[20] Mme Royale, the only daughter of Louis XVI, had become Duchesse d'Angoulême by her marriage to her cousin, the Comte d'Artois' elder son (q.v. later in this chapter). The Duc de Berry, his younger son, was assassinated in 1820. (Trs.)

I need hardly say that the army was even more violently annoyed. About midday I decided to write to M. de Nesselrode, asking him to bring my letter to the Emperor Alexander's attention. Three-quarters of an hour later, an order was despatched to all the Russian troops, and before long the ground was strewn with green sprigs, torn from their shakos and helmets. Their example was followed by the Prussians, which left only the Austrians, who persisted in retaining their cockades, with the result that they became the object of particular dislike, which continued to increase until they left the city.

I went out towards the end of the morning in order to judge for myself how things were going in the neighbourhood of the Tuileries. When I got back, I found on my desk a very short letter, in a hand that was then unknown to me; it was the King's. When sending my bulletin the previous evening, I had taken the liberty of asking His Majesty for his instructions as to the nature and extent of the relations that he authorised me to maintain with him. Was it his wish that I should occasionally wait upon him, as I had done with Monsieur, in order to report to him privately?

His answer was very simple. I was authorised to follow the procedure I had previously adopted, and I could wait upon him every day at eight o'clock in the morning. I availed myself of this permission the following day, and was received with extreme kindness. The King told me that we had been in correspondence for longer than I was aware; he said that, ever since his return to France, my bulletins had been sent on to him. He added that he had read them with interest, and urged me to continue to keep him informed on all matters with the same frankness and precision. He several times repeated that I should not worry about abusing his permission, as, particularly to begin with, he would be delighted to see me every day.

As I was leaving his study, I found a man waiting at the door with an air of impatience, plainly revealing by his expression that he was somewhat surprised at my having preceded him. It was M. de Blacas,[21] who immediately went in to see the King. The following day, when I repeated my visit, the King

[21] The Comte (afterwards Duc) de Blacas d'Aulps had been Louis XVIII's favourite since 1811. His rigidly Royalist views helped to make the formation of a united ministry impossible after the Restoration. Following the King's flight to Ghent during the Hundred Days, the dismissal of Blacas was made one of the conditions of his second Restoration. (Trs.)

told me, as I was on the point of leaving, to go upstairs to see M. de Blacas; he was anxious that I should, as far as possible, bring him up to date with the true state of affairs. He added that, in future, I should do well to see him either before visiting his study or after leaving it. It was not difficult to guess that this was the result of the ill humour M. de Blacas had displayed on meeting me there the previous day. I realised that he would prefer me to call upon him before I was admitted to His Majesty's presence.

Basically I had everything to gain, from the point of view of the service, by keeping on good terms with a man who enjoyed the King's confidence in such large measure. I therefore went upstairs to see M. de Blacas. At that time he lived on the floor above the King's apartments, and the only secretary he had was a miserable-looking Abbé, whose name I have forgotten. I was somewhat surprised to see him there, for we had got out of the way of employing ecclesiastics except in their capacity as priests. M. de Blacas, who had been reading my bulletins for the last ten or twelve days, was fully in touch with the matters we had to deal with. The disapproval implied in my comments, since they were directed at those who enjoyed Monsieur's private confidence and at the instructions they had given, were not likely to be displeasing to him, since he himself was on pretty bad terms with this Prince and his court. There had never been a full understanding between the two brothers, and on more than one occasion M. de Blacas had had to serve as the rather crusty interpreter of the King's wishes to Monsieur and his supporters. Thus here was I, thanks to circumstances which I knew extremely little about, to all appearances in a better position than the one I had just given up; in fact, as long as M. de Blacas remained in direct contact with the King, I never experienced the slightest discouragement. Right up to the last moment, I had reason to believe that my services were appreciated.

Eventually, however, the criticism of Pasquier by Monsieur, and more especially by the members of his entourage, carried the day.

'On the 13 [May], at eight o'clock in the morning, I arrived for an audience with the King, and was admitted as usual. After a short conversation His Majesty, as gracious as ever, said to me: "You have not been up to see M. de Blacas this morning. Be sure to do so as you go out, he has something to tell you." I thereupon left the King and, going

*upstairs, found M. de Blacas in a state of some embarrassment.
"Well, M. Pasquier," said he, "I have to inform you that it has been
decided to make a change, but that the King is very anxious that you
should not see it as in any way a sign of his disfavour. In the ministerial
reorganisation that has been agreed upon, you will not be keeping the
Police." Then, without giving me a chance to speak, he hastened to add:
"I have been instructed by His Majesty to ask you what place would
best suit you—you shall have it immediately."—"You could not have
had better news for me, Monsieur", I replied. "To have remained at the
Prefecture would have been a severe test of my loyalty . . . As to my
own inclination, there is one very easy way for the King to satisfy them.
The position of Director-General of Roads and Bridges is vacant. If I
were to be given it, I should be only too happy."—"You may regard it as
yours", said M. de Blacas, accompanying his promise with some very
civil remarks.*

'*. . . I was curious to know who was to take my place, and how the
police were to be organised. "We have taken your advice", he replied.
"In future there is to be only one appointment, which will combine the
duties of both positions;*[22]* and the King's choice has fallen upon M.
Beugnot." On hearing this name I was unable to suppress a gesture of
surprise. M. de Blacas asked me for an explanation. At first I refused,
then, as he insisted, I assured him that M. Beugnot was quite the most
unsuitable man to carry out the duties envisaged for him . . .*

'*I agreed that he had every conceivable attainment; that I knew no
one better educated and wittier than he, that I did not doubt his intentions
were excellent, but . . . I could not conceal the fact that he was by
nature utterly unsuited to administering the police. He was talkative
and indiscreet, and as a result easily gave himself away; in difficult cases
he lacked resolution, and his timidity almost amounted to pusillanimity.
M. de Blacas was flabbergasted; I withdrew . . .*'

*Beugnot himself fully realised how unlikely it was that the position
would suit him. He went to see Pasquier and begged him to respect 'the
natural order of things, that is to say, for me [it is Pasquier speaking]
to be in charge of the Police, and for him to take over Roads and
Bridges'.*[23]* A futile discussion ensued, which seems to have rather upset
Beugnot, who then 'rushed off' to see the Chancellor. 'I urged upon him*

---

[22] That is to say, both Minister of Police and Prefect of Police in Paris. As a
matter of fact Pasquier had recommended this reform to the Abbé de Montesquiou, in the course of the conversation referred to earlier.

[23] As Commissioner for Home Affairs in the Provisional Government, Beugnot
had arranged for this post to be left vacant, intending to reserve it for himself.

what was obvious enough, that M. Pasquier was much more competent
than I to direct the nation's police force since he had already been so
successful with the Paris police; that his flexible, ever-ready mind, his
experience and his reputation were of such value that they should not
be thrown away.' A further discussion that led nowhere, and Pasquier
remained in charge of Roads and Bridges, despite a last minute attempt
by the 'ultras' to get one of themselves appointed. He left the Prefecture
of Police on 18 *May, and a fortnight later the Allies evacuated Paris.*

I shall never forget the feeling I experienced when, before eight
o'clock on the morning of 3 June, as I was crossing the Place
Louis XV on my way home, I found it and the adjacent quays
on the north bank filled with Russian and Prussian troops,
getting ready to move off with their packs on their backs and
evacuate Paris. Fog was coming down, and whether it was the
bad weather or whether people were exhausted with all they had
seen, this great occasion was allowed to go by uneventfully and
without spectators. No one, or scarcely anyone, took the trouble
to watch it. It might have been some quite ordinary troop
movement, being carried out under quite ordinary conditions.

As for me, who could still see their entry into Paris, sixty-one
days previously, which had aroused in me as in many others
such painful emotions, and all the dangers and difficulties that
had at the time seemed to me almost insurmountable, I could
not get over the fact that everything was happening so peacefully, that so complete a solution had been reached in so short
a time. I felt I must be dreaming, and wondered whether all
this was only an illusion. I remained standing on the bridge for
half an hour, motionless, leaning against the parapet, watching
that crowd of soldiers, with all those weapons and horses and
cannons, flow past me; and as they began to disappear, I
breathed more freely. How remote from my mind was the
possibility of seeing again, after so brief an interval, these
formidable troops who had been such a crushing burden for us!

Next day the opening of the Legislative Body took place.
The whole royal family had assembled for this great ceremony,
for the Duc d'Angoulême had arrived eight days previously. Of
all the Princes, he was the one who had played the most useful
and brilliant part in the Restoration. His appearance attracted
all the attention due to one who had just achieved great success
in a bold enterprise. He had travelled through a considerable

part of the Midi, where he had visited the armies of Marshal
Soult and Marshal Suchet. Everywhere he had distinguished
himself by the integrity of his mind and that moderation in his
disposition which were later to lead him, at a time when
everyone's passions were aroused, to pronounce the famous
words: 'Unite and forget'. The King was welcomed with transports of joy; his venerable appearance, his noble features, his
voice, sonorous and pleasant though rather high-pitched, even
his infirmities, which he had learned to bear with dignity, won
all hearts. His speech, which he was said to have written himself,
was a genuine success. In it he recalled, in the happiest and
most moving way, the testament of Louis XVI.

The Chancellor Dambray's speech was less favourably
received; people commented on the fact that he used certain
old-fashioned words which had almost gone out of use. For
instance, when speaking of the Charter, what was the meaning
of the expression *ordonnance de réformation*?

Finally, the Charter[24] itself was read by M. Ferrand. The
preamble was skilful; it could not have been shown more
clearly how a constitution, freely granted by the King's wisdom
in response to the wishes of his people, offers a greater chance of
lasting than any concessions violently extracted from the weak.
The terms of the Charter are so well-known that it would be
pointless to enumerate them; I would merely note that, though
the Chamber of Peers was not yet constituted on an hereditary
basis, the hereditary principle was nevertheless asserted, the
King having reserved the right either to appoint peers for life,
or to make them hereditary, as he chose. Evidently they were
unwilling to commit themselves to making the peerage hereditary
in the families of certain Senators, to whom, as individuals,
they could scarcely avoid granting a peerage. A list of peers, to
the number of one hundred and fifty-four, which the King had
signed that morning omitted the names of several Senators,
especially those who had voted for Louis XVI's execution.

[24] This was the Constitution promised by Louis XVIII before his entry into
Paris. Based on the English model, it provided for a Chamber of Peers appointed
by the King and a Chamber of Deputies to be elected on a very narrow franchise,
but by discarding the contractual theory of sovereignty and retaining the principle
of legitimacy, it opened the way to a revival of absolutism. Nevertheless, by
guaranteeing freedom of worship, the revolutionary land settlement, the independence of the judiciary and the formal liberty of the press, it claimed to preserve
some of the major democratic gains of the Revolution. (Trs.)

Thus was the Restoration definitively achieved.

The King's government had not been appointed until the day when it was finally relieved of all the difficulties imposed upon it by the presence of the foreign princes. Henceforward, it would be standing on its own feet; both its successes and its failures could now only be attributed to itself.

At no time in my life have I felt happier than during the period I am now coming to. Above all I was utterly delighted that we had emerged from a difficult, even a dangerous, situation without serious mishap. I was in the position that suited me best. Responsible for one of the most interesting spheres of public administration, I found myself at the head of a body of men distinguished for their talent and intelligence, and who welcomed me with pleasure. The engineers had been afraid that they might be given a chief with no experience of administration and little disposed to recognise past services. They were satisfied that in me they would find a zealous defender of their rights; that I could be of use to them. I was treated by all the Ministers, especially the one I was responsible to, the Abbé de Montesquiou, with every mark of consideration. In all that I had done I had been inspired by my devotion to the country, with no thought of personal interest and no desire to fulfil my own ambitions. I had received no special reward; the position I occupied was equal in rank to the one I had held under the Imperial Government, though of less importance politically.

All my friends urged me to demand the title of Minister of State, which had been readily granted to M. Anglès. I was anxious not to show the least sign of wanting it. I did not even pay any attention to a remark by the Abbé de Montesquiou, which would have justified my asking for a peerage. In the event, when honours were being showered upon everyone else, I received none; I was not even promoted to a higher grade in the Legion of Honour.[25] For my own part, I admit that both my scruples and my self-respect rejoiced in the kind of distinction that arose from the moderation of my desires. Free of all political responsibility, I was ready to enjoy the present without worrying about the future; yet now and then my habits

[25] This was amply atoned for on 28 September 1815, when, on the resignation of the Ministry, Pasquier, still only an Officer of the Legion of Honour, was promoted to the position of Grand Cross without passing through the intermediate grades.

of observation, and some knowledge of men and affairs, occasioned me somewhat disturbing reflections. I dismissed them from my mind.

In the course of the summer, Pasquier was attached ex officio to the Committee of the Interior in the Council of State. 'The positive knowledge I brought to it and the one or two services I was able to render resulted very soon, and with little trouble to myself, in my achieving a reputation in the new government.' He prided himself on having been responsible for Corvetto—who was to play such a brilliant part in the financial reforms of 1815—retaining his title as Councillor of State. Indeed, his influence cannot have been negligible, for Monsieur confided a significant secret to him: 'Talking to me one day about the new form of government that the King had granted, he let slip: "This is what they want, so we shall have to give it a try; but the experiment will not take long, and if, at the end of a year or two, it's clear that it's not working properly, we shall have to go back to the natural state of affairs"—by which he meant, the Ancien Régime . . . I need hardly say what harm such an opinion was bound to cause.'

The relentless Baron Louis would not listen to the demands of the new Director of Roads and Bridges. 'Both roads and bridges were badly dilapidated . . . On the basis of the most rigorous calculations, I had asked for eighteen or nineteen million francs to defray the cost of upkeep.' All the Minister of Finance would agree to was fourteen millions, and not another sou, despite the efforts of the Abbé de Montesquiou who supported Pasquier. 'For several years the allocation for upkeep remained pretty much the same as Monsieur Louis had fixed it at in 1814. In addition to the very real harm that was caused by mistakes of this kind, one also has to remember the very unfavourable opinion of the royal administration to which they gave rise. There was a general slowing down of the work, which was in striking contrast to the activity that had distinguished the previous administration.'

Towards September . . . I visited Champagne, Picardy, Flanders and Normandy in my official capacity.

I have already said how much I enjoyed the duties I had been entrusted with, and to which I was determined to devote the most assiduous attention. Napoleon had always shown the greatest interest in them; with a little care the activities generated by him would persist for a long time. Accustomed to the energy that was demanded of all the heads of major departments under the imperial regime, I wasted no time in acquainting myself with everything I was responsible for, both men and things; and it was not long before I knew how matters stood.

The labour available for Roads and Bridges was not easy to organise. The great loss of territory had resulted in a considerable number of engineers returning to France; and those who did so were by no means the least able. Were they, too, to be retired on half pay? Or should I take the opportunity of dismissing the least efficient? I felt it would be against the interests of the government to impose this hardship on men so worthy of support, who had many friends and who enjoyed the esteem and respect of the public. A saving of two or three hundred thousand francs did not seem to me to offset the drawbacks of such a rigorous approach. I therefore decided to reorganise the service throughout the kingdom in such a way that employment would be found for practically everyone. If it had not been for the reduction of funds imposed upon me by M. Louis, everything would have been all right.

Within these narrow limits, I had complete control of what was allocated to me, and my authority was not subjected to any supervision. It might be supposed that it was very agreeable for me to be able to deal with everything like this, as I pleased. However, this large measure of independence had exactly the opposite effect on my mind; and all those who attained leading positions after me found it to be the same. Previously, the work of the Director-General of Roads and Bridges had always been one of those to which the Minister of the Interior devoted considerable attention. The Emperor used habitually to take the chair at meetings of the department whenever any important project was to be discussed or any decision taken about the allocation of funds; and he often used to call in the leading engineers to discuss with him their various plans, and report on how the work they were responsible for was progressing. This way of running things had now been superseded by utter indifference. The freedom to do as one wished was therefore more than offset by the decline in importance, and by the loss of what men always prize so highly, the satisfaction of seeing their work criticised and appreciated by the head of the State, whose approbation is often their highest reward. It was not long before everyone began doing the work entrusted to them without in any way putting themselves out. I myself, though still very active, and anxious to win esteem and consideration in my new post, could not help realising that I should have worked harder and better under the previous government; that I was often putting off to the next day work, which in the past I should certainly have completed at once. However, I think I am justified in saying that the administration of Roads and Bridges was not by any means the one where this inevitable weakness was most apparent.

The advisory board at Roads and Bridges consisted in the main of able men; listening to the discussions, it was almost always fairly easy for me to arrive at the correct conclusion, although I had no real technical knowledge of the subject. In this respect, there is one point which, though not always appreciated, I have often heard frankly admitted by engineers of outstanding ability: that is, that an engineer, however talented he might be, would make a bad Director-General. Too easily carried away by the desire to distinguish himself, by the pleasure of being involved in large and splendid enterprises, he would tend to neglect matters of real importance, while expenditure would seldom be soundly and wisely related to the results achieved. Besides, there is no organisation which is completely free from divisions of opinion, rivalries and even hatreds. If the Director was an engineer he would be bound to take sides; he would have friends and enemies, and could scarcely help favouring the former at the expense of the latter.

I began my tour of inspection along the banks of the Seine, the Marne and the Oise, in the part of the country that had been a theatre of war. Where I found bridges that had been destroyed, and that had so far only been replaced by frail, temporary structures, I gave all the necessary orders for them to be repaired on the spot. Then I decided to visit the Saint-Quentin canal, and the channel ports from Dunkirk to Le Havre. My visit to Champagne and Flanders helped me to realise how lively men's memories of the imperial government still were. Whether because of the military spirit that prevailed in these provinces, or because manufacturing interests dominated all others, people certainly felt on all sides disaffection towards the royal government and considerable distrust of it. The factory owners were afraid of English competition, by which they believed themselves to be threatened, and they greatly resented seeing their outlets in Belgium and on the other side of the Rhine completely closed to them.

The soldiers, large numbers of whom were now home again, inspired the warmest interest, and all their grievances were listened to with extreme sympathy. This last attitude was general; I encountered it wherever I went. This is what I had to say on the subject in the report I sent to the Abbé de Montesquiou: 'There is one matter that deserves serious attention, especially when one remembers the spirit that prevailed in France eight or ten months ago: the army, which was once the terror of every family, is becoming well liked and popular now that retirement, leave and desertion have restored to their families considerable numbers of officers and men who continually boast of its valour and heroic deeds, and tell endless stories of the dangers and sufferings it endured. It has become the object of the most lively feelings of admiration, even of affection. Everybody is talking about its rights; all the favours bestowed on those who never belonged to it are regarded as being at the army's expense. They share in its fame, which they look upon as belonging to the nation; every day they cling more closely to it; and this feeling is accompanied by a profound dislike of foreigners.' (This last feature was particularly noticeable in the northern provinces that I visited.) 'Quite inconsistently, they are conscious of all the advantages of peace, yet argue as though they wanted war. Finding their passions indulged in this way, the soldiers become increasingly difficult to handle and to satisfy; they complain bitterly about the slightest thing; they insist continually that the government has broken its word and has not fulfilled all its promises to them. Their jealousy at every favour granted to anyone but one of themselves is thus without bounds.' This description was written at the end of October, that is to say, less than five months before Napoleon's return to France.

The town of Saint-Quentin, where I stayed for several days, was one of those where I had the best opportunity of studying the attitude of the manufacturing class. It must be noted that this class owed the great development of its industries to the blockade of the continent, which had ruined the maritime towns; it was the blockade more than anything else that had led the town of Bordeaux to rise against Napoleon and fling itself into the arms of the Duc d'Angoulême. At Saint-Quentin, as in all the other industrial towns, feelings were very different. At Péronne, at Amiens, people were more favourably disposed. And when I reached Normandy the difference was even more noticeable. There the interests of those engaged in maritime trade exerted a powerful influence; the town of Le Havre, in particular, displayed great satisfaction with the new order of things. There the port was full of buildings, and there was plenty of commercial activity. They were no longer afraid of fortifications being built on the landward side. To be turned into a fortified town is almost always one of the worst fates that can befall a commercial city; and the fortifications planned by the last government would have involved sacrificing the finest properties in the neighbourhood, for they were to cover the whole Ingouville coast. One feeling, which did not at all fit in with the inclinations of the royal family and the cabinet at the Tuileries, dominated the friendly outlook of the people of Le Havre; this was their deep hatred of England, which was revived by the return of the sailors who had been prisoners of war, and by their accounts of their sufferings and the monstrous treatment they had endured in the English hulks.

I returned from Paris along the valley of the Seine; on the way I visited Louviers, where I had several law suits to settle; there the spirit of the industrial population was better than at Amiens or Saint-Quentin. When I got back, I made a summary of my notes for the Abbé de Montesquiou, but though he appeared to be considerably impressed by them, what use would he make of them? Even supposing there had, at that time, been anyone in the government prepared to listen to warnings, there was no one sufficiently enlightened to draw the necessary conclusions. I had particularly insisted upon the attitude and situation of the clergy and the ancient nobility. As to the clergy, though their activities appeared to be more prudent than those of the nobility, a rumour was beginning to spread that certain priests, particularly in Picardy, were using their authority in the confessional to disturb people's consciences about owning property as a result of the sale of land that had previously belonged to the emigrés or the clergy.

On the question of the nobility, here is what I had to say: 'From what I have seen of it, France is in favour of the monarchy as regards its feeling for the King's person, but in its tastes and inclinations it is democratic. Thus, far from the ancient nobility having regained the slightest influence, it is, on the contrary, the object of a marked distrust. So many interests are at the present time based on the abolition of the privileges it used to enjoy, on the possibility of attaining any position whatever one's rank, that there is a deeply rooted conviction that the nobility is anxious to see the revival of these ancient rights which are incompatible with modern society. Now, amongst these old noble families there are certainly some, who, by their imprudent language even more than by their deeds, encourage the suspicions and fears that we should be striving to dispel. To say that, since the Restoration, the nobility has lost more than it has gained in public opinion is sad, but it is nonetheless true. As a result of the criminal acts of violence committed by the Revolutionary party, people were prepared to feel sorry for the aristocracy, even to like them. But directly they believed that they were prepared to abuse their power, the whole position changed. It will need time, possibly much time, to set this matter right, but I believe it is important to take note of it in order that everything possible may be done to palliate it.'

The government changes which brought Marshal Soult to the War Office, Beugnot to the Admiralty and, apparently at Fouché's suggestion,[26] *d'André to the Ministry of Police, upset public opinion.*

All serious-minded men were struck by the state of confusion in the administration, by the government's lack of authority, and by the fatal consequence that this state of affairs was bound to have if it continued. The Abbé de Montesquiou, realising the truth of this, resolved to inform the King. But since it was no use pointing out what was wrong unless at the same time he could suggest a remedy, he wished to talk the matter over with a number of reliable people to whom he could speak with complete freedom. He chose MM. Royer-Collard, Becquey,[27]

[26] Fouché, 'at the time of the King's entry into Paris, had no hesitation about retiring to his country estate . . . This behaviour had borne fruit, especially with Monsieur. Those who belonged to the latter's entourage paid scant attention to anyone's antededents, provided they were prepared to accept his views and put themselves at his disposal. Thus, among certain Royalists who prided themselves on their breadth of outlook, it was generally accepted that M. Fouché was the cleverest man thrown up by the Revolution; and that, even if they could not employ him openly, they would be well advised to keep in touch with him and take advantage of his advice.'

[27] François Louis Becquey, with whom Beugnot had been friendly as a young

Guizot and me. He was anxious that our discussion should not attract attention. It was therefore agreed that our meeting should take place over dinner at M. Becquey's; if I am not mistaken the day decided upon was sometime during the first fortnight of January. When the Abbé arrived, we were surprised to see that he appeared to be ill at ease and in a bad humour; the reason for this was not far to seek since, as he informed us, far from being in a position to tell the King the truth, for the last three days he had realised that his own position in the government was threatened. His disapproval of Marshal Soult's admission to the Council had been ill concealed; M. Beugnot was equally unacceptable to him, and he had allowed it to be seen that he considered him to be quite unsuited for the Admiralty; and lastly, the bad terms he was on with M. de Blacas had continued to grow worse. The latter had made up his mind to get him dismissed, and was doing his best to persuade the King to replace him by M. de Chateaubriand. This was certainly one of the oddest choices imaginable, since there was nothing in M. de Chateaubriand's career up to the present to suggest that he was capable of handling public affairs; his gifts as a writer were by no means those that are requisite for administering a great country. I am strongly inclined to think that the truth of this must have struck Louis XVIII, and that the impression it made upon him helped to prevent the intrigue from succeeding.

Fundamentally the King would have been glad enough to get rid of the Abbé de Montesquiou, who, by his continual rows with M. de Blacas, upset the peace of mind which he valued above everything else. The Abbé was nonetheless hurt and very disheartened. He was more inclined to ask to be allowed to resign rather than to defend his position and, above all, to undertake that bold exposure of the existing state of affairs that he had discussed with us. We had considerable difficulty in persuading him to remain at his post, at least for some time. This was all that resulted from our meeting, though it made us realise that the split in the government was much more serious than we had supposed; that each of the ministers was acting on his own account, without worrying about his colleagues, without method and without any commonly agreed plan. In his resent-

man, had been a member of the Legislative Assembly, and was one of the seven Deputies who had had the courage to vote against the declaration of war in 1792. He never went back on his monarchist sympathies.

ment, the Abbé concealed nothing from us. We broke up sadly enough; for my part this was the first serious warning that disturbed the pleasant tranquility in which I like to live.

About this time, the eventuality of Napoleon's return began to take root in Pasquier's mind.

That same day, 21 January,[28] I could not refuse an invitation from M. Louis, who absolutely insisted upon taking me to dine quite informally at M. d'André's, who, he said, was most anxious to have a talk with me about the police, and about what could be done to help him bear a burden which was beginning to scare him. I had no intention of taking the responsibility for giving advice which I knew in advance would not be acted upon. I arrived, therefore, fully resolved to remain on the defensive; and this turned out to be easy, for the information M. d'André wanted from me never went to the root of the matter. I saw that his closest associates were ill chosen, and that he was relying upon people quite unworthy of trust; now there is no mistake that it is so difficult to get men to overcome, once they have committed themselves to the wrong choice. I spoke to M. d'André about the island of Elba as I had to M. Beugnot, and, like the latter, I found him to be completely confident about the situation there. To dispel his confidence, I should have had to produce positive facts, whereas my fears were inspired only by reason and experience. I later learned that M. d'André had been so excessively confident that he had decided to save the very small sum allocated by his predecessor to keeping the island under police surveillance. Thus the two or three agents who had been employed there were recalled. After the Hundred Days, he implored all those who were aware of this, of whom I was one, not to say anything about it. The secret of this mistake was kept until his death.

In the autumn of 1814 the political scene was dominated by the opening of the Congress of Vienna.

[28] On 21 January 1815 the King had ordered the ashes of Louis XVI and Marie-Antoinette to be transferred to the church of Saint-Denis, and had declared a public day of mourning. So strong was the suspicion of Royalist activities in the capital that this decision gave rise to the rumour that all those who had been involved in the Terror were to be massacred. (Trs.)

Many people had said that France would not be represented at the Congress. Our prestige, as well as interests of the first importance, demanded not only that she should be present, but that she should do her best to make her voice heard. Amongst all the questions that would have to be thrashed out there, there were certain to be some whose solution would be of the greatest importance for her. There was therefore not the slightest hesitation in the cabinet at the Tuileries about the necessity of sending a plenipotentiary to Vienna. The choice inevitably fell upon M. de Talleyrand.[29] He alone, by the part he had played in diplomatic affairs for fifteen years, and by his very close relations with the sovereigns and their principal ministers during the negotiations which had led up to the Restoration and the Treaty of Paris, was in a position to fulfil the infinitely delicate role that devolved upon France's plenipotentiary. He was under no illusion as to the obstacles of every kind that he would encounter, and, either from fatigue or ill-humour, or more likely from affectation, he showed little satisfaction with this mission, little eagerness to fulfil it. I saw him two or three days before he set out, and I was struck by the air of dejection he assumed.

'I am probably going to play a pretty sorry role', said he. 'For a start, how are they going to treat me? Will they be prepared to listen to me? As a result of the Treaty of 30 May, the Allied sovereigns made the King of France give an undertaking not to intervene in the partition of the countries won back from Bonaparte which they consider it right to make. If they mean this engagement to be rigorously adhered to, my position there will merely be what is very improperly called "an honorary one". Every now and then, for the sake of appearances, I shall get up to speak, but no one will pay the slightest attention to what I say. On the other hand, here at home I shall be blamed for everything that doesn't turn out just as they want it to. The folk here don't trust me, and for the last five months they haven't been at much pains to prevent me knowing it. In such a situation the best thing to do, if it were possible, would be to stay at home.'

For M. de Talleyrand to speak like this, whatever opinion one

---

[29] Talleyrand had been appointed Minister of Foreign Affairs on 13 May. As such, he signed the first Treaty of Paris on 30 May, which, though on the whole generous in its provisions, deprived France of most of her territorial acquisitions since 1792.

may have as to his sincerity, was nonetheless remarkable. Yet his words contained the key to his later behaviour. For my part, I have no doubt that, at heart, he was delighted to be going to Vienna, and that he had already made up his mind how he was going to act. But he was anxious that no one should suspect this, so that in the event of failure it would be easy for him to make excuses. What he said about his position was in many respects true. It cannot be denied that both at court and in the Council it had become extremely trying. After all he had done, after arranging everything during the very stormy time in April, once this crisis was over, he had found himself more or less pushed aside. Not only had his influence on the government's activities been almost nil, but he had been refused the few favours which he felt he had the right to demand for those in whom he was most interested. I had seen him, despite his most urgent insistence, unable to obtain the Prefecture for M. de Rémusat, who had shown the greatest devotion to him in the hour of danger.

Such a position would have been hard even for a man with less claim to his sovereign's benevolence, but to M. de Talleyrand it must have seemed intolerable. To extricate himself from it, he must certainly have considered making use of the opportunity that now presented itself. He had to take advantage of it, either to make himself more acceptable, or to become so useful that they would find themselves once more obliged to rely upon him. If he decided upon the latter approach, when he got to Vienna he would have to make himself the spokesman of France's true interests; if he failed to achieve these fully, he would at least save everything that could be saved. In this way, he would be so much the representative of the country that they would have to accord him the consideration to which he aspired. If he took the other line, he would simply have to consider the personal interests of the House of Bourbon, and make the most of these at every opportunity; maybe such obsequiousness would be more generously rewarded than the services he had already rendered, and which had been so poorly esteemed. I might add that, at that time, M. de Talleyrand's financial affairs were not in good shape. During the last years of the Empire he had lost a considerable amount of money; the failure of the firm of Simon in Brussels had alone cost him more than four millions, not to mention a very large sum which he had received, on what grounds I do not know, from the town of Hamburg, and which Napoleon had insisted upon his repaying.[30] His difficulties were so grave that, if the Duc de Rovigo had not had his house in the rue de Varenne bought from him at a very high price out of the Emperor's privy purse, he would have had difficulty in meeting his very serious obligations.

M. de Talleyrand reached Vienna at the end of September, accompanied by M. de Dalberg, M. de la Tour-du-Pin, French ambassador at The Hague, and Comte Alexis de Noailles, whom he had appointed as his assistant, with the title of Minister Plenipotentiary. He was quite confident that none of these dignitaries would interfere with his activities, nor venture to oppose him in any way.[31]

The following fifty pages or so, in which Pasquier continually allows his hostility towards Talleyrand to appear, are devoted to the deliberations of the Congress of Vienna. According to him, Louis XVIII's representative committed a capital mistake by uniting France 'with her two natural enemies, for her history attests that is what England and Austria have almost always been.[32] And against whom was this alliance directed? Against the two States (Prussia and Russia) from whom she had nothing to fear, with whom she had no common frontier, and whom it would have been easy to secure as firm allies because no conflicting interests existed between her and them.'

Napoleon's landing at the Gulf of Juan for a time put an end to these diplomatic conversations. Pasquier expresses surprise that 'during the whole course of the deliberations at this Congress, where all the principal politicians of Europe were gathered together, nothing was either said or

[30] Pasquier's memory is here at fault. Four million francs was the sum that the city of Hamburg had granted to Talleyrand, in the hope that its annexation to France might be prevented. As to the bankruptcy of the Simons bank (not Simon; the Chancellor did not worry much about the spelling of proper names), it would appear to have cost the Prince of Benevento only one million five hundred thousand francs. In any case, this was the amount of the loan for which, on this occasion, he unsuccessfully applied to the Tsar. Such were Talleyrand's financial difficulties that in 1811 he was obliged to sell part of his library.

[31] 'I am taking Dalberg', said the Prince of Benevento, 'so that he can spread the secrets that I want everybody to know about. Noailles is the Pavillon de Marsan's man; it's best to be spied upon by an agent chosen by myself. La Tour-du-Pin will do to sign passports.'

[32] On 3 January 1815, a Treaty of Alliance was signed between England, Austria and France. The purpose of this Treaty, which moreover was fulfilled, was to thwart Russia's desire to obtain the whole of Poland, and Prussia's to obtain Saxony, which for so long had remained faithful to Napoleon.

done in relation to Napoleon and Europe'. Only General Pozzo di Borgo, 'whose perspicacity was sharpened by hatred', would have been prepared to raise, in agreement with the Duke of Wellington and M. de Talleyrand, the proposal to send the Emperor to the Island of St Helena. 'Did Napoleon get to hear of this and did it in any way affect his decision in the month of March? . . . He made up his mind so precipitously and so suddenly that one cannot help feeling that there must have been some decisive motive for his acting as he did . . .

'In any case, one thing is certain. The attitude adopted with regard to Napoleon was superlatively inept and imprudent. The French government especially, and it was France who was most concerned in this matter, had made an unforgiveable mistake . . . They had seen fit not to pay any of the sums of money annually due to Napoleon and his family under the Treaty of 11 April.[33] The King of France had agreed to this. If they were considering changing his place of residence, sending him further away, they should have been at pains to keep him under conditions of the strictest security and scrupulously to fulfil all the terms of the Treaty'.[34]

Regrets were idle, however. Having reached the soil of France on 1 March, 'the eagle flew from steeple to steeple . . . ' The Emperor's occupation of Lyons on 10 March, made the position almost hopeless 'for anyone who was not prepared to deceive himself'. The defection of Marshal Ney and his army was the final blow. 'The official news reached the government on the evening of the 18th; on top of this they learnt that the old guard, under the command of Marshal Oudinot, had risen at Troyes and hoisted the imperial colours; and, finally, that the army drawn up on the road to Fontainbleau was disposed to follow the example of Marshal Ney's, and that several regiments were already on their way to join the Emperor.'

I was informed of these details early on the morning of 19 March by M. de Vitrolles, who also told me that a decision had been taken that the King should leave that evening. His Majesty

[33] The Treaty of 11 April 1815, granted Napoleon possession of the island of Elba with the title of Emperor, and an income of two million francs with reversion as to one half to the Empress. Napoleon's brothers and sisters kept their property, and in addition received an income of two and a half million francs. The Treaty, guaranteed by a declaration of the Provisional Government, had been ratified by Napoleon on the 13.

[34] Pasquier's version is entirely borne out by the most recent work on the question, Guy Godlewsky's *Trois cents jours d'exil: Napoléon à l'île d'Elbe*, Paris, 1961.

5 Louis XVIII enters Paris, 3 May 1814

6 Napoleon's landing at the Gulf of Juan,
near Cannes, 1 March 1815

was withdrawing towards Lille, with Monsieur and the Duc de Berry, in the hope that, if the garrison there remained loyal, it would be possible for him to hold on long enough for help to reach him from outside. The Duc de Bourbon, for his part, was leaving for the Vendée, where his presence would help to rouse the people, who would doubtless prove themselves on that occasion worthy of what they had been in the days of their heroic struggle against the Revolutionary forces. Much was also hoped of the influence that the Duc d'Angoulême and his Duchesse appeared to exercise in the Midi. Bonaparte would thus be surrounded in the middle of France; it would not be long before the foreign armies reached our frontiers; and he would then find himself in no state to continue his resistance.

Such was the plan that M. de Vitrolles expounded to me on the morning of 20 March! It was perhaps well enough conceived, but it was based on hypotheses in which I found it difficult to feel the slightest confidence. I knew France too well not to regard it as almost certain that all resistance, even in the most remote Departments, would rapidly be smashed by the occupation of the capital, and would be rendered useless by the complete defection of the army, the whole of which would be swayed by the same impulse. For my part, the whole question was to find out what decision the Allied armies would arrive at, and how energetically they were prepared to pursue the new war. Now, in this respect, while there was considerable probability that they would act, no one could be certain that they would.

M. de Vitrolles also informed me of his personal views. He reckoned to leave at the same time as the King, and to go to Bordeaux, where he would tell the Duchesse d'Angoulême whatever it was essential for her to know; then he would overtake the Duc d'Angoulême and set about organising around him a government capable of making active use of such resources as still remained at his disposal. He would, he assured me, be provided with very extensive powers, which the King would give him before leaving. In fact, he never obtained these powers. He strongly urged me to go with him, but I refused, first of all because I had little faith in his success, though I took care not to tell him so, for it was important not to discourage him; and furthermore, because, if I was to be of any use to the royal cause, it would in all likelihood be in that part of France where I was known, where I enjoyed a certain amount of respect, and where I had a certain number of friends. He could not deny that I was right, but he pointed out to me that I should perhaps be running a grave risk, and that Bonaparte's wrath might well weigh heavily upon me. 'I don't think so at the start,' I told him. 'But in any case I have ways and means of finding out.'

When I left him I was still far from certain as to what was the best thing to do. The one issue on which I was firmly resolved was that I would not leave France except as a last resort. It was a Sunday. I went to the Palace at the hour when mass was due to start. There was a huge crowd in the salon, some of them drawn thither by genuine concern, but many more in the hope of finding out what was happening. Few people knew that the King's departure was fixed for that evening; and those who did kept their mouths shut. I watched the King and the royal Princes pass through the salon as usual, on their way to the chapel. In spite of the great grief displayed on their countenances they put on a bold front. As he reached me the Duc de Berry stopped, and took me by the hand as though wishing to say farewell. He must have known that I was aware of the situation. M. de Blacas, who was in waiting upon the King and could not leave him, gave me a very significant glance, while the Abbé de Montesquiou engaged me to visit him after mass. This I did, and he confirmed everything that M. de Vitrolles had told me in the morning; the only difference being that, while the latter still thought of putting up a resistance, the Abbé considered the cause of the House of Bourbon as utterly lost, this time for ever. He told me to come and see him again in the evening at his niece's, Mme de Fezensac; he was reckoning on leaving the Ministry during the afternoon, and intended to set out from her house during the night.

I arrived promptly on time, and we talked for a long time with complete freedom. He told me all the reasons that had made him give up hope. I, in my turn, said that I did not know what would happen to the House of Bourbon, that this depended on what support it received from the Allied sovereigns; that it was quite possible that they would abandon their cause, which, indeed, would not surprise me; but I added that, as for Napoleon, he might well, despite his first swift and brilliant success, encounter much greater difficulty in re-establishing himself than many people thought, because, since his departure, men's minds had changed in a way he was not expecting; and that if he was energetically attacked by the coalition, I was extremely doubtful whether anyone would sacrifice much to maintain him in power. The Abbé de Montesquiou, however, was so convinced that there was nothing more to be done with the Princes, with whom he was throwing in his lot, that, when speaking to me of matters concerning myself, he strongly urged me to remain in charge of Roads and Bridges if I was able to. I replied that this was neither possible nor honourable, and that I should consider myself lucky if they were prepared to let me live in peace with my modest household.

The Chancellor [Dambray], before leaving Paris and also on his way through Rouen to the port where he was to embark, expressed a similar point of view to those magistrates who came to see him, exhorting them all to remain at their posts. Among these was his brother-in-law, President of the royal court of Rouen, who had no great difficulty in following the advice he had received from so high an authority.

I shall not attempt to describe the confusion that reigned in men's minds during the crisis that we had to face, from the moment when the King's departure was resolved upon until the Palace of the Tuileries was peacefully occupied by Napoleon. Once again everything was open to question. The whole of 19 March was spent in preparing to leave, or rather to flee. In the ministries and government offices, every precaution that there was time for was taken to prevent the newcomers from obtaining information on matters that it was most important to conceal from them; but everything was done in such a hurry that much was overlooked, with the most unfortunate results. They were so pushed that they even failed to remove from the King's study notes and correspondence which, it should have been realised, were of the most secret nature, and which, directly he arrived, Napoleon at once laid hands on.

M. Louis left behind about fifty million francs in the vaults of the Treasury. Whether this was intentional on his part, or due to negligence, he was nonetheless open to severe criticism, whichever assumption was correct. It would appear that only a small part of this sum was in cash, and that the bonds and securities would be difficult to realise once they had left the Treasury. Doubtless he regarded these funds as belonging to the State, and considered that they ought to remain at its disposal, to be used to meet government expenditure—for example, to pay the interest on the national debt—but even if this was so, he was still reproached for not having paid the interest in advance, which would have been one way of leaving less public money at Napoleon's disposal. I am not sure whether this would have been a practicable measure, since those to whom it was due had made no preparations for receiving it, and they could not be warned in time. What is indisputable, however, is that with a little more foresight it should have been fairly easy, in the interval between 5 and 19 March, to have had considerable sums transferred to one or two towns to which the King might retreat; to Lille, for instance, or to Rouen. All this goes to show what a state of illusion persisted, right up to the eve of the catastrophe. All the King was able to take with him was the funds available in the coffers of his civil list, and the crown jewels. He instructed the Treasury to pay one hundred thousand francs to each of his ministers, to help towards the expenses necessitated by their flight. The Abbé de Montesquiou refused to accept this money. Amongst the precautions that were taken, I must not forget to mention that M. de Maubreuil was released from prison; M. de Bourienne was afraid that he might make statements which, although they were lies, would nevertheless have been very unpleasant for the royal government.

The King set out during the night of the 19th–20th. It is easy to imagine the confusion that was bound to accompany this unforeseen withdrawal of the whole court, which two days previously had still been indulging in so many illusions. Still, they all managed to get away during the night, and by the morning of the 20th solitude reigned in the palace, in the courtyards of the Tuileries, in the neighbouring barracks, in the ministries and in many of the houses in the Faubourg Saint-Germain. There was something sinister about this solitude; the expression on everyone's face betrayed a feeling of anxious expectancy. Napoleon's supporters soon began to show themselves, but they were not yet numerous enough to have any appreciable effect in arousing the people.

VII

The Hundred Days and the Beginning of the Second Restoration
March–July 1815

UTTER DISCOURAGEMENT AMONGST LOUIS XVIII'S SUPPORTERS – NAPOLEON FORMS HIS GOVERNMENT – FOUCHÉ AT THE MINISTRY OF POLICE – PASQUIER EXILED FROM PARIS – MOLÉ REPLACES HIM AT ROADS AND BRIDGES – FOUCHÉ SCEPTICAL ABOUT THE NEW REGIME: CAULAINCOURT EQUALLY PESSIMISTIC – DEPARTURE FOR COULANS – PASQUIER'S BROTHER INVOLVED IN ROYALIST PLOTS – PASQUIER BACK IN PARIS – FURTHER CONVERSATION WITH FOUCHÉ – PASQUIER CONVINCED OF NAPOLEON'S DEFEAT – LIVES AT THE CHÂTEAU DU MARAIS – WATERLOO – HURRIED RETURN TO PARIS WITH MOLÉ AND BARANTE – FOUCHÉ'S INTRIGUES – PASQUIER AND HIS FRIENDS URGE HIM TO ACT – ABORTIVE APPROACH TO GROUCHY – RELIEF AT NAPOLEON'S GOING – LOUIS XVIII ARRIVES AT ARNOUVILLE – TALLEYRAND FORMS A GOVERNMENT – PASQUIER KEEPER OF THE SEALS AND TEMPORARILY IN CHARGE OF THE MINISTRY OF THE INTERIOR – HIS INDIGNATION AT FOUCHÉ'S APPOINTMENT AS MINISTER OF POLICE – DECAZES BECOMES PREFECT OF POLICE

Despite my firm intention not to leave Paris, I thought it as well to make a few inquiries. I wrote to M. de la Valette; I had not seen him for the last three weeks but I knew him well enough to be convinced that I could count on him. I therefore asked his advice. My intention was to retire to my estate near Le Mans, but it would be very helpful to me to spend a few days in Paris to put my affairs in order. Could I do so in safety? M. de la Valette replied that he would be with me in less than a couple of hours. The conversation that we had on this occasion is of such importance that I shall repeat it as literally as my memory permits.

Unwilling to assume the responsibility of advising me on so delicate a matter, he had been to see M. de Cambacérès, and, knowing the interest that he took in me, had not hesitated to show him my letter. After a few moment's reflection on the serious question I had raised they had both agreed that it was impossible to foresee what the Emperor would do; he would be well advised to behave with extreme moderation; this would certainly be the unanimous opinion of the people he would send for as soon as he arrived. It was not to be supposed that he would commit any act of violence especially in the early days; on these grounds these gentlemen were inclined to think that I could stay in Paris without danger; and, furthermore, they promised to pay the greatest attention to anything that might concern me and, if necessary, to warn me.

M. de la Valette added that, it I found myself in the least danger, I could always take refuge with him, and that he would then find some way of getting me out of Paris. After thanking him for this fresh proof of his friendship, and assuring him that in case of need I should not hesitate to take advantage of his offer, I went on to say that I should have all the greater confidence in his protection since he was bound to enjoy great prestige; that this could not be otherwise in view of the part he had certainly played in the great events that we had recently witnessed.

'What part are you referring to?' he replied—'But surely it was you who maintained the closest possible relations with the Emperor, who kept him in touch with everything that was going on? It was probably your advice that decided him to return.'—'You are utterly mistaken', he answered. 'If that were so, not only should I have no reason for hiding the fact today, I should pride myself on it. Now, I swear to you that since the Emperor left I have only written him one letter, and that was for New Year's day; and since I had no means of getting it to him, I sent it to the postmaster general at Lyons, assuming that he would find some way of sending it on. Whether or not it ever reached him, I have no idea, for I received no reply.'—'But who, then, if it was not you, was able to keep him supplied with the information that he has certainly been getting?'—'Undoubtedly, the Duc de Bassano,' said he, adding with a laugh: 'Don't imagine, however, that I was not a conspirator. It was because I was up to my eyes in conspiracy that I stopped seeing you; I was anxious not to be exposed to your probing, and still less to risk compromising you.'—'But surely that amounts to more or less the same thing? You will receive all the more credit for having plotted on your own initiative, and not under orders.'—'That would be all right, if indeed, as you assume, I had plotted in his interests; but that was something we scarcely considered.'— 'What! You didn't consider it! Whatever conspiracy were you mixed up in then?'—'The one in the north, with d'Erlon, Lallemand, and Desnoëttes.'[1]—'But surely all these generals intended to go over to Napoleon?'—'Not at all. Indeed, it was the news of his disembarkation and rapid advance that led to everything falling through, and completely upset everything.'— 'But what, then, were you hoping to do?'—'We intended to get to Paris, where we had good friends awaiting us, and then we should have seized the King, and all the members of his family that happened to be with him, and politely taken them back to the frontier.'—'And then what?'—'We should have chosen a King who would have owed his crown to France, not accepted it at the hands of foreigners.'—'But this King, where were you going to get him from?'—'Who knows? Perhaps the Duc d'Orleans,[2] if he had been prepared to behave intelligently and

[1] Generals Drouet d'Erlon, Lefebre-Desnouettes and Lallemand did in fact raise the troops under their command against Louis XVIII, but the movement came to nothing. It would appear to have been instigated by Fouché who, equally opposed to Napoleon and the Bourbons, hoped as a result of this military backing to set up his own government in Paris.

[2] Later to become King as Louis Phillipe (1830–48). His father, the wealthiest man in France, had supported the Revolution in its early days, when he was known as Philippe Egalité, but was guillotined in 1793 for his suspected complicity in a plot to put his son on the throne after the execution of Louis XVI. For the same reason Louis Philippe, who had fought as a youth in the revolutionary army, was exiled to America by the Directory. Returning to France after 18 Brumaire, only to find Napoleon firmly established in power, he became reconciled with his cousin, Louis XVIII (he was descended from Louis XIV's brother), but shortly after the Restoration his sympathy with the Liberal opposition led to his being again exiled. His chance came with the 1830 Revolution, when the middle-class Liberal majority in the Chamber, having overthrown Charles X, summoned him to the throne. Himself overthrown eighteen years later by yet another Revolution, he spent his last two years in exile as the guest of Queen Victoria. (Trs.)

reasonably. Of course, he would have had to accept the Constitution honestly, and then I don't think he would have frightened Europe, who certainly wouldn't have resorted to arms merely for the sake of Louis XVIII.'

There our conversation ended. The revelations it contains, made at such a moment, cannot be suspected of insincerity; unless I am mistaken, they throw a quite unexpected light on the attitudes and events of that period, even on the most obscure aspects of the position in which Napoleon was soon to find himself.

Le Moniteur, which appeared on the morning of 20 March 1815, was still under the editorship of the royalist government; it contained a proclamation of farewell, bearing the previous day's date, in which the King announced his departure from Paris owing to the defection of part of the army which had sworn to defend his throne. 'The present crisis will be overcome,' he said. 'We have a serene faith that the soldiers who have been led astray, whose defection exposes our subjects to so many dangers, will soon come to recognise their mistake. They will find the reward for their return in our forbearance and benevolence. Before long we shall be back in the midst of this honest people, to whom we will once again restore peace and happiness.'

Then the Chamber of Peers and the Chamber of Deputies were adjourned for 1814, and a new session was summoned for 1815. The Peers and Deputies were to meet again as soon as possible, wherever the provisional seat of government was established, but any meeting of either of the two Chambers which took place elsewhere would be declared invalid and illegal. When it came to signing this document, His Majesty must have regretted the rash declaration that he had felt it necessary to make three days earlier in the Chamber of Deputies, when, referring to his age, he spoke of ending his career by dying for his people![3]

All confidence had disappeared, everyone felt profoundly disheartened! During the course of the morning I saw many royalists and emigrés, but not one of those I spoke to was not convinced that everything was irrevocably lost and that the

[3] In his speech to the Chamber of Deputies on 16 March 1815, Louis XVIII had said: 'I have worked for the happiness of my people. I have received, and continue to receive every day, the most touching signs of their affection. At the age of sixty, what better end to my career could I hope for than to die in their defence?'

House of Bourbon had disappeared for ever. Three months later, many of them were not afraid to boast of the energy they had shown, of their attachment and loyalty to the King, of their unshakable faith in the triumph of legitimacy; had I then been called upon to give evidence, all I could have spoken of in good faith would have been their utter dejection.

During the morning, I was urged to withdraw from Paris without delay, and even to leave France. M. Mounier and M. Anglès,[4] having decided to leave that evening, did their best to convince me that it would be very dangerous for me to brave Napoleon's return. I replied that emigration was a course that I found repugnant, and that I should only agree to it in the last extremity. Moreover, I knew from my experiences during the most terrible period of the Terror that if one has friends, and I had many, it is not difficult to find ways of escaping pursuit, at least to begin with. However, I took advantage of M. Mounier's offer, who, still convinced that I should soon be forced to cross the frontier, was willing to help me obtain satisfactory letters of credit. To this end he took me to see a banker with whom he was on intimate terms. This was M. Casimir Périer, who, like himself, came from Dauphiné. M. Périer proved to be most obliging, and, without asking me to deposit any securities with him, sent me during the day letters of credit for Belgium, England and Holland. I never made use of them, but it was most gracious of him to have done me this good turn.

Before leaving, I felt I must go and thank M. de Cambacérès for all the kindness he had shown me in his conversation with M. de la Valette. He received me very kindly, but I found him in a state of great agitation, tormented by all the anxieties that beset a nature as timid as his when circumstances begin to be difficult. He had to make up his mind what part he was going to play; this frightened him, and he gave vent to his profound exasperation with the royal government with a violence proportionate to the efforts he had hitherto made to conceal it and keep it to himself. 'And would you believe it,' said he, 'they have even gone as far as to strike out my name from a statute relating to the composi-

---

[4] The Comte d'Anglés had been appointed Minister of Police in the Provisional Government on 3 April, 1814, after Pasquier had declined the post. 'As for M. Mounier,' says Beugnot, 'who did not like the Emperor any the better for having been one of his ministers, and who delighted in parodying the scenes that took place in the imperial household, he was by no means anxious to put to the test how far Bonaparte, now that he was back, would enjoy the joke.'

tion of the Académie Française, which had already been signed!'
What particularly annoyed him was that this last provocation
could only be explained on the assumption that the charge of his
having been a regicide had been revived, despite his continual
efforts to refute it. He thought he had succeeded in vindicating
himself. It will be remembered that, on this issue, the Abbé de
Montesquiou had been most helpful to him with the King; and
yet it was the Abbé de Montesquiou who had been responsible
for this business about the Academy.

The court's attitude had therefore become more hostile towards him. He had no difficulty in convincing me that he had
known nothing of the Emperor's plans; his prudence and cau-
tion were too well-known for them to have risked taking him
into their confidence; but it was clear to me that he felt considerable doubt about the future. 'All will be well', he said to me,
'if the Empress is restored to him. That will prove that Austria
is still ready to support him. But if she is kept away from him . . .'
I did not press him any further.

When I got home, who should turn up but that rascal Veyrat,
whom I had been at such pains to get expelled from Paris; which
had led to an unpleasant enough scene between Monsieur and
myself. His patrons at the palace had arranged for him to be
allowed to return shortly after I left the Prefecture of Police. But
they had not given him back his job, and he thought this was a
good opportunity of getting reinstated. He said that he had been
instructed by the Duc de Rovigo, the Minister of Police, to see
that the white flags which were flown on every government
building were replaced by the tricolour. By the time he reached
the Roads and Bridges office, he had already carried out his
orders at a number of others. Having impudently forced his way
into my office, he informed me in a lordly manner of the purpose
of his visit. I replied that if the Duc de Rovigo was Minister of
Police, then I was certainly no longer the Director of Roads and
Bridges, and was therefore in no position to give orders. The
Duc de Rovigo has since claimed that he had given no such
orders, but I find it hard to accept the truth of this disclaimer.

*After his triumphant arrival in Paris, Napoleon formed, though not
without difficulty, a government, the most striking feature of which was
the return of Fouché to the Ministry of Police. Pasquier, as Director-
General of Roads and Bridges, was replaced by Molé.*

Every day I used to go to see M. de la Valette, at seven o'clock in the morning, at the Ministry of Posts where he had taken up residence. He told me that there was already some question of an amnesty, from which a number of people would be excluded, though he felt certain that the exceptions would only affect those who had fled, and whom they knew they could not lay hands on. As for the other people who were more or less compromised, he still believed that for the moment they had nothing to fear. Possibly one or two of them might be banished and not allowed within a certain distance of the capital, but this also seemed to him to be unlikely. He spoke of M. Fouché's appointment as Minister of Police with regret, and could not help deploring the fact that the Emperor should still be prepared to trust a man of his stamp. He also told me that the Emperor had sent someone to see him the previous day to get him to accept the Ministry of Foreign Affairs, but that he had refused because he did not think that he had the necessary qualifications to fill such a difficult position. Thereupon, approaches to the Duc de Vicence had been renewed, and eventually his objections were overcome. Thus, the government had now been completed, but, as may be seen, not without considerable difficulty. For Napoleon to find that his highest marks of confidence were so persistently rejected, was a quite new experience, and he must have found it most disconcerting.

One morning, as I was chatting with M. de la Valette, it was easy to see that he was unusually upset. Twice within a quarter of an hour he had rung to find out whether the courier from the North had arrived. Trusting that my question would not be too indiscreet, I asked him to tell me the reason for this impatience. The King ought to have arrived at Lille; had something serious happened there, since the troops in the town had not yet come out for or against him? Here is M. de la Valette's answer, which I put on record because it is evidence of the loftiness of his feelings. 'My God,' said he, 'I have been informed that General Lion, in command of a regiment of Horse Guards, has had orders to pursue the King and his escort, the rearguard of which is, I believe, made up of "red companies". If, by any mischance, General Lion catches up with them, I know what will happen; he is one of these dashing cavalry officers without a trace of magnanimity, and he will wipe them out without pity. The young men that form these "red companies" are in no condition to stand up to him; they almost all belong to the best families in France; it would be a frightful tragedy, an affliction for the whole country. I shall not have a moment's rest until I know that they are safe.'

And yet, seven or eight months later, the very men for whom he had shown such generous concern were to be unmercifully demanding his head!

On the 23rd, M. Réal called upon me, but I was out. He had left word that he would come back because he urgently wanted to see me; and had gone on to the Place Vendôme, where M. Decazes lived.[5] I later discovered that he had called upon him for the same purpose that he had come to see me: when he returned a quarter of an hour later, he informed me that I was to be banished. I could go wherever I liked, provided it was not less than forty leagues from Paris. Throughout our interview he behaved with great concern and kindness, and appeared to be genuinely upset by what he had to do. I asked him whether I had to leave immediately, or whether I should be permitted to stay in Paris a few days longer so that I could find an apartment where Mme Pasquier could live during my absence. He replied that, as far as he was concerned, he would grant me all the facilities I could want, but that I should have to see M. Fouché, who would give me my passport, and who alone could decide whether I could remain.

My old colleagues on the Council of State showed no hesitation in displaying their sympathy for me. Next day, after they had paid homage to the Emperor, M. Regnault, their spokesman, told him before they withdrew that, speaking in the name of the whole Council, they had been deeply grieved to hear of the severe measures that had been taken with regard to M. Pasquier, a former colleague, for whom all those who had worked, with him felt both friendship and esteem. The Emperor, though without displaying much annoyance, replied that some examples

---

[5] Elie Decazes (1780–1861), who rose to be a judge under the Empire, supported the Restoration and remained faithful to the Bourbons through the Hundred Days. After the second Restoration he became the favourite of Louis XVIII in succession to Blacas, and took Fouché's place when the latter was dismissed from the Ministry of Police. In 1819, as President of the Council, he became head of the Ministry, maintaining his liberal position with difficulty against the democratic radicals on the one hand and the *Ultras* on the other. Accused unjustly of complicity in the murder of the Duc de Berry, the King reluctantly accepted his resignation and, having made him a Duke, sent him as French ambassador to London. (Trs.)

had to be made; that my defection, which had been one of the earliest, had also been one of those to cause the greatest stir. From this answer my friends concluded that Napoleon was not particularly angry with me, and that if I chose to make some approach to him and ask him for employment it was fairly certain that I should not be refused. M. Molé in particular insisted upon this strongly and proposed to undertake either to pass on a letter to him or else to speak to him on my behalf, but though he pressed me for a long time and used the most skilful arguments to convince me I persisted in my refusal.

M. de la Valette, whom I saw later and who knew me better, advised me not to accept my banishment without protest. 'You must not,' said he, 'by allowing yourself to be treated as guilty, give the impression of admitting that in fact you are so. To do so, might well have serious consequences later on. In your place, I should write to the Emperor and complain emphatically that you have been treated very unjustly, and in such a manner as to suggest that you have been singled out for a punishment that you no more deserve than all those others, who, like you, yielded to the force of circumstances.' I told him I would think about it, and then went off to M. Fouché's.

The conversation that took place on this occasion between M. Fouché and myself was of such interest that I am reporting it in full. As I had been kept waiting for some time in his outer office, he began by saying: 'Before I could ask you in, I had to get rid of one or two tiresome people so that we can talk at our ease. Let us go into the garden, where we shall be less likely to be disturbed.' We had scarcely left the house, when he turned to me and said: 'What do you think about all this?'—'That's a curious question to ask me for, although of course I have my own views, you can hardly expect me to confide in the Minister of Police.'—'You might, however, do a good deal worse, but since you don't wish to speak I can see that I shall have to open the conversation. So I'll start by telling you that this man has in no way improved and remains just as despotic, just as determined to conquer; in short, just as crazy as ever.'—'How can you expect me to believe that,' I replied, smiling, 'after what *Le Moniteur* told us the day after his arrival? Surely you must have read all the fine things he said at Lyons on his way through: We must forget that we were once the master of nations; my rights are no more than those of the people; whatever may have been done or said by individuals since the fall of Paris will be forgotten by me. After such assurances why should you suppose that I feel the least anxiety?'—'True, and having spoken all these fine words, scarcely had he got here than he banished you, you and plenty of others. Why, at this very moment, he may be signing a decree in which, on top of the measures he is taking against the House of Bourbon—and these are natural enough on his part—he is banishing to forty leagues from Paris all those who accepted any ministerial appointment under the royalist government, as well as all those who held any position, civil or military, in the royal household, etc. And what's more, all these individuals will be obliged to take the oath, which according to him, is demanded by law, as though an oath imposed in this way would be accepted as binding by any man in his senses! If they refuse to take the oath, then the whole lot of them will be submitted to police surveillance and any measures that are necessary for the safety of the State can be taken against them. And that just shows, as you must agree, exactly what he means by forgetting the past and respecting the freedom of the individual.'—'These are very serious matters,' I replied, 'which I must not venture to discuss.'—'Come on now, stop being so cautious. Haven't I set you an example? To sum up, let me tell you this: despite the assurances he has given, the whole of Europe is about to hurl itself upon him; it will be impossible for him to resist; and within four months they will have settled his hash.'—'If that happens I shall resign myself to it. But in all good faith, your Grace, I cannot see what purpose is served by the confidences you are entrusting to me.'—'Right! Then now I'm going to tell you. I ask nothing better than that the Bourbons should return, only this time matters must be arranged a little less stupidly than they were last year by Talleyrand; we are not going to have a position where everybody is at their mercy. We must insist upon properly thought out conditions, with good solid guarantees.'—'Excellent! I am not opposed to any of this; it would suit me as well as it would you. But what can I do about it?'—'For the present, nothing; before long, perhaps a great deal. When the decisive moment arrives I shall need able and reliable men to back me up, men who inspire confidence in everybody, even in the royal family. Above all, I shall need a man who can give a lead to the town of Paris, for, as you will realise, I shall be obliged to get rid of this idiot Réal that he has saddled me with. Well, you are that man. I am counting on you!'—'You do me great honour, but to tell you the truth I do not feel tempted to run such great risks and, for the moment, all I want is to take things easy. However, since you appear to be so kindly disposed towards me, I shall take advantage of the fact to ask a favour of you. Before I leave Paris I need a few days to put my affairs in order. I should be grateful it you would agree to this, and also if you would give me a passport so that I can go to my estate near Le Mans.'—'A few days? Why, take as long as you like. Although you have been pretending to turn a deaf ear to me, I'm sure you understand me perfectly. However, you are going to clear out. For the present that's the best thing you can do, but you must be ready to come back at the first sign from me. You are friendly with Mme de Vaudémont. Leave your address with her, and I will get her to write to you when the moment arrives.' —'Since you suggest this way of keeping in touch I shall make use of it in a month's time, not for any such serious reason, but simply to ask you for a permit to pass through Paris on the way to Mont-Dore, where my doctor has advised me to take the waters.'—'Splendid, whenever you like! So that establishes our means of communication. I will send you your passport and, as to the time you require before leaving, don't be in any hurry.'—'I shall avail myself of your permission, but in moderation, for, despite your protection, the Emperor, according to what you have just told me, might very well have me arrested, if he felt that by staying too long my presence here was becoming a nuisance. I don't at all fancy finding myself shut up within four walls. What I need above all else is freedom to move about.'— 'There I completely agree with you, as I know from experience. But why then are you letting yourself be banished?'—'You must be joking! How can I avoid it?'—'Very simply. Write to him, and ask to be readmitted to the Council of State! He will be only too happy to agree. Don't you realise that he hates me even more than you, and yet I am one of his ministers?'—'That's all very well for you; you are clever enough to maintain such a position. For my part I should be quite incapable of doing so.' —'Oh, I know just what you mean: you feel qualms, because you now pride yourself on your loyalty to the House of Bourbon. But surely, if you are to be of any real use to those you want to help, the first thing is that you should have a finger in the pie? I ask you, what use would you have been last April, unless you had been Prefect of Police?'—'Situations can change very rapidly', I replied. 'And my obligations today are very different from what they were last year. I have made up my mind irrevocably.'

Having thought the matter over, I could see no objection to following the advice M. de la Valette had given me: to write to the Emperor. My letter was handed to him by the chamberlain-in-waiting, M. de Beauvau, who had kindly undertaken to do so. In it I said that I had served him faithfully until I was convinced that the interests of my fellow citizens, whose safety had been entrusted to me, as well as those of the entire country, made it essential for me to do the one thing that might save them from utter disaster. I had done nothing that could injure him personally, nor had I ever forgotten the respect I owe to the man who had summoned me to undertake the most confidential duties. I received no reply to my letter. I had not hoped for one, and it certainly didn't worry me that there was none.

Having been 'fortunate enough to find a little house in the rue de Suresnes, which Mme Pasquier could move into immediately', Pasquier decided to leave Paris.

From what M. Regnault had told me of the friendly attitude towards me on the part of the Duc de Bassano and the Duc de Vicence, I did not want to leave without having seen them. Despite the air of confidence he affected, the Duc de Bassano struck me as being less resolute than I should have expected. Moreover he was as annoyed as his character allowed him to be: he made no attempt to conceal the fact that he was not at all pleased that M. Carnot and M. Fouché had been brought into the Council of State. It was also clear that he would have liked to take over the Ministry of Foreign Affairs again, but it had not been offered to him. Nor was he at all pleased with his position as Secretary of State, for the other ministers had made it quite clear to him that they had no intention of submitting their work to him so that he could modify and cut it about as he pleased. He was extremely civil to me, bewailed the fact that I had been banished, and assured me that he intended to see that the new Prefect of Le Mans respected my privacy. The Prefect was M. Lagarde, former Commissioner of Police. He did, in fact, receive the most formal instructions from the Duc de Bassano, and obeyed them implicitly. With the Duc de Vicence, the conversa-

7 Napoleon returns to the Tuileries, 20 March 1815

8 Bivouac of the Prussian Royal Guard
in the Luxembourg Gardens

tion was much more confidential; it took place on my last day in Paris. He talked to me open-heartedly, and concealed nothing from me. He was heartbroken, and could only foresee every kind of misfortune.

'What the Emperor is doing is mad,' he said. 'By this time, like everyone else, you will have seen the declaration against him[6] promulgated by the powers at Vienna on the 13th, and you have doubtless read the miserable comments that we are reduced to making about it. So he is going to have the whole of Europe on his hands, and they won't give him the chance to make any preparations. They refuse to listen to a word from him, and the couriers we send cannot even cross the frontier. He is bound to go under, but then what is to become of our poor country? It will be devastated, and perhaps partitioned, for we can no longer count on the slightest magnanimity from the Allied sovereigns. The one who was best disposed towards us last year, the Emperor of Russia, must now be the most exasperated. Is anything to be hoped for from the Bourbons? I am afraid that outside France there is little enthusiasm for their cause; they must be very angry with them for allowing themselves to be kicked out so easily. So what is there for us to hang on to? We are like shipwrecked men looking for a plank to cling to. As for the Emperor, he must realise that his position is very different from what he had hoped for. Everything has changed in France since he left; he has no idea of the direction men's minds have taken. Certainly there was great dissatisfaction with the royal government, but under it people enjoyed a degree of liberty that would make it intolerable for them to have to live today under the imperial government as understood by the Emperor, especially towards the end. In any case, you see, he is afraid to restore it openly, and he is equally afraid to grant the freedom that everyone wants. He only promises it. His old habits have proved too strong for him; that is why he has banished you, and plenty of others.

'Which road is he going to take then? He himself does not know. He appeals to the men of the Revolution, yet they are the ones he most fears. On the other hand, he no longer dares trust the more reliable men whom he had gathered round him in latter years; and as a result he is on the wrong course, a dubious, illogical one. He is completely out of his depth. Why, then,

[6] Napoleon had in fact been declared an outlaw by the Allies.

cannot he not see that the feeling he inspires in most people is simply fear, and that this fear could easily drive men into the arms of Louis XVIII if some favourable opportunity arose. What will be the result of this terrible war he is bringing upon us? Even the most resolute of the generals are afraid; the whole nation is terrified at the thought of it, and will blame him for all the suffering they have to put up with.'

This is a brief summary of a conversation that lasted more than an hour, and which gave me a deeper and wider insight into the situation than anything I had heard hitherto. 'Oh, how I wish I was in your place,' said he, taking my hand, 'and how I envy you your banishment. I only hope they will leave you in peace, but, in any case, if I can be of any use to you count on me"

'On 1 *April I set out for the Maine* [*his home at Caulons*], *leaving Paris without regret, but with a feeling of profound sadness; pre-occupied with the crisis which equally involved the peace of Europe and the future of my country.*

'*I spent April in a worried and painfully apprehensive state of mind, although I had no personal cause for anxiety* . . .' True, *the Emperor saw fit* 'to *insist quite illegally that all the principal officials who had served the King should take an oath of loyalty to him as a condition for their being left in peace* . . .' *Pasquier's brother, as a former Prefect of La Sarthe,* 'was *invited to send this oath in writing. He was in no mood to submit to this arbitrary demand; as for me, I regarded it as a formality of little importance, extorted by force and in consequence worthless* . . .' *Eventually the Prefect, M. Lagarde, to whom the future Chancellor had been recommended by the Duc de Bassano, who had since been appointed Secretary of State, arranged to drag things out as long as possible* . . .

On 1 *May, judging it opportune to dissociate himself from his brother, who was inclined to get involved in plots that he knew to be futile, Pasquier left Coulans. His pretext for going was to take a cure at Mont-Dore. As soon as he reached Paris he went to see Fouché, to ask permission to spend a fortnight in the capital. He found the Minister of Police in an even more cynical mood than he had been a month earlier. 'What's the use of a fortnight?' said Fouché. 'Stay as long as you like . . . Haven't you seen his* Acte Additionnel, *guaranteeing everyone's personal safety and protecting them from arbitrary banishment? We've got him a lot better tied up than he expected, just you wait and see.' Then he continued: 'Besides, what do you want to go off to Auvergne for? It doesn't make sense. Before the end of the month he'll be obliged to leave Paris to join his army. And, once he has gone, we shall remain in control. I daresay he may win one or two battles, but he'll lose the third, and that will be when we come into the picture. Believe me, things are going to turn out all right . . .' However, the prudent Pasquier pleaded ill-health in order to avoid modifying his plans.*

In his innermost heart, however, he was convinced that Louis XVIII's return was inevitable. 'There was only one issue on which opinion was divided: Was Napoleon in a strong enough position to resist the on-slaught he would have to endure? Many people believed that he was, and they formed the majority. But many others were dubious. I was one of the latter, and I was absolutely convinced that the only possible result of his defeat would be the re-establishment of legitimate authority . . .'

The first days of my stay in Paris were spent in seeing everyone who could throw any light on the situation for me. It did not take me long to discover that the *Acte Additionnel* satisfied no one, although it contained one or two provisions which might be regarded as an improvement on the corresponding articles of the Charter. But the disturbing intention underlying it was only too clear; and this was especially apparent in the omission of any provision for the abolition of confiscations, and this despite the example set by the Charter. It did not take me long to discover that this omission had been strongly opposed in the Council of State, and that Napoleon had obstinately insisted upon it in a most significant manner: it was only too easy to see that he had ulterior motives. In the final article, there was an attempt to get the French people to declare that it had never intended, nor did it now intend, to make it legal, even in the event of the imperial dynasty becoming extinct, to propose the restoration of the Bourbons, or of any prince belonging to that family, to the throne of France. How could anyone fail to realise that a man who dared to put forward such a claim was prepared to go to any lengths, would use every means, to maintain himself in power?

The semblance of agreement which was to sanction the re-storation of the imperial government should have misled no one; it was simply the most convenient method of avoiding any serious discussion. By means of this consultation, and the meeting in the Champ de Mai, the Emperor hoped to avoid the necessity of summoning a meeting of the Chamber of Deputies before leaving to join the army. Certainly it would not have suited him to leave behind an Assembly which he would be too far away to control. But he was unable to avoid this difficulty; his intentions had been seen through, and the evidence of discontent with which he was surrounded, forced him, on 30 April, to issue the decree for the convocation of the Electoral Colleges. In M. Benjamin Constant's work on the Hundred Days,[7] one can see how delighted he was when Napoleon was thus forced back upon his last position. Nothing could so effectively hinder him from carrying out his ulterior aims. Indeed, whatever the composition of the Chamber of Deputies proved to be, it was bound not to suit him completely; his enemies of every kind had a good chance of being elected, and, since he dared not resort either to threats or violence, he had no effective way of keeping them out. It may be added that, had it not been for the mistaken approach adopted by the royalist party since the beginning of the Revolution, which consisted in abstaining from all public office whenever the government was constituted against its principles, it would have been very easy for it to have won a large number of seats in this Chamber. And what a difference this would have made, when the moment of decision arrived! But in such matters, the most enlightened men are obliged to accept the feelings of the majority, under pain of incurring a dislike which it is very difficult for them to recover from later. Despite my banishment, many influential electors from Paris told me that if I chose to appear at the Electoral Assembly my nomination was assured. But I consulted one or two friends, and refused.

During this same period I had to refuse a most extraordinary order, which I was far from expecting. One fine morning, to my great astonishment, I was notified by some captain or other of the Federates, that my name had been entered on his muster, and that I must therefore turn up the following day at the Saint-

[7] *Mémoires sur les Cent-Jours en forme de lettres*, Paris, 1820–22. Born in Switzerland and arriving in France for the first time in 1795, Benjamin Constant is perhaps better known as the lover of Mme de Staël and later of Mme Récamier, and as the author of the brilliant autobiographical novel *Adolphe*. He was, however, extremely active as a liberal politician and propagandist. After defending the Directory against the counter-revolution he supported the *coup d'état* of 18 Brumaire, but proving too independent for Napoleon's taste, followed Mme de Staël into exile in 1803. During the Hundred Days he drew up the *Acte Constitutionnelle* on Napoleon's behalf, for which he was exiled once more when, Louis XVIII was returned to the throne. Later he was elected to the Chamber of Deputies, where he consistently advocated the freedom of the press; and, in 1830, was made President of the Council of State by Louis Philippe shortly before his death. (Trs.)

Denis parade ground in order to be enrolled and start training. This proved to be a wonderful opportunity for observing to what lengths human stupidity can go. The Mayor in my district was a certain Lecordier, a bill broker whom I had known, carrying on the same business, when I was Prefect of Police. Wishing to avoid the unpleasantness of seeing my home invaded by fusiliers, merely because I had refused without more ado to appear as instructed, I went to see M. Lecordier. He received me in the most disagreeable manner, assured me that there was nothing he could do about it, and that as my name appeared upon the muster I should have to report. 'What, sir?' I replied. 'When I am nearly fifty years of age, a former Councillor of State, Prefect of Police, Director-General of Roads and Bridges and, in addition, banished from Paris?' As he persisted, however, I withdrew, though not without telling him that I could only suppose he was crazy. (Incidentally, after the second Restoration, M. Lecordier discovered that he was a most devoted royalist!) The next day I went to see General Darrican, who was in command of the Paris Federation. He roared with laughter at the Mayor's stupidity, and immediately had my name removed from the muster.

Among the people I saw most of were M. Royer-Collard and M. Becquey. The former confided to me that, resuming his former habits, he had found a way of keeping in touch with Ghent, and was passing on all the information he thought would be of use to them. He was doing his best to provide a reliable picture of the state of affairs in France and of the general frame of mind, especially in the capital. Since it would have been extremely imprudent to write by post, his letters, or rather his notes, were taken each week by a reliable messenger, who, to avoid all suspicion, only returned to France a long time after and by a roundabout route. They had to have a fresh one each week, and since M. Royer-Collard, having previously been a professor at the university, was well-known amongst the students, he always managed to find one of them who was eager to undertake this dangerous mission. It would be difficult to describe the enthusiasm there was amongst these young people for the royal cause, which they identified with the struggle for freedom.

After the meeting at the Champs de Mai, as Napoleon was about to set off for the army, this correspondence assumed greater importance every day; M. Royer therefore decided to send M.

Guizot himself. Despite my intention of leaving Paris, I had to change my plans because of a dangerous fever, which made me seriously ill for nearly a month. I had occasion to see M. de la Valette again. The goodness of his heart had eventually overcome his doubts; he needed to renew his faith in the fortunes and destiny of the Emperor. From a genuine feeling of friendship towards me, he did his best to overcome my resistance and persuade me to make approaches to the master which he was convinced would prove effectual. 'You are deceiving yourself', he told me. 'I assure you the Emperor will triumph over his enemies. At the present time, you have nothing to fear from him and he would grant you anything; but if you wait until the hour of victory the situation will be completely different. Who, then, would dare to answer for it that his desire and need for revenge will not regain their ascendancy over his mind? Don't rely on this liberal Constitution that he pretends to want to grant; once he finds himself at the head of a victorious army, it won't be long before he throws off the feeble bonds with which today he has allowed himself to be bound. Didn't he make it clear enough, by his refusal to subscribe to the abolition of confiscations, what secret thoughts still remain at the bottom of his heart? And why insist on running a risk that you can so easily avoid?'

I thanked him as I was bound to do for his steadfast and friendly zeal on my behalf; but I did not attempt to hide from him in fact that the nature of Napoleon's new reign, if he succeeded in establishing himself on the throne, which is what he seemed to expect, certainly did not encourage me to enlist myself once more in his service. I added that perhaps I deserved less credit for rejecting his proposal than he imagined, because, fundamentally, I could not accept his estimate of the probable result of the war. From this we went on to discuss the real strength of the army that the Emperor was trying to raise; and, despite his desire to convince me how formidable it would be, he let fall one or two admissions which made it clear that his confidence was not as assured as he wished to make it appear. He agreed that the spirit of the soldiers was much better than that of the officers, especially those of higher rank; that the marshals were worn out, lacking either zest or energy. Moreover, while there were many regiments, it would be better if there were fewer of them but stronger, etc. In short, this discussion, far from shaking me, confirmed me in the opinions I had already formed. What had struck me particularly was his admission of what was to be feared from Napoleon, were he to come back victorious.

The opening of the session of the Chamber of Peers and the Chamber of Deputies, and the difficulties, both open and concealed, which immediately arose between both Assemblies and Napoleon, did nothing to increase Pasquier's confidence in the imperial regime.

I had scarcely recovered from a long illness when, at the beginning of June, I decided to go to the Marais before setting out for Mont-Dore. I was drawn to Mme de la Briche, M. Molé's mother-in-law, by many memories; good, gentle, always kindly, always concerned to promote the interest of others without ever thinking of herself, she occupied a place in society that no one else could fill. She had been lucky enough to survive the Terror without mishap. The Revolution had spared both her and her estates. This was all the more extraordinary since the château of Le Marais, by its elegance, luxury and the extent of its estates, was just what one would have expected to appeal to the popular appetite. When the storm subsided, she found herself in a better position than anyone else to bring together in her home all that remained of the old society; when she married her daughter to M. Molé, her salon became the resort of all those who were not resigned to frequenting the salons of the Directory and the society of newly rich contractors.

At Le Marais I found not only M. Molé but also M. de Barante, who, on 20 March, had resigned from the Prefecture of Nantes and had refused another post which the Emperor had offered him. He was a man who combined an upright heart, and all the charm of an accomplished man of the world, with a powerful and well-developed mind. The three of us agreed on most matters, and our hopes and fears were shared by all the inmates of the château. In times of political crisis such harmony of outlook and feeling, such reciprocal confidence, is especially comforting. I need hardly say that we awaited news of the opening of the campaign with the greatest impatience. We heard of the victory at Ligny on the 16th. Despite this brilliant start, however, we still considered it probable that the huge forces with which Napoleon had to contend would be victorious; though at the same time we felt that the end might be a long time coming. The battle of Waterloo, and its disastrous results, therefore took us by surprise.

On Wednesday, the 21st, at nine o'clock in the evening, one of the people staying in the château received a note from M. Saulty, the head of the tax office of the Department, who lived nearby at the château of Basville. The note had been written immediately after he received very definite news that the Emperor had lost a decisive battle, that the Imperial Guard had been destroyed, that the whole army had been put to flight, that Napoleon had come to the end of his resources and that everything was finished. My first impulse, and both M. Molé and M. de Barante felt the same, was to get back to Paris as quickly as possible. All three of us, therefore, piled into a small travelling barouche belonging to me. We borrowed horses to take us as far as the first posting station, and, as day was breaking, we reached the gates of Paris.[8]

The news of the disaster of Waterloo had caused a great stir in Paris. I remember the anxious curiosity we felt as we approached the Invalides, and looked out to see whether the tricolour flag was still flying. Mme Pasquier had sent a messenger who met us on the way, to inform me that the Emperor, defying all conjectures, had reached Paris the previous day, only a few hours after the news of his defeat. What had he come for? How had he brought himself to abandon his army, confronted by a victorious enemy, thus leaving the road to France open, and to rely upon his subordinates to collect the scattered remnants of his forces, when the only hope of reviving their courage was for him to remain with them? I was lost in conjecture; but here is what I soon discovered.

During the morning of the 21st, Napoleon could not make up his mind whether to appeal to the two Chambers with a view to obtaining their support, or whether to set up a dictatorship and 'declare France to be in a state of siege, summoning to his assistance all patriots and all honest Frenchmen'.

The Chamber of Deputies, by voting in favour of a motion moved by La Fayette, which declared the Assembly to be in permanent session and announced that any attempt to dissolve it would be high treason, convinced the Emperor that he could scarcely count on parliamentary support. At the same time, all the information that was reaching him excluded the possibility of an armed uprising.

[8] According to Molé, 'Joy shone on every face. M. Pasquier already saw himself raised to the Ministry, the one great ambition of his life'.

On the 22nd he abdicated in favour of his son and invited the 'Chambers to set up the regency as soon as legally possible'. The ministers in office were provisionally to form a Council of Government.

On 22 March, I chanced to see M. Fouché, who appeared to be pleased that we had met. 'Well', said he, 'so at last we have got him to abdicate. You must admit that's not a bad couple of days' work.'—'Certainly, but what are you going to do about the condition in favour of his son, whom he still hopes to force on the country. It's scarcely necessary to point out to you how dangerous that is. What we need above all is peace, and the only way we're going to get it, either at home or abroad, is through the House of Bourbon.'—'Do you think I don't know that as well as you? But we have been caught on the hop. He has been crushed so quickly that he has left us no time to make any preparations. But we can't expect people to change their minds from one day to the next. Besides we've got the army to consider; it's no good upsetting them, we must try to win them over, for they could still do a great deal of harm. If only people won't press me too hard, everything will work out for the best and everybody will be satisfied.'

He then told me that, during the day, the Chambers were going to set up a Provisional Government Commission; that he was sure to be a member of it, and that the others would all be his men with whom he could do as he liked. He had already drawn up a list of his friends in the two Chambers and he was convinced it would be approved. 'So you see I'm in a very strong position, for there's nothing like collective authority—provided it is controlled by one man!'

He made an appointment with me for the evening to let me know the result of the voting. I went to his house with M. Molé. He was in the salon surrounded by about sixty people. We managed to have a talk with him in the embrasure of a window, and he repeated his refrain: '*Don't hurry me*. If I am not allowed the time I require, the whole business will be ruined. You ought to understand this, M. Pasquier,' he added, 'for you were in a position to see what happened last April at first-hand. How would things have turned out, if, disregarding all the risks and dangers, everything had been jeopardised by seeking to achieve on 2 April what was accomplished some two days later without striking a blow?'

I readily agreed with him that in matters of this kind, much the most important things was to choose the right moment, and that it could be very dangerous to attempt to anticipate it. However, I also pointed out that the situations he was comparing were not at all similar. Last year it had been necessary to revive men's memories, to make them conscious of rights that had been forgotten for more than twenty years. Today, all that had to be done was to obliterate what had been done in three months. The course was set, success was assured, whereas a year ago the most dangerous experiments had to be made. Moreover, then the enemy was already at the gate of the capital, the blow had fallen, and all we could do was to extricate ourselves as best we could. Today we had to forestall a similar disaster, the results of which would be yet more terrible. Thus not a moment must be lost in checking the enemy's advance; the most effective way to prevent the invasion of the country was to recognise the former dynasty. I could not help feeling that the utmost diligence was required.

M. Molé supported me with every argument he could think of. We were deeply engrossed in our conversation, when one of the Deputies, M. Gourlay, arrived; he had come straight from the Chamber of Deputies to acquaint M. Fouché with the first two nominations that had emerged from the ballot. These were himself and M. Carnot. M. Fouché's disappointment was only too apparent. He had not been reckoning on M. Carnot, who had nevertheless topped the ballot. He was not a man that was easy to handle and might be a most awkward colleague.

His annoyance was still further increased when M. Gourlay informed him that the candidate who had won the next highest number of votes to himself was General Grenier, from which it was clear that he would go on to the second ballot. Despite M. Fouché's impassive expression, it was not difficult to see that these were scarcely the nominations he had told me he was so certain of a few hours earlier. His candidates, I believe, were Marshal Macdonald and either M. Lambrecht or M. Flaugergues.

He was more fortunate in the Chamber of Peers, where he managed to get the Duc de Vicence, whom he certainly wanted, and M. Quinette, who was, I believe, also nominated through his influence. He was a man over whom he had always had considerable ascendancy. It can scarcely have displeased him to have as a colleague a regicide like himself. Despite the setback represented by M. Carnot's election, it was clear that M. Fouché was going to have a majority on the government commission. The slowness with which he chose to act may perhaps be explained by the fact that it suited him to bring home to the royalists the difficulties he would have to overcome with his new colleagues.

From the start there was one question on which they all found themselves in complete agreement. This was the need to use every possible means to prevent either of the two Chambers from passing an act that recognised the rights of Napoleon II. It was certain that all the forces that the imperial party still had at its disposal were going to be brought into play to carry a vote on this point. M. Fouché was deeply concerned about it.

Next day, when I saw him again early in the morning, it was the principal subject of conversation between us. He told me that when, during the night, Napoleon had heard of the unsuccessful efforts that his brother Lucien, MM. de la Bédoyère, de Bassano, Roederer and his other friends had made in the Chamber of Peers to get his son's succession proclaimed, he had flown into a passion; his indignation was clear enough proof that he would do everything in his power to revive the enthusiasm of his supporters. We should therefore expect fresh efforts to be made to win support for this claim in both Chambers, but especially in the Chamber of Deputies. M. Fouché made no attempt to conceal from me that in this respect he was not without considerable anxiety.

'Can one ever tell', he said, 'what may happen in an Assembly as badly organised as this one is? A burst of eloquence, a feeling of weariness and the desire to get it all over with may result in a decision being taken, when one is least expecting it, which is quite contrary to the will of the majority. What would be the consequences of such a decision? It would certainly rally the army in support of Napoleon II, and that would be extremely serious'. —'I agree with you that, as long as an Assembly is not fully committed, it can go the way one least expects. Napoleon wants his son to be proclaimed, you should get Louis XVIII proclaimed at the earliest possible moment. If you are for the moment content merely to prevent the passing of an act recognising Napoleon II, it will always remain a threat.'—'It's all very fine for you to talk like that,' he went on. 'Undoubtedly I have some support in this Assembly, but I have not yet had time to prepare it for such an abrupt transition; I have been caught napping. If I try to push them too far and too fast they may well get completely out of hand. Look how they elected Carnot yesterday. The most I can do for the moment is to avoid disaster and ward off the most pressing danger; in this respect, I have neglected nothing, I have given my instructions to my surest and most capable friends. Amongst them, very fortunately for us, I have one man of outstanding ability, on whom I can rely. His name is Manuel.[9] Do you know him? I know no one better at swaying a meeting. I told him again just now that, at all costs, it is absolutely essential for him to prevent this child's claim to the throne being recognised. He told me not to worry, and that he would answer for everything.'—'I am not acquainted with M. Manuel', I replied. 'But who have you got in the army?'

He informed me that Grouchy was back in France with his army corps, closely pursued by the Prussians and the English, and that if he was in a position to make a stand at all it would only be at a considerable distance within the frontier. So far nothing at all was known of what had transpired at Ghent since the victory won by the Allies. He told me that, in the event of his having to be away, his secretary, Fabri, would always keep me informed of what was going on, and added: 'But how and when are we going to manage to get into touch with these people at Ghent? They are so maladroit! Oughtn't they to have had an agent here? Oughtn't they to have got in touch with me before this? They must know what my aims are; they are bound to have been informed about them from more than one quarter.'

I have reported this conversation because it shows what was going on in M. Fouché's mind and the very real difficulties of his position. The control he exercised over the Chamber of Deputies was more limited than he was prepared to admit.

Napoleon's departure for Malmaison on the 25th simplified the problems of the Provisional Government, for the Emperor seemed to have recovered some of his popularity. 'The Federates, and a large crowd that had come in from the suburbs, arrived during the morning in the Avenue de Marigny, which runs alongside the garden of the Elysée, shouting

[9] Manuel's hostility towards the Bourbons later became virulent. In 1823 the views he expressed in the Chamber of Deputies gave rise to violent debates. In 1827 his funeral was the occasion of mass demonstrations against the government of Charles X.

Long Live the Emperor! *Napoleon kept coming out and thanking them. I saw him one day on the balcony. It was the first time I had seen him since my last conversation with him in* 1814, *on the eve of his departure for the French campaign, and I could not help experiencing the most profound emotion at seeing him reduced to having to acknowledge so repeatedly acclamations from so humble a source ... His expression, naturally grave, had become gloomy; sometimes he tried to smile, but the look in his eyes betrayed the sadness filling his heart.'*

As I have already said, as soon as I returned from the department of the Sarthe, very intimate relations had been established between M. Royer-Collard and myself. He had done everything possible to organise a regular correspondence with Ghent, but, though letters were regularly despatched from Paris to Ghent, all too often they remained unanswered. Thus we received no instructions, no guidance, no encouragement, and we had to reassure ourselves by assuming that this reserve was dictated by their uncertainty as to what was going to happen and by their fear of compromising us.

On the 22nd or 23rd, M. de Vitrolles, whom M. Fouché had set free, came to see us, and I did my best to concert with him all the necessary steps to be taken in the interests of the royalist cause.[10] M. Fouché had decided to release him from prison, firstly at the instance of Mme de Vaudémont, and secondly because he thought that this would provide him with an intermediary between him and the Bourbons who was not only extremely skilful but also devoted to his interests. He was not mistaken: M. de Vitrolles, deservedly grateful, was always to be active on his behalf, and on one very important occasion even exceeded all bounds of discretion.

We did what we could to convince M. Fouché of the need to act; we told him that if he missed his opportunity events would prove to be stronger than he, and would deprive him of most of the credit to which he could lay claim. But our arguments were addressed to a man who, both by character and revolutionary experience, was only prepared to rely upon positive information based upon concrete evidence, and, in the present situation,

[10] 'MM. Royer-Collard and Pasquier assisted me in different ways', says Vitrolles, the agent of the Comte d'Artois. 'The former liked to give me advice, which he supported with all his dogmatic vehemence and sometimes paradoxes; the latter had a better understanding of my ideas, and helped to carry them out without substituting his own, and his intelligence was fertile in expedients.'

such were the precautions that he still felt obliged to maintain with the party opposed to the House of Bourbon that, although he was ready to release M. de Vitrolles, he insisted upon him remaining strictly incognito and never leaving the place where he was hiding except at night.

It was at this moment that I received a high mark of confidence that I was far from expecting, but which, at the time it reached me and considering the large number of other people to whom it was extended, could not be of great use to me. One morning, very early, a man turned up to see me whom I at first had some difficulty in recognising. It was M. Hyde de Neuville.[11] I thought he was abroad, but he informed me that he had come from Ghent with a mission from the King. According to reports that had reached him about the situation inside his kingdom, His Majesty had decided that it would be a good idea for certain trustworthy people to be invested with his authority and empowered to act in his name. He had charged M. de Neuville to bring these warrants (they were dated 1 June), and to hand them over to the people concerned, of whom I was one. It is important to note that this permission had been entrusted to M. de Neuville before the battle of Waterloo, and that this event might have altered the King's outlook.

The difficulty of getting into France without being recognised, and without running the risk of having his papers seized, had forced M. de Neuville to go a long way out of his way. He had first been to England, then returned to the continent, and had managed to cross the frontier either from Alsace or from Lorraine. As a result a great deal of time had been lost. Moreover, for fear of compromising the people who had been selected, it had been decided to leave all names blank; these were only to be filled in if he was able to hand over the documents to the people for whom they were intended. This was certainly an indication of how highly the King trusted him, for there was nothing to prevent him from inserting one name rather than

[11] Baron Hyde de Neuville never wavered in his loyalty to the royalist cause either during the Revolution or under the Empire. His devotion to the Bourbons was later to result in his being the only one of all the right-wing Deputies who, on 30 July 1830, dared to plead the cause of the Duc de Bordeaux (1820-83). The latter, more usually known as the Comte de Chambord, born seven months after the assassination of his father, the Duc de Berry, younger son of Charles X, thus became, on the latter's dismissal in 1830, the legitimitist pretender to the throne.

another. He assured me that mine was one of those they were most concerned about, and that Mme la Duchesse d'Angoulême had especially urged him to do his very best to find me. I took care, as was to be expected, to enquire the names of those I was to be associated with, amongst whom I remember the following, though several of them only received the powers intended for them much later: M. de Grosbois, M. Dubouchage, M. de Chabrol, the Prefect of Lyons, Marshal Macdonald, Marshal Oudinot, the Bailli de Crussol, M. Hyde de Neuville and M. de Vitrolles; that makes nine people, but I may well have forgotten some of them. I think Marshal de Vioménil may have been one of them. The fact that M. de Vitrolles' name was included almost made me suspect that M. Hyde may have made use of the very wide powers of discretion referred to above. How could they have given him, at Ghent, the name of a man known to be in prison? And, on the other hand, how can one explain that M. Royer-Collard's name had been omitted?

As to the contents of these warrants, they merely stated that the bearer was authorised to do whatever, in his view, might be of service to the King. The document was signed 'Louis' and counter-signed 'Blacas d'Aulps'. But what could be done with such powers? What possible use could be made of them? I at once gave the matter the most serious thought, but I soon realised that they would probably serve little purpose. Things were happening with such speed that difficulties had to be re-solved and solutions imposed by decisive actions. It could no longer be doubted that the enemy armies had crossed the fron-tiers. The King was known to have left Ghent and to be prepar-ing to return to France, if, indeed, he had not already done so. It could therefore be taken for granted that he would soon make his decisions known officially, and in a positive manner that would put an end to all uncertainty. In such a situation, what then could be said or promised by men invested with powers such as ours, which, although quite recent, were already almost out of date owing to all that had happened since the day the warrents were signed! To which I should add that, in a situation where so many people were equally entitled to act with the same authority, it would have been essential to establish agreement amongst them, in order to ensure that the steps taken by one should not conflict with those taken by another. Now, such pre-liminaries could not help but take time and it was by no means easy to obtain agreement when several of the people involved had never had the slightest connection with the others. Ought I to acquaint M. Fouché with the new role I had been called upon to play? Having thought about it a good deal, I was convinced that nothing was to be gained by doing so; he would perhaps want to make use of me, and so compromise me to no useful purpose. I therefore decided not to mention the matter to him.

The Provisional Government was in no mind to conceal the serious inadequacy of the means of defence available. The reverses suffered by the remnants of the French army and the daily advances made by the Alllied forces were accurately conveyed to the Chambers, and the public too was kept scrupulously informed; since nothing was hidden, everyone could form his own opinion in full knowledge of the facts. The need to talk over so many important matters brought together at my house a certain number of people, every morning and evening, all of whom contributed such information as they had been able to glean. What I personally managed to obtain from the Inspector-General at the Prefecture of Police, M. Foudras, the man I had appointed to replace M. Veyrat, was of the greatest significance. He kept me informed, day by day and almost hour by hour, of everything that was happening at Malmaison, of the projects entertained by Napoleon, of his continual desire to stake everything on the hope of regaining power, and of the relations that he maintained to this end with such devoted supporters as he still had in the army and in the Assembly.

The men I liked to exchange views with were MM. Royer-Collard, Becquey, Molé,[12] de Barante, de Tournon, Portalis and M. Alexandre de Girardin. This last had, to begin with, held a splendid cavalry command in the army that the Emperor had raised at the start of the campaign, but certain indiscretions on his part aroused suspicion, he had found himself on the point of being arrested and possibly of being condemned by a court-martial. He had been very lucky, in that, angry as he was,

---

[12] The Comte de Molé (1781–1855), to whom there are many references throughout these Memoirs, came from a very similar background to Pasquier's, though fifteen years his junior. Both their fathers had been President of the Parlement of Paris and were guillotined during the Terror; both began their administrative career as members of Napoleon's Council of State; both held office under the Restoration; and both achieved their greatest political advancement in the reign of Louis Philippe. Molé, after a period as Foreign Minister, became Prime Minister from 1836–39. (Trs.)

Napoleon had been content to deprive him of his command and send him back to Paris. He was an enterprising, ambitious man, with a thorough knowledge of the army (for a long time he had been first aide-de-camp to Major-General the Prince of Neufchâtel) and he was greatly concerned to distinguish himself by some service that would win favour in the eyes of the Bourbons.

One of the subjects of our daily discussions was our fear lest Napoleon, realising the mistake he had made in abandoning his army and knowing that a very considerable body of them had succeeded in regrouping, might conceive the idea of returning to take command of them and of challenging the abdication, which, according to him, had been extorted from him, and the main condition of which had not been fulfilled. Already on his arrival at Malmaison he had issued a proclamation bidding farewell to the army, and the terms in which this farewell were couched had clearly been intended to sound out the mood of the troops. Publication of this proclamation in *Le Moniteur* had not been allowed, and it had only been possible to distribute it by underhand means; nevertheless its purpose was unmistakeable, and one could only assume that Napoleon intended to escape at the first opportunity and rejoin his soldiers.

It was to forestall this danger that the Government Commission had decided to entrust General Becker[13] with the command of the château of Malmaison, thus making him responsible for the Emperor's personal custody. There was good reason for trusting him in such a position, since it was known that there had been grounds for personal hostility between him and Napoleon. In fairness to him, however, it must be admitted that this fact in no way prevented him, whilst scrupulously carrying out his duty, from behaving with all the consideration that such a situation demanded. It was on the 26th, I think, that he received his orders; on the 27th it was learned that the army had retreated as far as Soissons, where headquarters had been established, and where whatever remnants of the various corps had managed to rally were placed under the command of Marshal Grouchy. With the army so near, there was every reason to fear that Napoleon would be carried away by the desire to take com-

[13] General Becker's brilliant career had been interrupted in 1809, when the Emperor came to hear that he was expressing opinions hostile to the war in Spain, but he had been restored to the active list in June 1814. He fulfilled the unpleasant task entrusted to him by the Provisional Government in 1815 with the greatest tact.

mand of it, and would find some means of getting to Soissons.

We were discussing this possibility when M. de Girardin arrived. 'It is absolutely essential for us to try and find out what is the mood amongst the rank-and-file, as well as amongst the officers. Here's Marshal Grouchy, in command of the only organised units still left between the enemy and Paris. I know him, and so do all of you. We must discover what he intends to do.' M. de Girardin concluded by saying that, if I was prepared to go with him, he was confident that there was nothing to prevent us from seeing the Marshal. We should be there next day before nine o'clock in the morning, and all in all, even if our journey achieved nothing, there was no serious objection to it. I felt considerable hesitation. I was still in a poor state of health, and the fatigue of such an expedition scared me. However, in the end I yielded to their insistence, and at midnight M. de Girardin and I drove off. He had undertaken all the preliminary arrangements, had put on his General's uniform and was equipped with passports and travelling warrants. In addition to this, he was known at all the posting-stations on the way, and in consequence we should be sure of obtaining every facility.

We left Paris with his horses, but from the first stage travelled post. We were making good time, and were only a few leagues from Soissons, when we met a dispatch rider coming from the other direction. M. de Girardin decided that this would be a good opportunity of finding out what was going on, and, with that tone of authority which comes from the habit of giving orders, he summoned the courier, asked him if he was carrying dispatches for the Minister of War and, when he replied in the affirmative, demanded to see the inventory of documents contained in his saddlebags. M. de Girardin had for a long time been the first aide-de-camp to the Major-General, and was therefore particularly well-known to the army couriers, all of whom were used to receiving their orders from him. These dispatches had been sent by Marshal Soult.

'So you come from Marshal Soult, then?' said M. de Girardin. —'Yes, mon général, he's in command of the fortress.'—'And what about Marshal Grouchy?'—'He's still in command of his corps, and they say he's going to set up his headquarters at Dammartin; though other people say that all troops, even those belonging to his corps, are going to be put under the command of Marshal Soult.'—'Right, that's what I wanted to know', said M. de Girardin.

This news gave us serious food for thought, for it almost certainly meant that, if we went on, it would be Marshal Soult and not M. de Grouchy that we should meet. 'It would be most imprudent for us to go any further,' said M. de Girardin. 'If Marshal Soult disapproves of what we are doing, and thinks that it may in any way compromise him, he is quite capable of having us arrested.' We therefore decided to return to Paris. On the way back we turned off at a side road, which took us to his estate at Ermenonville. I did not know this delightful spot and, as the weather was magnificent, I spent the day most agreeably being shown over it; a very different kind of occupation from the one we had been prepared for. In the evening we made our way back to the main road and returned to Paris, knowing no more about what we had set out to discover than when we started. Both of us were home by midnight, so that, apart from our friends with whom it had been arranged, no one knew anything about our excursion.

Our state of uncertainty was not to last long. Almost as soon as he reached Paris, Marshal Grouchy, having handed over his command, set about finding some way of making it known that he was well disposed towards the House of Bourbon; and two days later I met him at M. de Vitrolles', whose hiding place he had discovered. There he was putting himself at his complete disposal, and imploring him to inform the Princes as soon as possible that they could rely upon him, and that all he asked was an opportunity to prove his devotion. As to Marshal Soult, it is clear from what he did later that, like his colleague, he too was seeking an opportunity to play some part which would entitle him to the gratitude of the dynasty which was bound to be restored once more to the throne of France. We had exposed ourselves quite uselessly to the dangers that might well have resulted from our expedition to the retreating army. Orders had just been given to the troops to proceed as rapidly as possible to Paris. This unexpected move had been rendered necessary by the swift advance of the enemy, whose advance guard had already reached Compiègne, and who, if they took the Senlis road, could thus arrive before the gates of the capital in a few days' march.

The next few days were a period of anxiety for those who, like Pasquier, regarded the return of the Bourbons as the only possible solution.

Napoleon's departure for Rochefort on 29 June to some extent re-assured them. But as long as the Emperor remained on French soil, who could tell what might happen? 'All we had to hearten us were M. Fouché's intentions, which we thought we understood. We knew his past record, and we certainly recognised the very real ability of which he had given proof in so many political crises. But what confidence could we feel in his honesty? In fairness to him, I must say, however, that he kept me very fully informed as to the real state of affairs, and that he very rarely misled us about what he was doing, or about his hopes. Having allowed things to reach their present position, he felt as strongly as we did ... the necessity of bringing things to a head, and acted accordingly ...

' *... Everyone flocked to his house: the most extraordinary collection of people crowded into the public rooms, both friends and enemies. As for Fouché himself, he moved about from group to group, as completely at his ease as if he were expressing the same opinion to them all. Many a time I have seen him leave a window recess, where he was chatting with his old comrade-in-arms Thibaudeau, a former member of the National Convention, with every appearance of intimacy, to join me and my friends in another recess to discuss some message sent to Courtrai ...* '[14]

The armistice of 3 July, foreseeing the French army's retreat to the Loire and the entry of the Allied troops into Paris, was a sign that matters were coming to a head. Three days later Pasquier managed to get a confidential note to the King, in which he suggested that a general amnesty should be granted (except for a small number of 'guilty men' to be banished immediately), that, though the army should not be disbanded, a considerable number of officers should be retired on half pay, and, above all, that the 'national colours' should be retained.

I have already mentioned the special powers with which I and several other people had been invested, and which had been brought to us by M. Hyde de Neuville. Concerned to see that no use had been made of them, he conceived the idea of arranging a meeting of all those to whom they had been granted. We were invited to be present, on the evening of the 4th, at Marshal Macdonald's. The question arose as to whether nothing could be done to hasten the surrender of Paris to her legitimate sovereign. Those present, in addition to Marshal Macdonald, were Marshal Oudinot, M. de Vitrolles, M. de Grosbois, the Bailli de Crussol, M. Dubouchage and myself. M. de Chabrol

[14] Where Louis XVIII had arrived on his way back to Paris.

had already left for Lyons, where he thought his presence might be of use.

Someone proposed that on the following day we should proceed to the Hôtel de Ville, present our warrants to the Prefect, and instruct him to hand over the administration of the capital to us. If he agreed to our demand, we would publish a proclamation calling upon all good citizens to unite, in order to put an end to the sufferings of the fatherland. We should then call a meeting of the Municipal Council, and propose that it send a deputation to the King begging His Majesty to honour the loyal city of Paris with his presence at the earliest possible moment. This proposal was opposed by the Bailli de Crussol, M. de Vitrolles and myself. It was easy to point out that to do this would be running the risk, without any real advantage, of arousing passionate feelings in the city that might well lead to brawling and bloodshed. What was especially important was to ensure that nothing of this kind should occur either before or at the time of the King's arrival in the capital, which was quite certain to take place within a few days under the mere pressure of events. What was the point, simply in order to prove our devotion, of running the risk of causing trouble at a time when there was every reason to hope that we might be able before long to preserve at least the appearance of unanimity? I added that, in my opinion, it would be stupid to attempt anything until the withdrawal of the whole army had been completed. M. de Vitrolles and the Bailli de Crussol made it clear that by so doing we should risk upsetting M. Fouché's plans, the only man who could take the necessary measures and carry them out at the appropriate time. This discussion was the only use we made of the great powers that had been entrusted to us.

Our meeting did however have one result which had not been foreseen; it struck me that it might be possible to do something about the Municipal Council, that there was at least a chance that they could be persuaded to make a declaration that would show the mood and intentions of the town in a good light. I therefore went to see the Prefect, M. de Bondy, one of my oldest friends. I pointed out to him that, apart from any personal consideration, it would be in the interests of all those under his administration if he at once took the necessary steps to obtain some expression of opinion which would help to further the reconciliation between them and the House of Bourbon which was universally felt to be necessary. Legally, any such declaration could only come from the Municipal Council. He understood this : in agreement with M. Molé, a member of the Council, he initiated a debate which took place on the 7th, and had the desired effect. But it came too late, for the issue had already been decided. This effort on his part therefore received scant appreciation.

The royalist party, which had been strongly curbed in Paris, began to bestir itself as soon as it was convinced that no military action was to be feared. For some days past, numerous pamphlets, like that written by M. Maleville,[15] had been in circulation, and several of the most respected journals had not been afraid to voice the same point of view. This had annoyed the enthusiastic Bonapartists, that is to say those who wished to see a new dynasty, and on a number of occasions they had demanded in the Chamber of Deputies that measures should be taken to suppress a movement which ran counter to their opinions and feelings. Their protests, however, were useless; the principle of the freedom of the press, which they themselves had imprudently invoked at the beginning of the session, was now turned against them.

The movement of opinion continued to gather strength, and was noticeably accelerated when, on the 4th, news arrived that the King had left Cambrai and arrived at Senlis the previous day. He spent the whole of the 4th there and, during the morning of the 5th, arrived at the château of Arnouville, a league from Saint-Denis, where he temporarily took up residence. From the evening of the 5th, and throughout the 6th, all those who had devotedly served the royal family were eager to hasten thither, to demonstrate their zeal and pay homage to their sovereign. But the town gates were still under military control, and the National Guardsmen who were on duty there objected to all this coming and going, and behaved pretty roughly; there were some sharp disputes, and one or two people met with considerable ill-treatment on their way back.

Several of the courtiers who had accompanied the King to Arnouville, particularly the military members of his household, attempted to enter the capital ahead of him, and turned up in uniform, or at least sporting a white cockade. This led to

---

[15] The title of his work was *Au Gouvernement provisoire et aux deux Chambres*, 27 June, 1815, calling for the restoration of Louis XVIII.

considerable commotion; they were seized by the National Guard and led off to the Prefecture of Police, where they were detained. The Prefecture was no longer occupied by M. Réal; taking advantage of his poor state of health, M. Fouché had hurriedly replaced him by M. Courtin,[16] the King's attorney, and completely devoted to him. M. Courtin soon released the prisoners, and provided them with all necessary facilities to leave the town. This was the only incident of any significance during his short period of office, during which I have never been able to discover any reprehensible act on his part which could justify the treatment that was nevertheless inflicted upon him very shortly afterwards by the very man who had promoted him, that is to say, by M. Fouché.

We have come to the moment when this extraordinary individual could no longer afford to waste any time if he hoped to gather the fruits of all the manoeuvres he had been involved in. He had sent more than one emissary to the Duke of Wellington since the one he had despatched to make arrangements for the armistice; as soon as this important question had been settled, the Duke and he had both wanted to meet one another. He had been sufficiently shrewd to convince his colleagues on the Provisional Government that a conference with the English general might be of considerable benefit in the common interest.

It was with their agreement, therefore, that he set out on the 6th for the English headquarters at Neuilly. It so happened that M. Molé arrived at his house just as he was getting into his carriage. He invited him to get in beside him, and this is how M. Molé came to be present at the interview.[17] M. Fouché's air of assurance, the offhand way in which he dealt with all questions

---

[16] Despite his devotion to Louis, Courtin opposed the restoration of the Bourbons, and shortly afterwards was dismissed by Fouché and exiled to Belgium. In 1818 he obtained permission to return to France.

[17] Molé recounts that Fouché obstinately defended those who, like Ney, were assumed to have been responsible for the events of 20 March 1815 (when Napoleon returned to the Tuileries) maintaining that it was in the interest of Louis XVIII and his policy to forgive everything . . . 'I was amused by the simplicity of the Duke of Wellington, who argued vehemently, but without the slightest suspicion of Fouché's real views. Talleyrand, who understood both of them, supported the Duke of Wellington in this discussion, but in a casual manner, more or less out of politeness, like a man who was fully aware of what Fouché was up to and where it was leading to . . . They broke up without having reached any conclusion.'

and guaranteed that the King's entry into his capital would be a brilliant success, provided they were prepared to take his advice and leave everything in his hands, so impressed the Duke of Wellington that he undertook to get the King to accept his services, while at the same time obtaining such credit for him in His Majesty's eyes that he would be able to achieve all the good that he promised to do. M. Fouché then handed him a letter that he had written to the King, which the Duke promised to deliver. I have not seen this letter, and I should be very wary about identifying it with the one included in the Memoirs published in 1814 under his name.

Back in Paris, he had no hesitation in informing his colleagues that, according to his conversation with the Duke of Wellington, all they now had to do was to make the necessary preparations for Louis XVIII's homecoming, which would take place in two or three days at latest. On hearing this, M. Carnot, General Grenier and M. Quinette strongly insisted upon an idea that they had already put forward more than once; that they should retreat with the army to the banks of the Loire, taking with them their phantom government. Supported by M. le Duc de Vicence, M. Fouché managed to get them to abandon this idea, which could only have led to further disasters.

On the morning of the 7th, hearing that it was once again possible to leave Paris by the gates on the Saint-Denis side of the town, I decided that I, too, would go to Arnouville to pay my respects to the King. I got there at midday. I found the avenues leading to the château, and the courtyard, full of carriages and people; Marshal Macdonald arrived at the same time as I. The first person we met was General de Pozzo di Borgo, who seemed delighted to see us and questioned us closely about the situation in the capital, asking what kind of mood predominated and how the King was likely to be received. Having reassured him on these points, we entered the château. The King was holding a Council at the time, and the anterooms leading to his study were so packed with people that it was almost impossible to get through the crowd.

I noticed that almost everyone was discussing the same question: Why didn't the King leave for Paris immediately? Surely it was more or less certain that he would be enthusiastically welcomed? And if any ill-disposed people dared to raise their voices would they not soon be brought to justice? In situations of this kind one always finds some people who consider that things can only be brought to a satisfactory conclusion by a display of force or, as they would say, of strength! I was listening in silence to everything that was being said around me, when the Chancellor came out of the room where the Council[18] was being held. He caught sight of me, waved to me, went back into the room and, a minute later, came out again to summon me in the King's name and to take me into the study. Thus I suddenly found myself, without the slightest warning, introduced into the middle of the Council, in the presence of His Majesty, of Monsieur and the Duc de Berry. I was greeted with signs of goodwill on all sides.[19]

The Council consisted of all those whose names I have already given. It did not take me long to realise that M. de Talleyrand had, with his usual ease, already assumed the leading position. At the time I was quite unaware of what had taken place at Mons and at Cambrai.[20] I only knew that M. de

[18] The Council consisted of MM. de Talleyrand, Dambray, de Feltre, de Jaucourt, Beurnonville and Beugnot.

[19] Beugnot, who was present when Pasquier was speaking, comments as follows: 'M. Pasquier had hurried from Paris to report on the state of affairs in the capital which no one was in closer touch with than he, having been Prefect of Police for a long time and having, during the Hundred Days, put the information that he had acquired as a member of the administration at the service of the King. He spoke to the King with all that art, which he possessed in the highest degree, of examining every side of a question without carrying it a step further forward; and as, on his side, the King was never particularly concerned to reach conclusions, although the premises were very clearly expounded, by the time M. Pasquier had finished speaking it had become rather less clear than it had been before whether it was more expedient for the King to go on to Paris or to wait at Saint-Denis. It is true that, obedient to his orders on this occasion, M. Pasquier managed to slip in a few words of praise for Fouché, and lightly stressed the services that he could render. And never had his talent been put to more skilful use, for, having freely sown doubts and difficulties, he nevertheless allowed it to be seen how they could be overcome. This was the most important thing: to show how it could be done, without upsetting the King.'

[20] Talleyrand, who was opposed to the King's immediate return to Paris and would have preferred him to remain at Lyon until the end of the occupation, went to Mons on 23 June to be with Louis XVIII. Anxious to dissociate himself from a decision which he did not approve, and feeling that the atmosphere was not very favourable to him, he asked the King's permission to go to Carlsbad to take the waters—a permission so readily granted that he was completely disconcerted. At the Duke of Wellington's instigation, if not on his orders, Talleyrand rejoined the King at Cambrai two days later. This time the manner in which he was greeted was as friendly as it had been offhand at Mons.

Blacas had been dismissed.[21] Amongst the numerous people present I could not help being struck by the singular appearance of M. Chateaubriand; I can see him now, accoutred with a huge Damascus sabre which, as I knew, he had brought back from his travels in Syria, and which hung at his side, suspended by a long red ribbon. It was the King who took the trouble, with the utmost graciousness, to inform me of the subject under discussion, upon which he was very glad to have my opinion. Here, as in the anteroom, it was a question of deciding whether to leave for Paris straight away, or whether to wait until the morrow. To arrive at a correct decision, it was necessary in the first place to know what the general frame of mind of the people was. His Majesty did me the honour of suggesting that nobody was likely to be better informed on this matter than I.

I replied quite frankly that I thought it would be much better to wait till next day. The rearguard of the army, which consisted of the Imperial Guard, had only set out towards the end of the previous night, during which there had been a great deal of excitement. Many people had gone to the Champs de Mars to see it off, and there had been very moving scenes of farewell. Twenty-four hours would not be too long for those who had been stirred by this scene to calm down. The entire National Guard was still wearing the tricolour cockade. Did the King wish it to be replaced by the white cockade? If so, it would be better to wait until the end of the day, in order to allow time to prepare for and carry out this changeover. I assumed that nobody wanted to risk what might happen if the two emblems were to be worn side by side. In short, if they decided to set out that day, I felt it was impossible to guarantee that the King's return to his capital would not be disturbed by some unpleasant scene. If, on the contrary, they agreed to wait for twenty-four hours, then I thought I could answer for it that everything would go off to the general satisfaction; that His Majesty would be met by nothing but the most favourable and enthusiastic acclamations.

[21] Yielding to the pressure of some of his supporters, notably those under the influence of Monsieur, Louis XVIII had broken with Blacas at Mons on the 22nd. 'It is said that this decision was extremely painful to him', Pasquier notes. As some compensation the disgraced favourite was appointed ambassador at Naples. Secretly Talleyrand must have congratulated himself on this decision. He could not stand Blacas. This may have been due to envy, for he used to say of him that, with a salary of 150,000 francs, he had managed to save eight million francs.

No one opposed this view and it seemed to please the King, who, after a moment's silence, said: 'Well, then, so be it! That is agreed, gentlemen. It will be tomorrow.'

There followed a few minutes discussion between the King and M. de Talleyrand, during which Monsieur and M. le Duc de Berry, whom I was sitting next to, both displayed the greatest kindness towards me. His Majesty then called upon M. de Talleyrand to read out again, for my benefit, the decisions that had been taken previously. One was to the effect that all administrative and judicial officials, as well as the commanders and officers of the National Guard who had been on active service on 1 March last, would immediately resume their duties; another restored the command of the National Guard of Paris to General Dessolle, who would be responsible to Monsieur.

Asked what I thought of these two decisions, I replied that as far as General Dessolle was concerned we knew from experience how well suited he was to this command, that therefore nothing could be better than to restore it to him, but that it was important that he should be informed as speedily as possible because he would have a great many preparations to make for next day. As to the reinstatement of all administrative and judicial officials in the positions that they had occupied on 1 March, I said that it would have a good effect to begin with, but that before long it would be necessary to suspend the execution of this measure, in view of the fact that it would be impossible to retain the services of certain of these officials, who had continued to carry out their duties after the Emperor's return, who were deeply compromised, and who could therefore not be entirely trusted, at least for some time.

When the Council was over everyone withdrew. M. Louis caught up with me when I was already in the yard, trying to find my carriage. He told me that M. de Talleyrand wanted me to go up to his apartment, as he had something to tell me.

'It is to let you know', he added, 'that you are to be a member of the government, with a choice of two ministries, Justice and the Interior.' I was completely taken by surprise and, not knowing what to say, allowed myself to be led off to the outbuildings of the château, where M. de Talleyrand had been accommodated. But, as we arrived, his carriage was just driving up and he invited me to get in with him, ordering mine to follow on behind.

'We can talk on the way', said he. 'I will drop you at Saint-Denis, because I have to go to see the Duke of Wellington at Neuilly.' He at once confirmed what M. Louis had just told me. Taken unawares, rather scared by the burden that was going to be placed on me, though at the same time flattered that, in such difficult circumstances, the choice had fallen upon me, I did not know what to reply. M. de Talleyrand put an end to my uncertainty by assuring me that it was simply a question of which choice I was going to make, and pretending that this was the only thing he had any doubt about. I decided in favour of the Ministry of Justice, which seemed to me much the least onerous. 'That's that, then,' he replied. 'The matter is settled.'

'Yes,' said I, 'but only on one condition.' Whereupon, obeying a sudden impulse, I asked that the post of Director-General of Roads and Bridges, which I should be leaving and should much regret giving up, should be left in the hands of M. Molé, who occupied it at present. His immediate reaction was negative. 'Yes,' I insisted. 'He only took this position because he was unwilling to accept either of the ministries which were offered him; and on top of this he refused to become a member of the Chamber of Peers. His opinions are perfectly sound, and I myself will answer for them. You will need to reassure a lot of people, many interests, and there's nothing you could do which would be more directly to the point. After all, isn't M. Molé's name one that it is worth while associating with the House of Bourbon?'

He agreed with all this, but added that it would be very difficult to get the King to understand it, because, at the time of his first return to France, he had had many prejudices against M. Molé. That was the difficulty. 'Don't forget,' I insisted, 'that the granting of this favour is a condition that I feel entitled to make in return for giving up the pleasantest and happiest position I have ever had in order to accept one which is bound to be risky.' He promised to do what he could to obtain this satisfaction for me.

It was at this point that M. de Talleyrand announced that M. Fouché was to be the Minister of Police. Seeing my expression of profound astonishment, he said: 'What could we do? Everybody insists upon it. The Duke of Wellington, whom he has completely won over, declares that he is the only man who can guarantee the surrender of the capital, and therefore of France.

He himself came to implore the King not to refuse to have him in his government, and, since we are at present under such obligations to the Duke of Wellington, it is impossible to refuse his request. And that's not all. The whole Faubourg Saint-Germain swears by M. Fouché, and all the letters and emissaries that have reached the King and the Princes during the last fortnight can talk of nothing but him, and the great services he has rendered to the royal cause. Finally, the Bailli de Crussol arrived yesterday evening at Arnouville, and so successfully indoctrinated Monsieur that this morning he went to see the King, and expressed himself so strongly in favour of M. Fouché that he managed to silence all objections.[22] For the moment, therefore, we have just got to accept him as inevitable.'

'I can see that', I replied. 'I know also that for the moment this appointment will remove certain difficulties, but at the same time I very much fear that it will continually give rise to a great many more. God knows, I realise that M. Fouché deserves to be well treated; it is essential to find some way of satisfying him. But I cannot believe it was necessary to make him a member of the Council, or to allow him to be on such intimate terms with the King. There are certain things that can never be forgotten, and there are some associations that can only be indulged by wounding susceptibilities which deserve to be respected. I pity the King for having such a minister, as much as I pity myself for having such a colleague. However, since the matter has been decided, and the King is resigned to it, we shall just have to accept it and put as good a face on it as possible'.

Naturally, I wanted to know who would be the other members of the new ministry. M. de Talleyrand was to preside, as Minister of Foreign Affairs, M. Louis was in charge of Finance, Marshal Gouvion Saint-Cyr was Minister of War, M. de Jaucourt

---

[22] Talleyrand's words are fully supported by Beugnot. The Bailli de Crussol, says he, 'asked the King in the name of the Faubourg Saint-Germain to keep Fouché at the Ministry of Police . . . I could not believe it. What! The Bailli de Crussol, the last of our knights, the prototype of loyalty! . . . I reproached this honest man pretty severely, and his only reply was: "What else do you expect? Since the King left the country Fouché has saved us all; it is only thanks to him that M. de Vitrolles has not been shot; and, fundamentally, who are the enemies of the royal family in France? The Jacobins. Well, he holds them in the hollow of his hand, and once he has come over definitely on to the King's side we shall all be able to sleep soundly. My dear Beugnot, in the Faubourg Saint-Germain we are all getting on; we have been through too much; what we need now is to feel safe." '

at the Admiralty, the Duc de Richelieu[23] was responsible for the royal household, M. Fouché for the Police, and myself at the Ministry of Justice. Apart from M. Fouché, I had no comment to make about any of the others, though the presence of M. de Richelieu pleased me immensely and was some consolation for that of M. Fouché. As to the Minister of the Interior, he had not yet been appointed. M. de Talleyrand told me that a number of names had been considered in the event of my refusing this position, and that we would talk about it again tomorrow. This conversation had brought us as far as the Révolte turning, near Saint-Ouen, where I got into my own carriage to return to Paris, since M. de Talleyrand had to meet M. Fouché at Neuilly, at the Duke of Wellington's, who had expressed the wish that their first interview should take place in his presence. As everything had been agreed in advance, it proved to be neither a long nor difficult interview, and M. de Talleyrand immediately took M. Fouché to Arnouville, where he kissed hands and was sworn in as Minister of Police.

M. Fouché was later to boast that, in the course of this first interview, he made His Majesty listen to some home truths, and gave him some very salutary advice which was unfortunately not acted upon. I have reason to believe, however, that all he did was to mumble a word or two of thanks and a few protestations of loyalty. His delight at having attained such a position after so many intrigues and dangers certainly would not have left him with the necessary presence of mind to make a long speech. What I have since been told of his confusion on this occasion leaves me with no doubt whatsoever in this respect.

He was back in Paris before five o'clock that evening, but though he already regarded himself as one of the King's ministers, he said not a word about it, especially to his colleagues in the Provisional Government Commission, with whom he had one last point to clear up. He called them together and informed them that the Allies had decided to restore Louis XVIII

---

[23] The Duc de Richelieu (1766–1822) emigrated during the Revolution and from 1803 to 1814 served with distinction in the Russian administration in the Crimea. After the Restoration, having refused Talleyrand's offer of a place in his Ministry, he succeeded him as Prime Minister, but resigned in 1818 after the refusal of his colleagues to support a reactionary modification of the electoral law. After the murder of the Duc de Berry and the enforced retirement of Decazes, he again became President to the Council, in 1821, but shortly afterwards, resigned once more owing to the attacks from the *Ultras* on the one hand and the Liberals on the other. (Trs.)

to the throne, and that, as he was to make his solemn entry into Paris next day, the only decision that remained for the Commission to take was to dissolve itself and apprise the Chambers of the fact.

The need to adopt this resolution became even more obvious, if that is possible, as a result of a most unhappy incident. That morning, the town gates had been handed over to the foreigners, and the Prussians, impatient to assert themselves as conquerors, had promptly advanced as far as the Luxembourg gardens and the garden and courtyard of the Tuileries, which they occupied militarily. Any further resistance was therefore impossible, and M. Carnot could not refuse to sign a message to the two Chambers which read as follows:

'Monsieur le Président, until now we had reason to believe that the views of the Allied sovereigns, as regards the choice of the Prince who is to reign over France, were not unanimous. This was confirmed by our plenipotentiaries on their return. However, the ministers and generals of the Allied powers declared yesterday, in the meetings which they had with the President of the Commission, that all the sovereigns had pledged themselves to restore Louis XVIII to the throne, and that he would be entering his capital either this evening or tomorrow. Foreign troops have just occupied the Tuileries, which is the headquarters of the government. In these circumstances all we can now do is to pray for our country. Since our deliberations can no longer be free, we believe that we should disband.'

I reproduce the exact words of this message because it was to become the first cause of complaint, on the part of the King, the Court and the royalists, against M. Fouché.

As one of the King's ministers, he should never have signed a document which gave substance to so many doubts about important facts, and represented the restoration of the legitimate King as such a calamity that the only thing left to do was to pray to heaven for the welfare of the country. He defended himself by maintaining that it was most important that the Government Commission should agree to dissolve itself, and that only by making this concession had he been able to get them to do so. To this it might be replied that, since the Commission, like the Chambers, would next day have simply disappeared of its own accord, all he had achieved was to commit a pointless breach of manners; but such refinements of feeling were unlikely to make much impression on M. Fouché.

It would appear that there had originally been a sentence in this message, which had only been cut out in proof, implying that new guarantees would be added to the Charter, and that the tricolour would be retained as the national flag. On this last point in particular he had certainly received no authorisation whatsoever to promise anything. The truth of the matter is that he never scrupled to lie if he saw the slightest advantage in doing so! The Chamber of Peers received this message with complete indifference, and immediately broke up. Its chairman, M. de Cambacérès, was scarcely the man to encourage useless resistance. In the Chamber of Deputies, however, there was considerable feeling. Once again it was M. Manuel who took it upon himself to express the views of his colleagues. He maintained that such a communication should in no way prevent the Chamber from continuing its work on the Constitutional Bill, and he concluded his speech rather awkwardly by quoting Mirabeau's famous words: 'We are here by authority of the people, and we will not leave unless we are driven out by bayonets.' It is always an indication of coldly calculated feeling when, in such circumstances, a man quotes someone else's words; and the better known they are the more unfortunate their effect. Nevertheless, his advice was accepted, and they went on with their debate, which was concerned with a clause relating to the hereditary powers of the peerage. This was the last clause in the Bill to be endorsed, for the President then vacated the chair, despite a certain amount of shouting from some of the more violent Deputies who would have liked to remain in permanent session. In the midst of the tumult that ensued, the only decision to be taken was that the Chamber should meet again next day at eight o'clock in the morning. Thus ended the Provisional Government which had replaced Napoleon's.

On the morning of the 8th, the leading article in Le Moniteur, which was on sale very early, was as follows: 'The Government Commission has informed the King that it has just dissolved itself. The Peers and Deputies imposed by the late Government have received notification to this effect. Both Chambers are dissolved; the King will enter Paris towards three o'clock this afternoon, and His Majesty will proceed to the palace of the

Tuileries.' This article had been drawn up jointly by M. de Vitrolles and M. Fouché. It was followed by the two royal decrees, reinstating the public officials who had been in office on 1 March, and restoring the command of the National Guard of Paris to General Dessolle. Then came an order of the day, worded as follows: 'By order of His Majesty the King, Lieutenant-General Dessolle today resumes command of the National Guard of Paris. Signed: Marshal the Prince of Essling; Baron Borelli, Chief of the General Staff.'

At the same time an order of the day from General Dessolle was handed out and affixed to public buildings. It contained a very skilfully worded message of congratulation to the National Guard on the excellent spirit it had constantly displayed and on its zeal in the maintenance of law and order; the formal command, that henceforward only white cockades should be worn, was explained so tactfully that it was accepted without difficulty.

A certain number of Deputies, faithful to the previous day's decision, did not hesitate to turn up at eight o'clock in the morning at the Chamber. But the doors were shut, and guarded by a detachment of the National Guard, who, despite their protests, refused to let them enter. Thus there was nothing left for it but to go home. The officer in command of this detachment happened to be M. Decazes, an Appeal Judge during the first Restoration, whom Napoleon had banished at the same time as myself. He had hurriedly returned at the first news of the disaster of Waterloo, and was anxious to adopt an attitude towards the royalist party that would inspire confidence. A very intimate relationship with a member of M. Louis' family had enabled him to maintain a correspondence during the time that the minister was at Ghent. It will be seen later on how greatly he was to benefit from this association.

There was extreme excitement in the town throughout the morning, but it calmed down. One feeling predominated over all others; joy at being once again safe and at peace, after having miraculously escaped so many dangers. When the King entered the town at three o'clock the welcome he received from the vast crowd that had gathered to meet him was far beyond our wildest hopes, and completely upset all sinister predictions. It must be agreed, however, that for anybody who had taken careful note of the attitude displayed only the previous day, especially by the National Guard, this represented an amazing transformation. The Guards carried out their duties with the utmost devotion, maintaining perfect order, while the feelings they displayed were all that could be desired.

At four o'clock, M. de Talleyrand summoned a meeting of all the members of his Government. As I was one of the first to arrive, he took me aside and told me that it was essential for me to take on the Ministry of the Interior for a few days, in addition to that of Justice. I protested that the burden would be too great. He assured me that I should not have to bear it for long. He explained to me very confidentially why it was not yet possible for the King to make known his choice for the Department of the Interior. 'It is most important for us to win over the Emperor Alexander,' said he, 'and to get him in one way or another to associate himself with our affairs. To ensure this, I have had what seems to me an excellent idea, that is, to give the Ministry of the Interior to General de Pozzo di Borgo. He is of French nationality, since he was born in Corsica, and his qualifications are beyond dispute since he used to be a member of the Legislative Assembly. He is a man of considerable intelligence. He has already rendered great services to the House of Bourbon, and no one stands higher in the Emperor Alexander's estimation. If only this can be arranged, we shall be able to do whatever we like with the Emperor, but we must first get his agreement to M. de Pozzo, who, as he is employed by him as his representative with the King, cannot and will not do anything without his consent; indeed, without his orders. So, you see, we must have a few days to carry through the negotiations successfully. I hope it will not be long, but I shall soon know where I stand.'

I raised all the objections that naturally suggested themselves, but in the end I simply had to resign myself and agree.

At the time, I was not aware of everything that had happened at the Congress of Vienna [. . .] and I had no idea how the French Cabinet stood with regard to the Emperor Alexander; this very tiresome aspect of the political horizon was completely unknown to me. I only recalled the excellent relations that had existed between the Emperor Alexander and M. de Talleyrand in 1814. I was therefore basing my highest hopes on the continuation of this admirable understanding, so that the cruellest disappointment was in store for me, for which I did not have long to wait. Our first ministerial meeting was short, and of little account. The names of the Ministers who had been appointed had not yet been officially published. Nothing had yet been signed.[24] Nevertheless, M. Fouché did not hesitate to join us, and owing to his presence everyone felt uneasy. We discussed one or two important posts that would have to be filled straight away. M. de Talleyrand said that the King had agreed to M. Molé being in charge of Roads and Bridges, which seemed to please everybody, while M. Beugnot was to take over the Post Office. Something had to be done for a man of genuine ability, who had been a minister till 20 March, who had followed His Majesty to Ghent, and who, moreover, during the Mons crisis had firmly stood by M. de Talleyrand.

There remained the Prefecture of Police; it was important that it should be in safe and experienced hands. It was agreed that it should be given to M. Anglès, who had for a long time exercised comparable functions and had also given proof of his devotion by going to Ghent in order to be with the King. Once this delicate matter had been decided we broke up, having agreed to meet that evening at eight o'clock.

During the interval M. de Talleyrand sent for M. Anglès and announced our decision to him; he declined the proposal, basing himself on his position as Minister of State, which, according to him, was higher than the post that he was being offered. The fact of the matter is, he did not wish to be under M. Fouché's orders; this was the only motive for his refusal, from which he would not budge. We found M. de Talleyrand very disconcerted and hurt by this incident. I can still almost hear the ensuing dialogue, which proved to be the starting-point of a great career. 'Well, then, what are we going to do about the Prefect of Police?' he asked, in a noticeably ill-tempered tone of voice.—'What about M. Decazes?' M. Louis

[24] It was eventually Beugnot who presented the order appointing Fouché for Louis XVIII's signature. 'The King glanced at it and dropped it on the desk, at the same time laying down his pen. The blood rose to his cheeks, his eyes darkened, and his whole body collapsed as though suddenly overcome by the thought of death. Our conversation, which until then had been easy and charming, was suddenly interrupted by a dreary silence. The silence lasted some minutes and then, heaving a deep sigh, the King said to me: "Oh well, I suppose it's got to be done . . . " He picked up his pen, then stopped yet again before writing his signature, and uttered these words: "Oh, my wretched brother, if you could see me now you would have forgiven me . . . . " At last he signed the document, painfully and with a trembling hand, while at the same time tears rolled down his cheeks and fell onto the paper . . . '

at once suggested.—'Decazes? What about him? Does anyone know him?' Whereupon M. Louis replied that M. Decazes was an Appeal Judge, that he was a very intelligent and talented man, that on 20 March he had given proof of his devotion to the cause of the Bourbons, that as a judge he had opposed every attempt to recognise the usurper, that the latter had revenged himself by banishing him, and that during the recent crisis no one had sent more reliable information to Ghent than he. M. de Talleyrand then asked me whether I knew him. 'Very little,' I replied. 'He is the son-in-law of M. Muraire, who introduced him to me when I was at the Prefecture of Police, though I saw very little of him. I have never had any conversation with him, and all I know is that on several occasions he has presided at the Assizes with distinction.' When the same question was put to M. Fouché his answer was: 'Decazes? Oh, he's a decent enough fellow. We shall get on splendidly.'

This was how his appointment was decided upon. M. Talleyrand got the King to sign that evening, and it was published next morning in *Le Moniteur*, together with M. Molé's and M. Beugnot's and the announcement of the other members of the Government.

Conclusion

Thus Pasquier had completed his apprenticeship to political life. The future Chancellor still had forty-seven years ahead of him, thirty-three of which were to be spent in leading positions, thirteen in retirement.

Whether in power or not, what kind of life did he lead? An inveterate worker,[1] his daily timetable is known to us thanks to the recollections of his secretary.[2] Up at seven in the morning, by ten o'clock he was already at his desk. Files and interviews occupied the greater part of his day, whether as a leading civil servant or as a minister, though towards the end of his life their place was taken by reading and conversation. His correspondence always took up a great part of his time. 'He never allowed a day to elapse without thanking anyone who had done him the slightest service.' He always dictated both letters and speeches, which he often tried out on himself. 'Even in old age he rarely went to bed before midnight; he slept for two hours, then got up and walked about his room, chewing over the next day's work. You would hear him declaiming and arguing as though he had an audience . . . Sometimes he rested for a while in an armchair, but he only went back to bed towards four or five o'clock. An hour's sleep and he was perfectly alert . . . With him the regularity of his insomnia was a sign of good health . . . he had a real horror of being in bed . . . '

Obsessed by paper work, he was at least equally dependent upon social life. 'Gifted with extreme facility,' says Barante, 'conversation had done even more to form his character than work . . . Chatting around the drawing-room fire had been his apprenticeship for the Council of State and as a speaker . . .' Charles de Rémusat, who often met him at his mother's, reproached him for only talking about himself.[3] But this defect

[1] Proof of his labours are to be found in the archives at Sassy. In addition to the works already referred to in the Introduction, these include an essay on the *Life and Reign of Louis XVI;* another on the *Life and Character of Louis Philippe;* and, above all, eight large folio volumes containing his notes on an extraordinary variety of subjects. All these remain unpublished.

[2] Louis Favre: *Étienne-Denis Pasquier,* 1870.

[3] 'Get him away from stories of things he has actually seen, which he describes

277

was probably only apparent to those who knew him intimately. Listen to this charming description of him by Louis de Loménie: 'Anyone who saw him enter a drawing-room, his tall figure still lithe and perfectly upright, his head rather small but well poised, his expression mobile and lively rather than imposing, his quick gestures and elegant bearing, sitting down beside a lady or negligently resting his head against the back of an armchair, crossing his long legs and swinging one foot aristocratically at ease, or standing in front of the fire, he was prepared to make himself agreeable to everyone, charming his audience with the facility and eloquence of his speech, with his subtle discerning mind, with his vivid memory, full of serious and entertaining facts and piquant anecdotes, combining with an unusual happiness of thought and expression the grave and the gay, the agreeable and the severe—anyone who has seen him like this must agree that that sixteenth-century Étienne Pasquier who reveals himself in his letters as so witty, so gracious, so young in spite of his eighty years, was neither younger nor more lovable than his illustrious descendant,[4] who has just reached the age of seventy-seven.'

Yet though he had all the qualities likely to appeal to women, at least of a certain social background, it seems doubtful whether love played much part in Pasquier's life. The *History of my Times* contains no trace of it. In any case, it was certainly not with Mme Pasquier that the future Chancellor experienced the ravages of passion. At the age of twenty-six, 'he married a widow older than himself', says Charles de Rémusat, 'and also wealthier; still fairly good-looking, but utterly boring. She was a tiresome, priggish woman, with a dignified, equable disposition, whom he continually neglected, though always treating her with the greatest respect . . .' In less forthright terms his faithful secretary, Louis Favre, conveys a similar impression: 'On ceremonial occasions she was a queen, quite superb! But she had a lack of with more intelligence than imagination, and he is a fastidious conversationalist. He is worth a great deal more than his conversation would suggest . . .'

[4] Pasquier's family had always prided itself on its descent from the sixteenth century lawyer. The Chancellor himself felt the most intense admiration for his 'ancestor', whose portraits and works were to be seen wherever he lived. Writing as a secretary who knew his job, Favre went so far as to find a likeness between the two men: 'In old age,' he says, 'wearing his black skull cap and purple silk dressing-gown, he might easily have been mistaken for the Étienne Pasquier whose portrait is preserved in the Museum at Versailles.' In fact, the relationship has not been proved.

interest in everything, a coldness, either real or apparent, that froze you . . .'

Did her husband seek consolation elsewhere? Here again is what Charles de Rémusat has to say: 'He was said to have been always in love, and odd stories were told about him. People maintained that his love, easily inspired and agreeable to cultivate, was even more easily satisfied, and that the women who loved him, once they had given him their hearts, had nothing further to offer him . . .' Sentimental friendships certainly played a part in his life. 'His relations with women of distinction had always been . . . one of M. Pasquier's main sources of happiness, and amongst them he found most sincere and devoted friendships', comments his devoted companion, not, one feels, without some compunction.

Three women in particular retained his affection. During his years in the Council of State and at the Prefecture of Police, Mme de Vintimille:[5] 'Throughout my childhood', notes Charles de Rémusat, 'they were inseparable. They spent their life with us . . . She was an intelligent rather than a witty woman, a reliable and devoted friend and a sensible advisor, but high spirited and passionate even in her friendships . . . M. Pasquier was certainly in love with her, though she was never his mistress. . . . Then suddenly, about 1811 or 1812, he decided that my aunt was younger, more attractive, more tender . . . It was now she to whom he had to write every morning, she whom he had to see every day . . .'

Thus it became Mme de Nansouty's turn, a Vergennes by birth. She too, if Rémusat is to be believed, was not Pasquier's mistress. But this did not prevent her from taking Mme de Vintimille's place in the future Chancellor's life. Her sister, Charles de Rémusat's mother, 'ventured to offer some advice. M. Pasquier was somewhat annoyed at listening to his behaviour being scrutinised in this way by a witty and self-possessed woman. Perhaps it dawned upon him that she was surprised that he should be the object of so lively a contest between two women. . . . By the time of the Restoration my aunt had definitely won; all resistance was over, and Mme de Vintimille was left, sadly gnawing the bone of friendship that was thrown to

[5] Known for her correspondence with the novelist, Joseph Joubert (1754–1824). Pasquier's letters to her are to be found in the Sassy archives, still unpublished.

her . . . .[6] She re-established relations with M. Pasquier on a calm and enduring basis . . .'

Her role was a minor one, however, compared with that of Mme de Boigne. It was in her that the Chancellor really discovered a twin spirit, who brought happiness to the last years of his life. He used to see her, if he could, daily, and if not, would write to her twice a day. Though he was twenty-two years older than she, they were drawn to one another by their sociability and their delight in the art of conversation, by their enquiring minds and, perhaps, also by a certain fellow feeling, since both of them were writing their Memoirs; and she only survived her old friend by four years.

Thus the years rolled by, in Paris during the winter, in summer at Coulans, and later at Sassy, or at Mme de Boigne's house at Trouville.

The honours heaped upon Pasquier by the July monarchy must have appealed to his vanity. The President of the Chamber of Peers was a fine sounding title, but how much more splendid that of Chancellor of France! He was appointed to this position in his seventieth year and no reward could have been more gratifying to a man who had once been a Counsellor in the Parlement of Paris. He must have felt that he was made for the position. The magnificent portrait of him in his robes of office, painted by Horace Vernet, produces an extraordinary effect of dignity and majesty.

But ambition does not decrease with age. Five years later the new Chancellor's eyes were fixed upon the Academy. Doubtless his opponents objected that he had never written anything, but the opportune publication of four volumes of his parliamentary speeches proved that however that might be he had at least talked a great deal. The election (as successor to Frayssinous) took place on 17 February 1842. Pasquier won a triumphant victory over Alfred de Vigny, with twenty-three of the twenty-nine votes in his favour. The papers were critical of the result: only Mme Emile de Girardin gave it her blessing. She even explained the meaning of it. 'If M. le Baron Pasquier has been

---

[6] She was probably afraid to behave towards the future Chancellor in the curious manner described by Sainte-Beuve: 'Mme de Vintimille, whenever she saw one of her ex-lovers enter her drawing-room, seemed to be unable to help opening the windows, even if it happened to be in mid-winter.'

elected,' she wrote, 'it is because he is one of the most intelligent men of our times, because his intelligence is a type, his conversation a model, for us; the ideal of good taste . . .'

Chateaubriand's reason for voting for Pasquier was an all too common one. 'M. Pasquier,' he confided to Vigny, 'is in no way connected with literature, but I have known him for the last forty years; he often calls on Mme Chateaubriand, and is very friendly with us.' And in his speech of welcome Mignet insisted on explaining the significance of the ballot. 'Our choice,' said he, 'is not only for the illustrious friend of literature. Modesty, as you yourself have just told us, may have suggested this to you. By electing you, we are above all welcoming to our midst the political orator who, for fifteen years, has shed lustre upon the tribunes of both chambers . . .'

In 1844, not long after his wife's death, Pasquier was granted a dukedom. He had graciously accepted the title of Baron of the Empire, though recalling that his family had already enjoyed a barony under the Ancien Régime. But this new honour created problems. Louis-Philippe had not made his Chancellor a duke merely to see the dukedom extinguished with his death. Yet Pasquier had no children. He therefore decided to adopt a great-nephew, the grandson of his brother Auguste, Gaston d'Audiffret, who married a 'wealthy heiress', Mlle de Fontenillat. The young couple took the name of Audiffret-Pasquier, and came to live in the Luxembourg Palace, which was the Chancellor's official residence. Eventually he presented them with the Château de Sassy,[7] where the coats of arms of the two families may still be seen on the pediment.

Pasquier survived his wife by eighteen years, retaining his iron constitution to the end of his life. 'He reached the age of ninety six without having suffered from any more serious illness than colds and catarrh . . .'[8] He died during the night of 5 July 1862, at one o'clock in the morning. At that time he was living in the rue Royale-Saint-Honoré. The funeral service was held in the church of the Madelaine on the 8th, and he was buried in the

[7] The arms of Audriffet and of Pasquier may still be seen side by side on the pediment of Sassy.

[8] Was this due to his diet? His secretary maintains that 'he never ate any vegetables . . . ' Be that as it may, he had a famous chef, who described himself as 'a pupil of the Talleyrand school', and whose father had been chef to the Duc de Penthièvre and to Grimond de la Reynière.

Audiffret-Pasquier chapel at Saint-Christophe le Jajollet, near Sassy.

Is it necessary to add that Pasquier attracted the attention of his contemporaries? In the first place, by his physical appearance. Listen to what Charles de Rémusat has to say! 'Étienne Pasquier was a tall, thin, dried-up man, loose-limbed and ungainly, who, without ever being really graceful, always kept his brisk and lively bearing. He had not lost it even when he was ninety-two years old. . . . He can never have been handsome. He had a long face, crooked nose, thin lips, and eyes that were neither lifeless nor animated. His expression revealed a certain coldness, yet at the same time kindliness, vivacity, even intolerance, and a slightly disdainful self-complacency. The women he loved say that his glance could become tender, that he was easily aroused and had a most affectionate manner. . .' Not a very flattering description, but the man who wrote it was always prone to be critical. The Chancellor's secretary, despite his bias, is probably nearer the truth, if we are to judge by his portraits. 'M. Pasquier,' says he, 'was tall, slender and very upright; always elegantly dressed and well groomed. His voice was powerful and resonant, his expression agreeable; his hands and feet had an aristocratic delicacy . . .' And to sum up: '. . . In short, he had an air of distinction.' This was probably so, but it was hardly likely to reduce the number of those who were jealous of him; and there were plenty of these. Pasquier's name figured in the *Dictionary of Turncoats*, and it was fashionable to say of him 'that he carried more spare oaths of loyalty in his pocket than any man in France'.[9]

Was the witticism justified? Remember the stages of his career. During the Revolution, no political activity; none either during the first six years of the Consulate and the Empire. Then eight years in the Emperor's service, but that was a time when there were very few Frenchmen for whom Napoleon did not represent France. True, in 1814 Pasquier went over to the Bourbons: everything urged him to take this step—heredity, beliefs, temperament.[10] On the other hand, during the Hundred Days,

[9] When he was elected to the French Academy he was supposed, according to his enemies, to have made the famous remark: 'As a child I used to swear to myself that I would be a member of the Academy. It is the only vow I have ever kept.'

[10] He detested the Revolution. On 8 July 1813, Napoleon said to Cambacérès: 'If the Duc de Rovigo wants to expel from France all those who took part

he was honest enough—clever enough perhaps—not to make a second volte-face; and this enabled him in 1815 to adapt himself without difficulty, and to his own considerable advantage, to the Second Restoration. From then until 1830, what reason did Pasquier have to make use of one of his 'spare oaths'?

The most that can be said is that he displayed considerable alacrity in transferring his allegiance from one party to another, and this doubtless upset his contemporaries, who were as yet unaccustomed to parliamentary acrobatics. In 1830, it is true, he made no bones about deserting the cause of legitimacy, and was rewarded for doing so in rather too conspicuous a fashion. At the same time, he had made no attempt to conceal his opinion when he refused to take part in the Polignac ministry. Besides, for a 'moderate' like him, what a temptation to serve under 'a bourgeois king'! For the next eighteen years he was untroubled by conscientious scruples; and in 1848 his age—he was then seventy-one—spared him from having to take sides. Thus in forty-two years of administrative and political life, only twice did he break his oath of loyalty: in 1814 and in 1830. This was not much in a period when it was often difficult to distinguish between treachery and loyalty.

How is so well-established a reputation to be explained? In the first place, Pasquier's personality was sufficiently powerful to enable him to attain the highest positions, though it did not compel unquestioning recognition, in the same way as Talleyrand's for example. Many of his contemporaries must have felt, when considering his career as Councillor of State, Minister, Peer of France, Chancellor, Member of the Academy, Duke: 'Why him, and not me?'—An attitude of mind not very conducive to benevolence. Yet those who resented his success would have been quite mistaken if they had assumed that his career was only attributable to luck. That would be a complete under-estimation of Pasquier's remarkable ability. Guizot, who knew him very well—he was his chief assistant at the Ministry of Justice in 1815 —drew a striking portrait of him, every word of which is worth considering:

'He has been accused,' says he, 'of fickleness; in my opinion

in the Revolution there will be nobody left . . . You can also tell him that if he allows himself to be influenced by Prefect Pasquier or men of his type, who don't understand the situation either in France or in Paris, it won't be long before he sets the whole place on fire and shakes my government to its foundations, for it is based on the acceptance of all points of view.'

he laid himself open to this reproach more than is actually warranted by his conduct.[11] Having no fixed principles or definite plan of action, M. Pasquier, it is true, fluctuates wildly between the two extremes. . . but on either side there is a limit beyond which he will not go; and, within these limits, the very nature of his opinions allows him to shift his position without going back on his word, since it consists precisely in not tying himself down to any rigid line of action. . . . He is a commonsensical man, and though commonsense rarely enables anyone to surpass the bounds of prudence, at the same time he never falls below them; he is an intelligent man, whose intelligence is satisfied to maintain a position when it is tenable and to escape from it when the pressure becomes too heavy; he is a man of the world, devoid of any general principles but not of a practical morality which does not allow his political conscience to compromise his private character.'

'The most judicial of politicians and the most political of judges', Guizot describes him elsewhere, more concisely. Or, as Baron d'Haussez spitefully puts it: 'Character and natural disposition, with M. Pasquier everything is flexible. . . . One meets him everywhere, and always loyal to the prince he is serving so long as this prince remains on the throne; well-adapted to the posts he accepts, and skilful in the performance of the tasks entrusted to him.'

There is no reason to suppose that these estimates would have angered Pasquier. His mind was essentially conciliatory. 'He would have liked to govern by agreement', Charles de Rémusat remarks wittily. 'In the fullest sense of the word, he was an honest man. He combined justice and benevolence with complete probity. Capable of prejudice, of becoming exasperated, even of hating, he never sought for revenge.' He disliked extremes. 'He could always find good reasons for the least compromising line of conduct', and, with him, this was much less from fear of taking responsibility than from an aversion to systematisation. 'He never belonged to any party, he followed no flag' says Barante. 'He believed in law and order, which to him meant believing in freedom'. Such qualities of restraint and objectivity were of major importance in the troubled times in which he lived; and to these may be added an integrity that no critic ever dared to dispute.

[11] This was written in 1821. Would Guizot have expressed the same opinion twenty years later?

'One must live with the times', Pasquier often used to say, 'and not lag twenty years behind them.' This was the secret of his weakness, but also of his greatness.

He succeeded in adapting himself to changing circumstances, and in doing so he exposed himself to the charge of inconsistency, if not of disloyalty: an inevitable risk, when the legitimate authority is continually in dispute. The author of *A History of my Times* did not regard this instability of political life as justifying absention from it. 'What is the point of condemning oneself to a life of dissatisfied egotism?' he used to say. 'What can it lead to? Impotence, nothing but impotence.' Will anyone assert that he was wrong? For what would have become of France during the first unstable fifty years of the nineteenth century had she not been served by men as determined as Étienne-Denis Pasquier?

Index

Doctrinaires, the, 166 f.n.
Dubois, Comte de, 83-4, 87, 92, 102-8, 117
Dubouchage, M., 255, 260
Ducos, Jean-François, 26-7, 34, 38
Dudon, M., 83, 195
Dupont, General, *see* Étang, General Dupont l'

Elba, 220, 224
Emigration, the, 29-32, 46
Emmery, M., 186-8
Empire, the, xiii, xiv, 18, 48, 88, 104 f.n., 106, 110 f.n., 146, 236 f.n.
Enghien, Duc d', 44 f.n., 49, 80, 126 f.n.
Éprémenil, M. d', 14
Erlon, General Drout d', 231 and f.n.
Essling, Marshal the Prince of, 273
Étampes, M. d', 5
Étang, General Dupont de l', 45, 177, 197, 202 and f.n.
Eugène, Prince, *see* Beauharnais
Eylau, battle of, 75
Extraordinary Domain, the, 87 f.n.

Fabre, M., 186
Fabri, M., 252
Fain, A. J. F., 118 f.n.
Fauche-Borel, Louis, 103-4 and f.n., 105
Favières, M. de., 12
Faubourg Saint-Antoine, riot in (28 April 1789), 23
Favre, Louis, 277, 282
Federation, the, 34 f.n., 35, 245, 252
Feltre, M. de, 265 f.n.
Ferrand, M., 12, 14, 172
Fesch, Cardinal Joseph, 48, 97
Fezensac, Mme de, 226
Fiévée, Joseph, 103 and f.n.
Five Hundred, Council of, 42 f.n., 45 f.n.
Flaugergues, M., 250
Fleury, Cardinal de, 17
Fontainebleau, 85, 92, 93, 165, 175, 224
Fontanes, Marquis de, 45 f.n., 47, 48, 81
Fontenay, Mme de (Princesse de Chimay), 34-5
Fontenillat, Mlle de, 281
Fouché, Joseph (Duc d'Otrante), 47, 50, 51 f.n., 52, 76-9, 84, 88, 120, 218 and f.n., 234-5, 236 and f.n., 237-40, 242-3, 249-56, 260-1,

263-4 and f.n.s, 268-9 and f.n., 270-3, 275 and f.n., 276
Foudras, Inspector, 176, 256
Fourcroy, Comte de, 12, 17
François, Jean-Marie, 92 f.n.
Frochot, M., 89, 109, 113, 129, 130, 135
Fronde, the, 15, 18
Fructidor 18 (Napoleon's first coup d'état), 42-3, 46, 103

Garnier, Comte Germain, 74 and f.n.
Gaultier-Despréaux, Anne-Thérèse-Nicole, *see under* Pasquier
Gendarmerie of Paris, 137, 152, 161, 195
Ghent, 207, 245, 252-5 *passim*, 273, 275, 276
Girardin, Alexandre de, 256-9
Girardin, Mme Emile de, 280-1
Girondins, the, 34
Godlewsky, Guy, 224 f.n.
Grenier, General, 250, 264
Grimaldi, Abbé, 7
Grosbois, M. de, 255, 260
Grouchy, Marshal, 252, 257-9
Guidal, General, 121, 123, 125, 130, 131, 133
Guizot, François, 166 f.n., 219, 283-4 and f.n.

Haiti *see* San Domingo
Hardenberg, M. de, 186
Harpe, M. de la, 12
Haussez, Baron d', 284
Hauterive, M. d', 74, 77
Hauterive, Ernest d', 92
Holland, Crown Prince of, *see* Bonaparte, Louis
Hortense, Queen, 75 f.n., 171 f.n.
Hulin, General, 126 and f.n., 144
Humboldt, Baron Alexander von, 46
Hundred Days, the, 51 f.n., 158 f.n., 207 f.n., 220, 236-253, 282-3

Imperial Council, 52
Imperial Guard, 118, 119, 127, 128, 129, 155, 206, 248, 266

Jacobins, 35 f.n., 51 f.n., 131, 176, 177, 269 f.n.
Jaucourt, Marquis de, 171, 174, 265 f.n., 269-70
Jena, battle of, 83 f.n.
Jerome, King, *see* Bonaparte, Jerome

THE MEMOIRS OF CHANCELLOR PASQUIER

Rovigo, Duchesse de, 93, 129
'Royal Session', 20 f.n.
Royer-Collard, M., 166 f.n., 218, 245,
253 and f.n., 255, 256

Sabatier, Abbé, *see* Cabre, Sabatier de
Sacken, General de, 171, 173, 179, 202
Saint-André, Jean Bon, 71 and f.n.
Saint-Cyr, Marshal Gouvion, 269
Sainte-Beuve, M., 280 and f.n.
Saint-Fargeau, Louis-Michel Lepele-
tier, Comte de, 32 f.n., 33, 39–41
passim, 42 f.n., 172
St Helena, 224
Saint-Martin, M. de, 74
Saint-Mauris, Prince de, 36, 37
Saint-Roman, Mlle de, *see* Pasquier,
Mme
Saint-Simon, Duc de, 178–9
Sanhedrin, the Grand, 60, 61, 65, 68
sans-culottes, 27 f.n., 35
Saron, President Bochart de, 12
Sassy, archives of Château de, xiii f.n.,
105, 277, 279, 281
Saulnier, M., 88, 125, 126, 128, 131
Saussure, Mme de, 47
Savary, General (Duc de Rovigo),
79 f.n., 83 and f.n., 84, 86, 88,
91–3, 99, 105, 118, 123, 125, 126,
129, 131, 132, 134, 135, 137, 140,
145–9, 153–4, 165–6, 223, 234, 282
Sceaux et Titres, Conseil des, 69–75, 83
Schwarzenberg, Prince of, 84, 109,
157, 158–9, 166, 173, 185
Séjour, Dionis du, 12
Sémallé, M. de, 172, 196 and f.n.
Sémonville, Marquis de, 85 and f.n., 93
Senate, the, 45 f.n., 51 f.n., 131, 169,
171, 172, 174, 177, 180, 186–9
passim, 194
Sergent-Marceau, Antoine François de,
35 f.n.
Siéyès, Abbé E. J., 28, 39, 130
Souham, General, 185
Soulier, General, 129
Soult, Marshal, 211, 218, 219, 258–9
Staël, Mme de, 24 f.n., 26, 46, 47, 244
States General, 14–16, 20 f.n., 23, 24,
26, 33
Suchet, Marshal, 211
Swiss Guards, 23, 36, 37

Talleyrand-Périgord, Charles-Maurice
de (Prince of Benevento), xiii
f.n., 46, 47, 50, 51 f.n., 52–3,
75–80, 85 f.n., 139 and f.n., 147–8,
150–1 and f.n., 166–7 and f.n.,
171 f.n., 172–80 *passim*, 186–9,
191–2, 196, 200–4, 221–3, 238,
263 f.n., 264 and f.n., 266 f.n.,
267–70 and f.n.s, 283
Tallien, Mme, *see* Fontenay, Mme de
Terror, the, xi, 34–42, 47, 90, 110, 124,
220 f.n., 233, 247, 256 f.n.
Thibaudeau, Antoine, 75 f.n., 260
Thiébault, General, 78–9 f.n.
Tour-du-Pin, M. de la, 223 and f.n.
Tubeuf, 5, 8, 9
Turgot, M., 13, 110 f.n.

Ultras, the, 190, 198, 210, 236 f.n.,
270 f.n.

Valette, M. de la, 47 and f.n., 77–8, 100,
139, 140, 176, 229–30, 235, 237,
240, 246
Varennes, flight to, 31, 42 f.n.
Vaudémont, Princesse de, 46–7, 239,
253
Vendémiaire 13 (Royalist rising against
Convention), 42, 43, 106 and f.n.
Vernet, Horace, 280
Versailles, 22, 27 f.n., 149, 151, 178
Veyrat, Inspector-General, 88 and f.n.,
102, 104, 105, 150, 234, 256
Vicence, Duc de, *see* Caulaincourt
Victor, Marshal, 70–1, 177
Victoria, Queen, 231 f.n.
Vienna, Congress of, 51 f.n., 220–3,
241, 274
Vigny, Alfred de, 280–1
Vintimille, Mme de, 47, 145, 279 and
f.n., 286 and f.n.
Vioménil, Marshal de, 255
Vitrolles, Baron de, 191, 194, 198 and
f.n., 199, 201, 224, 225, 226, 253
and f.n., 254, 255, 259, 260, 261,
269 f.n., 273
Voltaire, François, 2, 59

Waterloo, battle of, 247–8, 254, 273
Wellington, Duke of, 224, 263 and f.n.,
264 and f.n., 268–70
Westphalia, King of, *see* Bonaparte,
Jerome
Westphalia, Queen of, 197 f.n., 198,
200, 203
Wolkonski, M. de, 162, 163
Würtemberg, Princess of, *see* West-
phalia, Queen of